Studying at a Distance

This book is due for return on or before the last date shown below.

Studying at a Distance

A guide for students

Fourth edition

Christine Talbot

Mc
Graw
Hill
Education Open University Press

Open University Press
McGraw-Hill Education
McGraw-Hill House
Shoppenhangers Road
Maidenhead
Berkshire
England
SL6 2QL

email: enquiries@openup.co.uk
world wide web: www.openup.co.uk

and Two Penn Plaza, New York, NY 10121-2289, USA

First published 2003
Second edition published 2007
Third edition published 2010
First published in this fourth edition 2016

A catalogue record of this book is available from the British Library

ISBN-13: 978-0-33-526254-0
ISBN-10: 0-33-526254-6
eISBN: 978-0-33-526255-7

Library of Congress Cataloging-in-Publication Data
CIP data applied for

Typeset by Aptara, Inc.

Fictitious names of companies, products, people, characters and/or data that may be
used herein (in case studies or in examples) are not intended to represent any real
individual, company, product or event.

Printed and bound by CPI Group (UK) Ltd, Croydon, CR0 4YY

Praise Page

"This is a book which I have been long waiting to see; thoughtful, considered information which will help all distance learning students, and their tutors. The sections on motivation and keeping going as well as that on planning and time management make the book worth the money alone. As a distance tutor, I would agree wholeheartedly about the need for the student to make the course their own and to take on the responsibility of learning, even to force the tutor to answer your questions as they arise to get the most from this way of learning. Anyone studying with the Open University or the Open College of the Arts (the art school equivalent and lesser known sister organization) would do well to read this before they even open up a course unit."

"This is a detailed handbook for all those who choose to learn at a distance for whatever reason. Even those who learn via traditional means will also find the information useful. This book is divided into sections with condensed chapter summaries which are not subject specific so are useful for social science to engineering students. Included is approaches to learning, practicalities of time management, life balance and getting support along with sections of resources for studying, essays and exams. All things that learners both distance and traditional can need help with. I recommend this book for anyone starting to study at a distance particularly after a break."

"This book is ideal for anyone who wants to embark on a distance learning course. Not having studied for many years and being something of an online novice I found this book invaluable for guiding me through areas such as the use of search engines; a glossary of terms; tips on reading and note taking skills. The details on 'research' are particularly useful. It makes an excellent reference book for dipping into if you reach that point during a course when you feel you can't cope."

"I recently decided to pursue a course with the Open University, and have little experience of studying. I was looking for practical tips to motivate me, help me organize myself and give me a decent overview of the whole e-learning experience from an academic perspective, and this book didn't disappoint. I'll be referring to it on a regular basis during my studies and would recommend it as an invaluable resource to anyone either studying from home or even considering it as in my case, it was the deciding factor as I now have the confidence to pursue this path...I won't feel as isolated or lost at sea with this book to dip into when needed."

"I have not been in education for a while and have decided to start an online course. I highly recommend this book, it is informative, easy to read and has given me many helpful hints and tips on studying away form a campus."

"*This book is invaluable for the first time, or even the long term, distance learner. Areas covered include motivation for studying, the learning process, note taking, tips on e-learning, in fact everything up to, and including, preparing for exams. Excellent for dipping into when you hit an obstacle to your studies. Highly recommended.*"

"*Most of my post 16 education has been carried out by 'distance learning'. Even so I have found this book to be very helpful, in particular, the chapters which discuss 'on line learning' or 'e' learning. This has opened a new part of learning for me. The sections on note-taking and relationships with tutors are also very good.*"

This book is dedicated to my grandson Louie who, at the age of three, has already discovered the delights of learning.

Contents

List of figures and tables   *xvii*

Foreword to the third edition   *xix*

Foreword to the fourth edition   *xxi*

Preface   *xxiii*

Acknowledgements   *xxv*

INTRODUCTION   1

    Purpose of the guide   1
    Who is it for?   1
    How and when to use the guide   2
    Responses   3
    What's included in the guide   3
    What's not included   4
    A note on terminology   4

1   ON BEING A DISTANCE LEARNER   5

    Introduction   5
   1.1 Studying at a distance: what is it?   5
   1.2 Studying at a distance: who is it for?   6
   1.3 Studying at a distance: who will succeed?   7
   1.4 Life as a student   7
    You belong to your institution   8
   1.5 Why are you studying?   8
   1.6 Motivation/goal-setting   8
   1.7 What qualities do you need to be an effective distance learner?   9
   1.8 Potential pitfalls and how to avoid them   10
    Demands on you   12
    Demands on others   13
   1.9 Experience counts   14
  1.10 Learning and the workplace   14
    Chapter summary   16

2   HOW PEOPLE LEARN   17

    Introduction   17
   2.1 What is studying?   17
   2.2 What is learning?   18
   2.3 How will you learn?   18
   2.4 Levels of learning   19
   2.5 What will you learn? Learning outcomes/objectives   20
    The cognitive domain   20

	What's expected of you?	21
	The affective domain	22
	The psychomotor domain	22
2.6	Characteristics of distance learning	23
	Learning by doing	23
	Learning by assessment	24
	Learning by reading and responding to feedback	24
	Learning by attending study days	24
	Learner autonomy – taking control of and responsibility for your learning	25
	Learning by reflection	25
2.7	Sources of learning	26
	The workplace as a resource	28
	What about your own experience?	28
2.8	The learning process	28
	The Experiential Learning Cycle	28
2.9	Approaches to learning	30
	Surface and deep learning	31
	Strategic learning	31
2.10	How do you prefer to learn?	32
	Learning Styles Questionnaire	32
	The VARK Questionnaire	33
2.11	The impact of technology on learning: a brief survey of the literature	33
2.12	The future of distance learning	36
	Chapter summary	37

3	**PRACTICALITIES OF STUDYING**	**38**
	Introduction	38
3.1	Place of study	38
3.2	Getting organized	39
3.3	Pace of study	41
3.4	Time of study	41
3.5	Periods of study	42
3.6	Time management	43
	Study schedule	44
	Weekly planner	46
	Keeping the balance	49
3.7	How will you use your time?	49
3.8	Course-specific information	51
	Programme/course information	52
	Contacts for support	53
	Tutorial details	54
	Attendance requirements	54
	Hardware/software requirements	55
	Electronic learner support systems	55
	Assessment specifications	55
	Progress	58
	University/college information	58
	Your feedback/module evaluation	58

	A note on rules, regulations and complaints procedures	59
	A note on registration and payment of fees	60
	And finally…	60
	Chapter summary	60

4 GETTING SUPPORT — **61**

	Introduction	61
4.1	Coping strategies	61
4.2	Support from your tutor(s)	63
4.3	Support from other students	64
	Why do you need other students?	65
	How can you keep in touch?	67
4.4	Support from the course administrator	68
4.5	Support from family and friends	68
4.6	Support from those at work	69
4.7	Support from other agencies	70
	Disabled students	71
4.8	Taking a break	73
	Chapter summary	74

5 TECHNOLOGY FOR LEARNING — **75**

	Introduction	75
5.1	What do we mean by e-learning and m-learning?	77
5.2	What skills are needed for e-learning and m-learning?	79
5.3	Glossary of terms	80
5.4	Online learning	84
5.5	Email and mailing lists	85
5.6	Mobile learning (m-learning)	86
	Protecting others	87
	Protecting yourself	87
5.7	Virtual learning environments (VLEs)	88
5.8	Discussion rooms/conference boards/bulletin boards	89
5.9	Self-assessment questions (SAQs)	91
5.10	Lectures, demonstrations and podcasts	91
5.11	Videoconferencing	92
5.12	Blogs and vlogs	92
5.13	Wikis	93
5.14	RSS feeds or news feeds	94
5.15	Other forms of e-learning	94
5.16	Viruses, security and backing up work	95
5.17	Health and safety issues of technology use	96
5.18	Help with technology for blind and partially sighted people	96
5.19	Accessibility of electronic learning materials	97
5.20	A cautionary tale	97
	Conclusion	98
	Chapter summary	98

6	RESOURCES FOR STUDYING	qq
	Introduction	99
6.1	Course materials	99
6.2	Library resources	100
6.3	Library catalogues	103
6.4	Bookshops	105
6.5	Periodicals/journals in various subject disciplines	106
6.6	Abstracts and indexes	106
6.7	Electronic resources	106
	Information literacy	107
	Author's note	108
	Databases – bibliographic and full-text	108
	E-journals	111
	E-newspapers	112
	E-books	113
	Searchable lists of web resources	113
	Search engines	114
	Search strategies	115
	Current awareness services for resources	118
	Electronic networking	120
	Evaluating websites for quality	121
6.8	Managing references	122
	Keep a record	122
	Styles of references	123
6.9	IT support	124
	Computer services helpdesk	124
	Chapter summary	125

7	READING AND NOTE-MAKING	126
	Introduction to Chapters 7–10	126
7.1	Reading	127
	Relevance	127
	Cover	127
	Abstract	128
	Contents	128
	Index	128
	Bibliography	128
	Introduction	128
	Conclusion	128
	Chapters	129
	Double check	129
	Take stock	129
	Order of reading	129
	Speed reading	130
	Critical and analytical reading	130
	More help	132
	A note on academic criticism	132
	Stopping reading	133
	Key points to remember when reading	133

7.2   Note-making from reading 133
      Highlighting 133
      Copyright 133
      Additional notes 134
      Physical means 134
      Summarize your thoughts 134
      Design 134
      To use or not to use 136
7.3   Recording and using sources 136
      Bibliographical details 136
      Cite your sources/plagiarism 137
      Quotations 138
      Chapter summary 139

8   ESSAYS AND WRITTEN EXAMINATIONS 140

      Introduction 140
8.1   Essay writing 140
      Created not born 140
      Start early 141
      Assessment criteria 141
      How many words? 141
      Read the question 141
      Read the literature 142
      Make notes 142
      Make a plan 142
      Make your points 143
      Link it all together 143
      Conclusion 143
      Introduction 143
      Critical and analytical writing 143
      Use of first person 144
      Use plain language 144
      Understand what you write 144
      Use drafts 144
      Reviewers 145
      Read the feedback 145
      Practice for exams 145
      Key points to remember when writing an essay 146
      More help 146
8.2   Revising for examinations 146
      Planning 147
      When to revise 147
      What to revise 148
      Reading 148
      Making notes 149
      Key points to remember when revising 149
8.3   Sitting examinations 150
      Assessment criteria 150
      Handwriting/spelling/grammar 150
      Planning for the exam 150

Beforehand 151
Write your name or number 151
Read the whole paper 151
Read each question 152
Planning each answer 152
Writing your answer 152
At the end of the exam 153
Key points to remember when sitting an exam 153
Chapter summary 154

9 OTHER FORMS OF LEARNING AND ASSESSMENT 155

Introduction 155
9.1 Working with others 155
What skills do you need? 156
Causes of concern, anxiety and frustration 158
Group working strategies 159
Multicultural group work 161
9.2 Report writing 164
9.3 Maths and data collection and analysis 165
Mathematics 166
Data collection and analysis 167
9.4 Labs, workshops and field work 167
Labs and workshops 168
Virtual field work 169
9.5 Posters, presentations and literature reviews 171
Posters and presentations 171
Literature reviews 171
Chapter summary 172

10 DOING A RESEARCH PROJECT 173

Introduction 173
10.1 Preparing to do research 174
What is research? 174
What is 'good' research? 174
Approaches to research 175
Methodological approaches 176
Your project proposal 177
Choosing the topic 177
10.2 Ethical issues 178
10.3 Feasibility 179
10.4 Literature searching and reviewing 179
Current research 180
Grey literature 181
Theses and dissertations 182
10.5 Evaluating other people's research projects 184
10.6 Managing your research project 185
Plan/do/review 185

	Managing your time	186
	Research schedule	186
	Record-keeping	188
10.7	Reporting your findings	190
	Your audience	190
	The content of the report	191
	Writing the report	191
	Citations and references	192
	Disseminating the findings	193
	Getting published	193
	Chapter summary	194

APPENDIX ONE	195
APPENDIX TWO	197
APPENDIX THREE	199
FURTHER RESOURCES	201

Note	201
General study guides	201
Guides for disabled students	202
Guides for international students	202
Subject-specific study guides	203
Guides to learning technology	203
Guides to reading, writing and referencing	203
Guides to sitting examinations	204
Guides to mathematics, statistics and science	204
Guides to doing research	204
Study guides on the web	206

REFERENCES AND AUTHOR INDEX	209
INDEX	213

List of figures and tables

Figure 2.1	Continuous Learning Cycle	29
Figure 3.1	Course study schedule	45
Figure 3.2	Weekly planner	48
Figure 5.1	Glossary of terms used in e-learning and m-learning	81
Figure 7.1	Mind map 1	130
Figure 7.2	Mind map 2	135
Figure 7.3	Quiz on understanding when to reference	138
Figure 10.1	Research schedule	187
Table 9.1	Differences between reports and essays	164

Foreword to the third edition

So – you're thinking of taking a distance learning course? Or maybe you're already studying at one of the many distance learning institutions now available to students both by correspondence and online? Or maybe like my daughter you're taking or about to take a distance course as one of your options whilst studying at a conventional face-to-face institution? Or perhaps you're a relative or friend of such a student, keen to help them as much as you can (my research suggests that support from families and friends is one of the most important factors in distance study success).

Well, you, your relative or friend are making a good choice. Distance learning is not only the fastest growing educational method in the world today but one of the most cost-effective for both students and the institutions providing it. My calculations suggest that a distance degree costs the student as little as 5 per cent of the cost of a full-time degree, for example. And institutions can offer qualifications for only around 30 per cent of the full-time cost.

Part of this huge saving in costs is due to the other enormous advantage of distance learning – its flexibility. You can fit distance learning around the rest of your life. You can carry on working whilst studying, you can carry it with you as you travel, you can study from almost anywhere in the world.

But – there's a downside to distance learning. It's the higher chance of failure and dropout. There's little doubt that failure and in particular dropout rates in distance learning are higher – sometimes much higher – than conventional education. Researchers argue about the reasons for this. Some of the reasons may be due to the external demands made on distance students that don't usually affect conventional students, such as job and family demands. Between devoting time to study or a sick baby there's little choice, for example. Other reasons probably have to do with the isolation that distance students can experience – isolation from other students, their tutors and the institution itself.

Whatever the reasons for dropout, there are things you or your student relative or friend can do to increase the chances of success. One is to ensure that you're on the right course for your needs – right content, right level, right media (correspondence or online) and right kind of support. Another (as I suggested earlier) is to ensure that you've got as much support from around you as possible – from families, friends, other students and tutors.

But the most important thing you can do to ensure success in distance learning is to make sure that you're as ready as possible for what you're about to take on. And one of the best ways to do that will be to buy this book. Christine Talbot has years of experience in supporting students and has written an immensely practical and accessible guide on how to succeed in distance learning. It's a mark of its success that it's now in its third edition. It is not only an excellent introduction to the delights and difficulties of distance learning but is an ongoing resource throughout a student's studies. I recommend it to you, or your student relative or friend unreservedly.

Ormond Simpson

Foreword to the fourth edition

Looking back at what I wrote for the third edition of Christine Talbot's important and highly successful book, I find myself re-emphasizing the advantages of distance study, both in terms of cost and flexibility, but also reminding myself of the disadvantage of the higher levels of dropout in distance education. Then again I'm also struck by the changes that have occurred even in the few years since that edition in terms of the increased use of technology in distance education in the form of e-learning.

Perhaps the most obvious example of this development is the MOOCS – Massive Open Online Courses such as *Coursera* or *FutureLearn* – whole courses available free, entirely on the Web, which can be taken at any time and are available to any number of people. In some cases they can lead to a qualification for the payment of a fee.

But even in ordinary accredited distance education there is increasing use of online technologies such as Virtual Learning Environments (VLEs), computer forums, podcasts, blogs, vlogs, wikis, social media and so on (if you're not familiar with some of these terms you will find them ably explained in Christine's book). Many of these are designed to overcome some of the disadvantages of distance education such as isolation.

However, like many technological advances, there are downsides as well as benefits. Computers can facilitate learning but they can also impede it when they fail through bugs, viruses, malicious software, Internet connection failures and so on. When connection is lost, learning stops. All the more reason then to be prepared for both the opportunities and the challenges that distance education offers by reading Christine Talbot's supportive and essential text. I warmly recommend it.

Ormond Simpson

Author of *Supporting Students for Success in Online and Distance Education* (2013)
Visiting Professor Open Polytechnic of New Zealand; Visiting Fellow University of London Centre for Distance Education; Previously Senior Lecturer in Institutional Research, Open University.
www.ormondsimpson.com

Preface

This book has a long history, dating back to the end of the last century, when email was in its infancy and self-assessment questions (SAQs) were completed by circling numbers on a sheet of paper. It has its origins in my facilitation of several face-to-face sessions at the University of Leeds as part of residential induction courses for postgraduate distance learning students. Positive feedback from students and academic staff led me to develop a written version of those sessions for distance learners whose course did not incorporate a face-to-face induction. This in-house version was revised annually, incorporating university-specific information. In the meantime, it became apparent from discussions with colleagues in other universities that there was a need for such a guide for their distance learners too. Various alternatives about how this could be achieved were discussed and, whilst it had to be, by its very nature, a more generic publication, the Open University Press book was born in 2003.

With the developments in distance education in general, and in e-learning in particular, it is not surprising that it was recognized by reviewers, by the publisher and by myself that new editions were required in 2007 and again in 2010. Now with mobile learning increasingly influencing how education both on campus and especially at a distance is being delivered, the time for a fourth edition has arrived. Whilst the technology for learning is shifting, the key concerns to distance learners, such as time management, communication with tutors and peers, motivation, accessing resources and completing assignments remain the same. These issues and many more continue to be covered in the new edition, and the overall structure of the book is unchanged. However, Chapter 5 has been extensively revised to reflect the changes in technology, Chapter 9 has been extended to include even more forms of learning and assessment, and the whole book has been thoroughly updated. I trust that these improvements mean that this book will provide the help and encouragement that you need to successfully complete your distance learning course. I wish you well with your studies.

Christine Talbot
July 2015

Preface

Acknowledgements

As I have made clear in the Preface, this book owes its very existence to the University of Leeds. My work there in the role of Learning Development Officer over a period of nearly nine years brought me into contact with scores of people from across the institution. Many of those people made a direct contribution to this book, and I should like to express my thanks to them. They include, in particular, staff from: the Library; Skills@Library; the Staff and Departmental Development Unit; course administrators; distance learning tutors; and, of course, the students themselves who not only provided feedback on earlier drafts of the guide, but also contributed many of the comments included throughout the guide. They are too numerous to mention, but you know who you are – thank you.

In addition, tutors at the University of Manchester contributed some of the extracts from student course guides; Phil Morgan, LUMS IT Services Manager, Information Systems Services at Lancaster University, provided me with up-to-date information about technological support for mobile learners in UK universities; and John, Paul, Barbara and Geoff provided useful insights into being a distance learner in the twenty-first century.

I should also like to express my appreciation to Alison Hughes and Debbie Prescott, University of Liverpool, and to Paul Chin, University of Hull, for reviewing the Leeds version of the guide; and to these and other colleagues in the Lancashire and Yorkshire network of Open, Distance and Flexible Learning Officers (ODFLOs) who encouraged the production of the original Open University Press edition of the book.

I should also like to record my thanks to Colin Neville, formerly of the Learning Development Unit of the University of Bradford and learning area consultant for the referencing learning area of *LearnHigher*, for permission to include (as Figure 7.3, in Section 7.3) his really useful 'Quiz on understanding when to reference' and the answers provided in Appendix One. These are taken from: Neville (2010) *The Complete Guide to Referencing and Avoiding Plagiarism*, page 15 and Appendix 1, page 195. Thanks also to the staff of *LearnHigher*, for permission to reproduce the material included in Table 9.1 (Section 9.2) 'Differences between reports and essays' taken from the *LearnHigher* 'Report Writing' online materials. And thanks to staff at the Higher Education Academy Subject Centre for Geography, Earth and Environmental Sciences (GEES) at the University of Plymouth for the details of the case study in Section 9.4.

My grateful thanks to Ormond Simpson, formerly of the Open University (UK) and now Visiting Professor of the Open Polytechnic of New Zealand and Visiting Fellow of University of London Centre for Distance Education, for permission to include his '3S model on how to catch up' in Section 3.7, and, of course, for writing the Foreword to the second, third and now fourth editions of the book. That may well be some sort of record!

For the extensive updating for this fourth edition I have needed to consult a large number of resources, and I have been greatly helped in this by the Library staff at Northumbria University and at Newcastle University.

And finally, my thanks are due to Chris Waterston, formerly of Newcastle University, specifically for his contribution to the two mind maps in Chapter 7, but also for his constant support and patience during the many stages of writing the various editions of this book.

Introduction

Purpose of the guide • Who is it for? • How and when to use the guide • Activities • Responses • What's included in the guide • What's not included • A note on terminology

Purpose of the guide

This guide is intended to help you to study by distance learning. It is meant to encourage you. It is also an attempt to provide you with the benefit of realistically anticipating potential difficulties of studying at a distance, and with the opportunity to consider suggestions as to how to overcome them. It aims to reassure you that, with the right attitude and necessary commitment, you should succeed in the task ahead.

Studying at a distance for the first time brings with it its own sort of culture shock, since the differences between this and following a traditional face-to-face taught course can be significant. That said, there are many aspects of studying at a distance that are now very similar to studying face-to-face. For instance, with developments in technology for learning that are increasingly incorporated into on-campus courses as well as distance learning courses (videoed lectures, VLEs for course materials, and so on), the differences are becoming less pronounced.

The guide incorporates numerous quotes (as in the box below) from distance learning students who have been there before you – and succeeded. Some voice the difficulties they encountered, reflecting the reality of their situation, and others also share the strategies employed to overcome those difficulties. Be encouraged!

'...what a feeling when it is all finished, and you look back and see just what you have achieved. I know now the study...has widened my thought, knowledge and understanding, and given me confidence to develop opinions and contribute, even in areas less familiar.'

Who is it for?

Whether returning to studying after a break of some years or embarking upon your first higher-level course of study, this book will provide you as a distance learner with the tools that you need. It is appropriate for full-time and part-time students, undergraduates and postgraduates, whether studying at home or within the workplace. It should be seen as complementary to your programme-specific guide, which will give you a lot more information on issues such as assignments, references systems, and so on, for your specific course.

How and when to use the guide

The guide will be most beneficial if you read as much as possible of it before the start of your programme of study. However, if time is already limited, you will find it useful to read at least the first five chapters, and to look carefully at the contents pages, so that you know where to find the help you need as you progress through your course. When you come to prepare your first assignment and, perhaps, plan and carry out a research project, you will find material here that will provide the support you need to succeed, and to complete your course.

I have attempted to present the overall content of the book in a logical order. I appreciate, however, that for many of you some chapters will be more pertinent than others. Having read through the first five chapters, there is no reason why, thereafter, you shouldn't use the guide in the order of chapters that best meets your own needs. For some, of course, there may be sections or even whole chapters that, after a quick skim, you will decide are unnecessary for you to read in detail because the content is already familiar to you.

The format of this guide introduces you to the style you may come across in the learning materials (whether in print or electronic form) provided by your module tutor. As I cannot be present with each of you as you work through this guide, I have tried to anticipate some of your questions or reactions to what you read and have spelt out some things in detail. Inevitably things are included that you personally don't need, but others might. The beauty of such materials is that you can skip through those sections at your own pace without waiting for others to catch up with you. Conversely, there may be some parts with which you are unfamiliar and so find difficult. You can, in the privacy of your own home or workplace, re-read the material as many times as necessary until you grasp a particular idea – a typical characteristic of learning in this way, and the reason why some people perform better using the distance mode of delivery. For those wanting more in-depth materials on any aspect covered in this book, there are plenty of suggestions provided within the text and in the Further Resources section to other materials.

Activities

Several self-study activities, some of which are followed by commentaries, have been included throughout the guide. You are strongly advised not to miss these out, as they are an essential part of the guide and introduce the crucial element of *active* (rather than *passive*) learning that is typical of studying at a distance. However, as I point out from time to time, it may be more appropriate for you to undertake some of the activities once you have started your course. Try not to read the commentaries until after you have given serious thought to (and in some cases taken action on) the activities.

Responses

Some study materials incorporate blank spaces in the text for your responses to activities but it is not possible to do that within this book. I would suggest that you keep a separate notebook or electronic file specifically for noting down all of your responses. You can then use this for easy reference whenever you refer back to this guide in the course of your studies.

What's included in the guide

After a brief look at what 'studying at a distance' is, who it is for, and who will succeed, you will look at your reasons for studying and at goal-setting. You will then be encouraged to identify the qualities needed to be an effective distance learner, the difficulties you are likely to encounter and the strategies available to help you to cope. You will also reflect on the qualities you already have and consider the relevance of your learning to your workplace. You will look at what studying and learning are, and at the ways in which distance learning is different. You are also given the opportunity to examine various approaches to learning and different styles of learning. You are then encouraged to get to know yourself better as a learner, and to work out the details of how, where and when you are going to study. A checklist of all of the information you need to obtain in advance about your course is provided, with examples from real student handbooks and comments from both distance learning students and tutors.

You will look at coping strategies, and you are offered suggestions about getting support during your studies, especially if you are a disabled student (there is particular emphasis on support for those with dyslexia). You are introduced to the various elements of e-learning (including online learning) and m-learning that you may be expected to use on your course and given extensive guidance about the resources (including electronic resources) you will need to find to complete your studies and your assignments.

For those of you who need something of a refresher regarding some basic study skills, there are two chapters to help you do this: the first on reading and note-making and the second on writing essays and written exam answers. A third chapter looks at other forms of learning and assessment you are likely to encounter on a distance learning course, including a section on working with others when studying at a distance (for those of you who have not had much experience of working collaboratively with other students before), writing reports, using skills in maths and data collection and analysis, and participating in labs, workshops and field work as a distance learner, as well as information on posters, presentations and literature reviews. For those of you who will have to engage in a significant project and to write some form of dissertation as part of your programme of study, you will find the chapter on doing a research project helpful. I have included this so that you can begin thinking about your project at a very early stage. No doubt you will need to return to the chapter several times as your course progresses and the reality of doing a research project begins to dawn.

I am confident that all of you using this guide will find much to support and encourage you in your studies.

What's not included

Although this guide does contain some information on developing your reading skills, making notes, writing essays and sitting examinations, some of you may require more detailed guidance. There are many excellent books and other resources available that provide this, and the final section of this guide (Further Resources) contains details of other resources (paper and electronic) that can help you further develop such skills, should you need to do so.

While there is a chapter on doing a research project, it does not attempt to provide everything you need to know about doing research, but there are many excellent and comprehensive books available to help you. Some of these are also included in the Further Resources section at the end of this book. In particular the chapter does not look at specific methodologies or techniques for actually doing the research. Rather it is an attempt to provide the practical framework within which you will need to work to successfully conduct and report on your research.

This guide does not provide specific information about your course: the course handbook or student handbook provided by the institution where you register for your course will do that.

A note on terminology

The terms 'course' and 'module', and 'course' and 'programme' have been used interchangeably in the guide since different terms are used in different institutions. In general, the term 'programme' is used to mean a whole series of smaller units of study, such as, say, six 20-credit modules.

1 On being a distance learner

Introduction • Studying at a distance: what is it? • Studying at a distance: who is it for? • Studying at a distance: who will succeed? • Life as a student • Why are you studying? • Motivation/goal-setting • What qualities do you need to be an effective distance learner? • Potential pitfalls and how to avoid them • Experience counts • Learning and the workplace • Chapter summary

'Completing the course is a wonderful experience. Passing the [course] was one of the highlights of my life so far. I am able to analyse and use written information in a way that I could not do before. I am able to apply those skills to every aspect of my life.'

Introduction

With the necessary drive and determination you will succeed as a distance learner, just as millions of others have before you. There are, however, many issues that it is good to consider *before* you actually start your course. Doing this helps you to get things clear in your head, be more organized and generally feel far more prepared to begin studying. In this chapter, after a general introduction to studying at a distance, you will look at your own reasons for studying and at what your goals are for your course. You will then look in greater detail at how you can be an effective distance learner. You are very likely to have already given some thought to some of these issues, but it is worth giving a little more thought to them now that you are about to embark upon your course.

1.1 Studying at a distance: what is it?

Distance learning or distance education, as the word 'distance' implies, takes place when you, the student, are geographically remote from the educational institution at which you are registered. You will also be remote from your tutor and other students for most or all of the time. You may be studying when at home or at work or while you are temporarily living away from your usual home, perhaps in another country.

Some of you using this guide may well be on a distance learning course that includes elements of face-to-face contact with your tutors and fellow students. These elements may take place 'on campus' of the institution itself or at a study centre closer to where you live. For example, you may occasionally be required to travel to your institution or study centre for tutorials or study days or to take part in an assessment. On the whole, however, you will largely be studying on your own, away from your college or university and from other people. Others of you may be following a 'hybrid', 'blended' or 'mixed-mode' course that will include a combination of both face-to-face and distance study. You will therefore experience first-hand the similarities and the differences between the two modes of study. You will probably be studying using a variety of different media, which may include radio, television, printed materials, a computer, or a tablet, such as a *Kindle or iPad*, or a mobile or smartphone, such as a *BlackBerry or iPhone*.

> '...getting back into the academic world after years of earning a living...has been like a breath of fresh air...For anyone who went to university but, like me, wasted a lot of their time (even if they had a good time wasting it!), distance learning is a great opportunity to do the things I should have done, or forgot to do.'

1.2 Studying at a distance: who is it for?

Many different kinds of people decide to take the opportunity to benefit from the flexibility of studying by distance learning: parents looking after small children at home; people living in remote rural areas; professional people who cannot attend a face-to-face course at set times; mature students who left school with few qualifications; people in prison; retired people with time for exploring new subject areas; and increasingly (in the UK, for example) school leavers who choose to combine part-time studying with embarking upon their career. Whatever your own circumstances, as a distance learner you are in good company.

Millions of people around the world have now successfully completed courses of study by both mixed and fully distance modes and have experienced the pleasures that learning can bring. There are specialist distance learning institutions, such as the various 'Open' and other universities in Africa, Australia, Canada, China, Germany, Hong Kong, India, Ireland, Israel, Malaysia, South America, the UK, the USA and elsewhere. (More than 2 million students have studied with the Open University in the UK alone.) In addition, many 'mainstream' colleges and universities around the world and some professional bodies offer programmes of study by distance learning, including short courses, MOOCs (Massive Open Online Courses), first degrees, higher degrees (such as MBAs), courses for continuing professional development (CPD), and courses leading to professional qualifications, for example in marketing, human resource management, nursing, teaching, accountancy and so on. Studying may be for as short as ten weeks or as long as ten years (although some institutions do impose a shorter time limit for completing their courses).

'Distance learning isn't for the faint-hearted – it requires self-discipline and motivation and an ability to work on your own with little contact with others.'

1.3 Studying at a distance: who will succeed?

You will! Just as with any programme of study, it is acknowledged (by me and others) that studying at a distance can be a mixed blessing: a great opportunity and a lot of hard work. The good news is that people perform at least as well studying as distance learners as they do studying face-to-face, and some people perform better. Many find that the advantages of being able to progress at their own pace, and choosing where and when they study, far outweigh the disadvantages associated with distance learning. Others have succeeded in spite of experiencing difficulties, and still others have not completed their course because the challenges have been too great. Many of those who have dropped out have said that the main reason for lack of success was that they just had not known what to expect and never quite came to terms with the demands placed upon them. It is my belief that this guide will help you to be better prepared for the task ahead and better able to succeed in your studies because you will have realistic expectations about the experience that awaits you.

1.4 Life as a student

Many of you using this guide will previously have had the experience of being a student and will feel prepared for the experience ahead. For others, this might be the first time that you have studied since leaving compulsory school education and there are many new and exciting things to get used to. Any study experience provides many new opportunities and challenges, not only in the process of studying itself, but also in terms of fitting your studying into the rest of your life. Being a distance learner is no different.

Your work/life/study balance may vary from full-time on-campus students and the methods of communication with others may differ when you are not regularly attending your educational institution, but the issues will be similar: time; money; socializing (more difficult, but not impossible as a distance learner); relationships with others involved in the course (course administrators, tutors and students); getting hold of resources; the excitement of learning new things; changing attitudes and beliefs; learning difficulties; assignment submission deadlines; achieving your goals; and so on. As with any student, you, as a distance learner, will need to give yourself time to adjust to this new experience. What follows in this chapter helps you to prepare to do this.

You belong to your institution

Remember as you work through this guide that, once you are registered for a specific course, you are a bona fide student member of your study institution. As such you are just as entitled to the provision of services and support as any other student. While the form of those services and support may differ from those provided for on-campus students, they should be equivalent.

1.5 Why are you studying?

This might seem a strange question at first, but it is important for you to be quite clear why you have made your commitment to study. When the going gets tough, it is helpful to remind yourself of your reasons for starting studying and why these reasons are important to you. It's not very wise to start a course because someone else wants you to do it – *you* have to put in the hard work, not them, so you must want to do it for your own sake. Some of your reasons may relate specifically to why you are studying by *distance* learning.

'Be sure of the reasons why you are undertaking the course. I had to be sure that my motivation would last the two years the [course] took to complete.'

Activity One

Note briefly *your* reasons for wanting to begin (and complete!) your distance learning course.

Commentary

Clearly your answers are specific to you, but there are usually certain themes in the reasons people specify. For some people the reasons are related to their present job or their career aspirations, for others it is a personal ambition to study for a particular level of qualification, and for others it is a more general desire for personal development, including 'improving the mind'. For many it is the flexibility that distance learning brings that is the main attraction. This may be because you may prefer to be an autonomous learner or you may want to combine studying with work and/or other commitments in your life. Whatever *your* reasons, it is important to keep these in mind for those off days that we all have. Your reasons may well change as you progress in your studies but it's important to be sure of what they are now, to give you the motivation that you need.

1.6 Motivation/goal-setting

Self-motivation isn't always easy – you need to have goals to provide a driving force. As well as knowing *why* you want to study, effective learning also depends upon your knowing *what* it is you want to study. You are probably using this guide after enrolling on your course of study, but you may yet have to make decisions about which non-compulsory modules you are going to study. Although your ideas may only evolve as you work through the earlier parts of the course, you probably have a general idea of the knowledge and skills you would like to possess by the end of your studies.

Activity Two

Take a few minutes now to note down what knowledge and skills you want to develop by the end of the course.

Commentary

Returning to this list from time to time may help boost your motivation when it is flagging, by refocusing on your goals and providing you with direction. It is also possible that you will need to reset your goals for studying on, say, a three- or six-monthly basis. You may also need to reset your broader lifestyle goals in the light of experience, especially with regard to the balance between work, study and relaxation. (We will consider this in more detail in Chapter 3.)

'I enjoyed studying at a distance. I now have the confidence to work independently and can explore my own subject matter in a systematic, logical way.'

1.7 What qualities do you need to be an effective distance learner?

Activity Three

Make a note of those personal attributes and skills that you think you need if you are successfully to complete your distance learning course. Two suggestions are:

- Motivation
- Initiative

'I could go up to six weeks and not have to be physically present for lectures – I found it hard to be disciplined enough to keep working in between taught sessions.'

'I found that I was disciplined, as I knew I would be penalized for failing to meet deadlines.'

> **Commentary**
>
> Many personal attributes and skills needed for studying at a distance are the same as those required by any other learner, but some take on greater significance when learning at a distance. The following have been suggested by students who have studied at a distance:
>
> - Self-confidence
> - Perseverance/resilience
> - Determination
> - Self-discipline
> - Time management skills
> - Forward planning
> - Effective communication skills
> - Ability to take responsibility for your learning
> - A balanced learning style
> - Critical reading and note-making skills
> - IT skills
> - Information literacy skills
> - Effective record-keeping
> - The ability to ask for help from the most appropriate source
>
> You may well have thought of others. As you work through this guide there is the opportunity for you to look at some of the attributes in the above list and to consider suggestions offered on how to acquire or develop any of those that you feel you do not yet have.
>
> It is worth noting at this stage that employers value the attributes that distance learning students bring to the workplace. They appreciate the dedication and hard work that are involved in studying in this way. A good employer will also recognize that someone who has committed to a course of distance learning will be motivated and confident to work independently.

> 'The light at the end of the tunnel is a great motivational factor (and the one that has kept me going), whether the course is for a job-related qualification which will achieve promotion, advancement or a pay rise! Or even just the personal satisfaction and pride that completion will bring.'
>
> 'I feel self-directed learning also means asking for help when you need it, rather than working in isolation.'

1.8 Potential pitfalls and how to avoid them

This section is, in some ways, complementary to the previous one. Even with all or most of the qualities specified above, it is likely that you will have obstacles to effective learning that need to be overcome. It might seem a rather negative approach to take, but unless you acknowledge potential problems you cannot take evasive action or prepare yourself to solve those problems that cannot be avoided. Almost everyone faces difficulties in starting a distance learning course, so you are not alone. Some problems are common to lots of students, but some may be specific to you.

Activity Four

In the light of what you have read so far, what difficulties do you expect to have to deal with if you are successfully to complete your distance learning course? Some of them are likely to relate to your personal/life circumstances (for example, domestic responsibilities) and others to the actual process of studying and learning (for example, writing essays).

'Before commencing on my distance learning course with the university, I had a number of unfounded fears (now I look back on the experience). I wondered if I would fit in, think quickly enough, and whether the breadth of my experience would be wide enough to contribute to the topics being studied. I wondered if I would find the tutors would talk in an academic language I would not understand. Other fears I had included my ability to be organized and keep to a study programme and have my assignment in on time.'

Commentary

You may have included some of the following:

Personal/life circumstances

- Coping with the conflicting demands of studying, work and home life
- Getting away from home/work for the residentials
- Not being supported practically or emotionally by family/friends/work colleagues
- Cost of travel and overnight accommodation

Studying and learning

- Finding time to study
- Having the confidence to start studying again after many years
- Writing essays again
- Coping with stress at the time of the examinations
- Being motivated enough to persevere when not attending university or college on a regular basis
- Feeling isolated because of not seeing fellow students regularly
- Feeling disheartened or unsure of progress because of not seeing the tutor regularly
- Keeping a balance between the work required for the face-to-face and distance learning elements of the course (if on a mixed-mode course)
- Not having the self-discipline to get down to doing the work
- Finding somewhere quiet to work
- Finding the level of the course too high to be able to complete it
- Coping with learning a whole new vocabulary relevant to the course
- Using the Internet to communicate with others and submit assignments
- Working/learning according to the rules of a different academic/educational culture

'Just concentrate on one thing at a time. Distance learning does not mean isolation. A small group of students exchanged telephone numbers, email addresses, and we did use them to contact each other regularly. At the height of the loneliness of the dissertation, I was in contact with one friend every day.'

It is quite normal for students new to learning at a distance to have some anxiety about doing so. It could even be seen as a good thing, since the desire to overcome the anxiety might provide the motivation that you need to begin. It is good to acknowledge fears about learning if those fears (and often misconceptions about learning) are to be lessened. However, too much anxiety is not helpful to positive learning. If you have serious worries about the whole process, it would be wise to get in touch with the course tutor to talk things through sooner rather than later. Hopefully though, you will feel better prepared for the experience once you have worked through this guide.

'Take regular breaks, keep up physical activity and arrange to see friends and go out occasionally. It is important to look after yourself, but still retain a focus and determination to complete the study healthily and in one piece.'

We will be looking at issues of time management and sources of support, in Section 3.6 and Chapter 4 respectively, to help overcome some of your anticipated difficulties. Even when studying at a distance it is possible to put support mechanisms in place and many of these are likely to have been anticipated by your course tutor. Chapters 7, 8 and 9 provide you with a refresher in basic study skills and, as mentioned in the Introduction to this guide, there are some further excellent guides to the process of studying and completing assignments, sitting exams and so on, listed in Further Resources at the end of this book. By the time you use this guide you will have probably already been accepted onto a course. This means that your tutors believe that you *will* be able to succeed in your studies, so once again – be encouraged.

Demands on you

'I miss lectures where I can hear others' comments and questions and realize that I am not alone in missing the point. I do not enjoy studying in a bubble.'

No one finds it easy when they first enter a new field (in studying or at work) or move into a higher level in a familiar field. Hopefully your course material will ease you in gently and get the brain going again. Many course materials include a glossary of new terms and a list of abbreviations and acronyms, so that you can turn to these as many times as you need until new vocabulary has 'sunk in'. If there isn't such a glossary, it is probably a good idea to create your own, adding new terms and their definitions as you come across them.

There is, however, no escaping the fact that studying is hard work and you need to be fully committed to the whole process. But you mustn't let it take over your whole life. What is potentially a rewarding and enjoyable experience can easily become only a chore if you don't maintain a healthy balance between studying and other aspects of your life.

> Difficulty: 'Balancing work, home, family and studying commitments.'
>
> Strategy: 'Prioritizing and planning, i.e. day for studying; day for time with family (important to keep everything in balance).'

If you decide that you are taking a few hours off (or even a whole day) with no studying and no work, then do it and don't feel guilty, otherwise you will not feel the benefit. And don't feel that you have to fill your time off with 'doing' things – sometimes it is good just to 'be'. Likewise, if you set aside a time for studying, worrying about domestic chores will be counter-productive. This might make it sound as though every day you plan as a study day will be a very positive experience and very productive but, of course, this isn't always the case. We all have our 'off' days when no amount of perseverance will help us learn anything. Although you need the self-discipline, it might occasionally be as well to cut your losses and go off and do something completely different – you will probably come back refreshed and ready to learn after all. Beware of too many 'off' days though – if this starts to happen too frequently, you may need to talk things over with your tutor.

> 'Don't forget home/family/friends. They also need to be timetabled and don't feel guilty for giving them time.'

Demands on others

> 'You need a supportive partner who can listen to tales of hardship and woe. My wife had to get used to me disappearing upstairs to work. When we had days off together I often had to work at an essay. Distance learning can impose a strain on partners that may be unappreciated by the student who is worrying about an essay reference list.'

There is no doubt that any form of studying, and distance learning in particular, makes demands on those around you – at home, at work and at play. Only you can judge how interested and supportive your family, colleagues and friends are likely to be, and the degree to which you should discuss your studies with them. Embarking on a new course of study might be very important to you at the moment, but others may see things differently. It is important to discuss with your friends and family that there will need to be a shift in the balance between your work, your studying and your time spent with them.

> **Tutor comment**
> 'Students need to balance their personal, work and study lives and this can be a difficult challenge.'

> 'Don't expect other people to automatically understand what you are doing the course for. It may even be difficult for you to explain it to them. I had an underlying conviction that this is what I wanted to do.'

Practical issues such as a quiet place to study or time to do so have to be resolved by you and those you live and work with. Most people find that if they set out what they are going to need and when they are going to need it clearly but firmly in advance, their 'demands' are better received than if they make them aggressively and expect instant response. Asking for the TV to be switched off 'now' so that you can have peace and quiet for studying, or wanting to take time off work for studying 'today', understandably won't make you popular with most people. The best advice is simply to keep the channels of communication open – keep people informed.

1.9 Experience counts

Whether you have recently finished a course of study or are returning to study for the first time in many years, you will already possess many skills needed to be a successful distance learner. Many of the skills outlined in the Commentary to Activity Three are acquired simply through life's experiences. Your earlier studies and work situations will have been valuable training grounds. In addition to learning skills, as an adult learner you will bring other relevant skills, knowledge and experiences, opinions and ideas to your studies. Although there will be new knowledge, understanding and skills to acquire, your main task will be to fit these into your existing ways of thinking. This will result in your reassessing and possibly revising some of your current views, but the learning process will be an enriching one for you. (You will explore the learning process more fully in Chapter 2.) Although studying at a distance is challenging, you almost certainly already possess what is needed to have a very positive learning experience.

1.10 Learning and the workplace

Many of you will be working towards a qualification that will be associated with your career and, in some cases, with your current employment. As you will see in Section 4.6, support from your employer and work colleagues can be a very important factor during your studies. In addition, the workplace might very well provide the ideal (quiet) place for you to study after the end of the working day, especially if you have to conduct practical exercises as part of your course.

It is widely accepted that learning takes place in a number of settings, including the workplace. A distinction is sometimes made between 'work-based' learning and 'work-related' learning. These terms have been defined in different ways, depending upon the context. What follows is my own interpretation of the two terms.

If you are engaged in 'work-based' learning, your course will be directly related to and form a compulsory and integral part of your current employment. Some learning is likely to actually take place within the workplace itself and it will be designed to increase the knowledge and skills that are needed in your job. You may need to use resources (colleagues, information resources, equipment) within the workplace to complete some of your assignments. You may be issued with a 'workplace learning contract' that specifies exactly what you are expected to achieve during your studies, within a given time frame. Remember that a contract is a two-way thing and that your employer will have various responsibilities under the contract too, perhaps by providing time off for studying, paying towards the cost of course and examination fees, and so on. This is perfectly reasonable, since the projects you undertake as part of your work-based learning will bring benefits to your employer.

If your course is 'work-related' it is less likely to be a compulsory element of your job, and will not necessarily be a part of your day-to-day duties in your place of work, but will nevertheless be related to some aspect of your current or future work. Maybe you are looking ahead to some sort of career move, or your course is relevant to obtaining promotion within your current workplace. You may be less well placed to ask for financial support from your employer in this case, but any reasonable employer will be glad that you are undertaking further studies and will want to support you, if only by giving moral or emotional support to encourage you in your studies.

In either case ('work-based' or 'work-related') it is important to discuss your situation with your line manager, so that if any issues arise that are related to your studies they are more likely to be supportive than if they were hearing about them for the first time. You may be studying at a distance for only part of your course of study, whilst you have to undertake an extended period of work experience on a placement for example. (This is common practice for those training to be teachers, nurses, lawyers, accountants and so on.) Even though your workplace may be a temporary one, it is vital that you make the most of the opportunity of being there.

Whatever form of workplace learning you are involved in (if any), you can draw on the experience of work colleagues, and obtain the support of your employer, workplace manager or mentor to help you to better understand your study materials and/or to complete assignments. (See also Section 4.6 for more about support from those at work.)

As will be seen in Chapter 9, with developments in technology for learning, most types of learning and assessment are possible, even when studying at a distance. The key to success is getting to know yourself as a learner, making the most of what you have and knowing how to acquire what you need. This, essentially, is what the whole of this guide is about. The process begins in the next chapter in which we look at how people learn, and you are encouraged to get to know yourself better as a learner.

Chapter summary

In this chapter you have:

- Looked at the likely experience of being a distance learning student
- Considered why you are studying
- Thought about what it is you want to achieve by following this course
- Identified the qualities you need to be an effective distance learner
- Recognized that there will be difficulties ahead
- Begun to consider what strategies to put in place to cope with the demands that studying is likely to make upon you and those around you
- Received reassurance that you can do this
- Been encouraged to make the most of the opportunity of learning in the workplace

2 | How people learn

Introduction • What is studying? • What is learning? • How will you learn? • Levels of learning • What will you learn? Learning outcomes/objectives • Characteristics of distance learning • Sources of learning • The learning process • Approaches to learning • How do you prefer to learn? • The impact of technology on learning • The future of distance learning • Chapter summary

Distance education is based on the premise that students are at the center of the learning process, take responsibility for their own learning, and work at their own pace and in their own place. It is about ownership and autonomy.

(Wheeler 1999)

Introduction

This chapter provides a structure by which you can carry out some self-reflection about yourself as a learner. You will find that taking time to work through the chapter will be time well spent. By understanding more about the learning process and about your own approaches to learning and preferences for learning styles, you will be better equipped to make the most of your learning experience. You will also be able to make appropriate choices (where available) from the various kinds of learning on offer. (Guidance for developing specific skills for studying is provided in Chapters 7, 8 and 9.)

First you will consider what learning actually is and the characteristics of distance learning. This will be followed by a consideration of what your sources of learning will be. You will then look, in some detail, at the learning process and at the different approaches people take to learning. You will also be encouraged to explore your own learning preferences. Finally, you will consider the impact of technology on learning, now and in the future.

2.1 What is studying?

This can simply be described as the process by which you learn.

The aim of any studying must surely be that you, the student, are able to learn effectively. Although studying is hard work, you will hopefully also be able to enjoy your learning experience. Learning has its own intrinsic rewards, potentially bringing you enormous satisfaction. There are the extrinsic rewards too: perhaps a new job is on the horizon, or promotion within your present job.

2.2 What is learning?

Learning is essentially the acquisition of new skills, knowledge and attitudes, and the recognition of how they relate to the skills, knowledge and attitudes you already possess. But learning is also the process of understanding what has been acquired, and applying it to both familiar and new situations. As Karen Rawlins (1996) suggests, 'learning is a process of self development' (p. 21), and 'students learn most effectively by relating knowledge to previous and current experience' (p. 20).

Learning is not just about collecting information – from your tutors, your course materials, library resources or the Internet – it is about your engaging with and making use of that information in a creative way. You cannot be a successful student if you expect to be passively 'taught' – you need to be prepared to actively 'learn'. Your course will equip you with the means to do this – by providing materials, yes, but also by giving you the opportunity to develop your own ideas by trying them out with your fellow students and your tutors. This will take place informally through discussion (face-to-face or virtually) and more formally by expressing your ideas in assignments and receiving feedback on them from your tutors. The learning process will take time. Don't expect to get great marks for assignments straight away. Do read the feedback from your tutors so that you can improve your performance in subsequent assignments.

2.3 How will you learn?

If you are new to studying on a higher level course, it may take time for you to adjust to the ways of learning that are expected of you. This will show itself especially by the fact that you have to take a lot more responsibility for your own learning than before, including having to find a lot of your own sources of learning (see Section 2.7 below). The teaching and learning methods may be quite different from those you were used to in a school setting, or when you previously studied in a college or university (not least because of the developments in learning technology in recent years), but you will adapt in time. You may be expected to do a lot of work in small study groups, which can be a mixed blessing. We will look in detail in Section 2.6 (below) at how you are likely to learn as a distance learner, in Chapter 3 at the practicalities of studying, and in Chapters 7, 8 and 9 at specific study skills you may need to develop (for example, group work in Section 9.1). It is important to emphasize at this stage that different people have different ways of studying and learning. You need to discover the ways that are best for you and to be able to recognize if/when those ways are no longer working and to be ready to adjust your learning strategies. There will, however, be times when the way you learn will be imposed by the requirements of the course.

You will need to be able to demonstrate how successful you are at learning. This will be judged by your tutors (and sometimes by other students) through various kinds of assignments. They will use various means to assess how much you have learned by measuring your abilities against a set of intended learning outcomes for each part of your course.

2.4 Levels of learning

Some of you starting your distance learning course may be unfamiliar with the current set-up in education and what is meant by academic terminology about levels of learning and degree type. You may have studied some time ago for a first degree and things have changed or perhaps you have come into education via a professional route rather than an academic one. This short section should help you place your current course of study within the wider context.

In many countries (for example, Australia, Ireland, New Zealand and different parts of the UK) levels of learning and the qualifications with which they are associated are increasingly being placed within a 'qualifications framework' (see, for example, the UK's Quality Assurance Agency for Higher Education website at www.qaa.ac.uk (which links to the 2008 update of the Framework for Higher Education Qualifications – FHEQ) or the Australian Qualifications Framework at www.aqf.edu.au/aqf.htm). The purpose of such frameworks (as well as attempting to assure quality in all educational institutions, amongst other things) is to provide guidance to learners about pathways through and progression within the educational and training system in which they are studying and working. The range of qualifications within 'tertiary' (third sector, after 'primary' and 'secondary' schools, sometimes also known as 'further') education is too great to enumerate here, but in 'higher' education something similar to the following five levels (based on the UK model) seems to be common to many countries:

FHEQ level	Typical qualifications associated with each level
Level 8	Doctoral degree (for example PhD)
Level 7	Master's degree (for example MA, MPhil, MRes or MSc) (Incorporating Postgraduate Certificate and Postgraduate Diploma)
Level 6	Bachelor's degree with or without honours (for example BA or BSc) and Graduate diploma and certificate
Level 5	Diploma of Higher Education (DipHE) and Foundation degree (for example FdA, FdSc) and Higher National Diploma (HND)
Level 4	Certificate of Higher Education (CertHE) and Higher National Certificate (HNC)

Students studying on courses at levels 4, 5 and 6 (leading up to a first or 'bachelor's' degree) are known as undergraduates. Those following level 7 courses and above are postgraduates. Within the qualifications framework for the European Higher Education Area the term 'cycle' is used to describe different levels within which all European higher education qualifications are located. The first cycle corresponds to level 6 in the table above, the second to level 7 and the third to level 8.

Many students do not wish to complete several modules and obtain a certificate, diploma or degree. Instead you may be following a short course (perhaps just one or two modules) to update your knowledge and skills in a subject relevant to your employment or potential employment. This is known as continuing professional development, and is particularly common at postgraduate level.

The implications of different levels of qualifications, in terms of what is expected of you, are dealt with in the next section about different levels of learning outcomes.

2.5 What will you learn? Learning outcomes/objectives

What you will learn will be determined by the syllabus for your particular course. A syllabus, however, while providing a useful list of topics to be covered within a course or a specific module of a course, does not spell out in detail exactly what a student should be capable of by the end of the course. In most educational institutions, in order for a course to gain official approval, these capabilities have to be expressed in the form of a set of learning outcomes. This is not a new concept, but the use of learning outcomes has increased in recent years.

Bloom et al. (1956) classified the outcomes of learning into three areas or domains:

1 **Psychomotor**   to do with skills
2 **Cognitive**   to do with thinking abilities: comprehending/understanding information, that is, what we know and what we do with what we know
3 **Affective**   to do with attitudes and approaches

Within each of these domains we can identify a number of stages of learning that can be viewed in a hierarchical way.

The cognitive domain

Since your learning will be largely to do with the cognitive domain we will look at that first, in some detail. The outcomes of *cognitive* learning can be categorized under a number of headings, in terms of what the learner can do, from the lowest level (knowledge) to the highest level (evaluation):

1 **Knowledge** can recall what has been learned
2 **Comprehension** can recall what has been learned and it has significance
3 **Application** can apply what has been learned in a familiar or a novel situation
4 **Analysis** can tease out the threads of meaning from a range of information
5 **Synthesis** can weave the threads together in a new way
6 **Evaluation** can judge the significance and value of what has been learned

What's expected of you?

In some countries and cultures it is common for 'direct "word for word" memorization and recall [to be] seen as an expression of ability and highly valued'. However, 'In the British context it is often seen as intellectual immaturity' (Introna et al. 2003: 42).

Generally speaking, in the UK, the USA and other western educational institutions the higher the level of course you are taking, the higher the level of learning outcome (as defined by Bloom et al. 1956) you will be expected to demonstrate, but any course will expect you to go well beyond memorizing facts and being able to recall them.

Assessment

Assessment on any course is essentially the measurement of the extent to which you have achieved the learning outcomes for that course. A minimum requirement in any assessment will be that you can demonstrate that you have understood the knowledge you have acquired (Levels 1 and 2), and most courses will expect you to be able to apply that understanding of knowledge to a situation that is new to you, or to your existing situation in new ways (Level 3). You will certainly be expected to demonstrate learning outcomes at Levels 4, 5 and 6 for a bachelor's degree with honours or a master's degree. (At doctoral level you will be expected to move beyond Level 6 and actually contribute original material to the body of knowledge in your chosen subject area.)

In order to demonstrate learning outcomes at Levels 4, 5 and 6, you will need to develop your critical and analytical thinking, reading and writing skills. We will look at these in more detail in Chapters 7, 8 and 9. But for now, one example of assessment to measure learning outcomes on a master's degree in accounting might be:

1 Analyse a set of corporate accounts (if possible from your own workplace) and prepare a presentation to post on the online discussion room. The presentation should highlight those elements of the accounts relating to environmental accounting (Level 4 – analysis).
2 Read the theoretical articles provided (items 12, 13 and 14 on the course website). Identify three common themes in the articles and at least two points of conflict between the arguments put forward in the articles. Use these common themes and conflicts as a framework to identify best practice in the set of accounts analysed in part 1 (Level 5 – synthesis, and a bit of Level 3 – application).

3 In the light of your answer to point 2, prepare a report outlining three possible courses of action open to the company to improve the environmental reporting. Justify which course of action would be the most appropriate (Level 6 – evaluation).

For other examples of questions at the six levels of learning (within the context of anthropology), see www.ion.uillinois.edu/resources/tutorials/assessment/ bloomtest.asp.

> 'The university is more interested in analysis and synthesis than descriptive accounts that demonstrate a wide but superficial knowledge base.'

The affective domain

Similarly, hierarchies can be constructed for the affective and psychomotor domains. For the *affective* domain the range would be from:

1 Not realizing/being unaware of an attitude, approach or value, through to
2 Being conscious of not having this attitude, approach or value, through to
3 Adopting the attitude, approach or value, and it eventually becoming a part of your everyday response

The critical approach to reading or the problem-solving approach in science and medicine serve as useful examples. The affective domain can also be described as someone's attitude or approach developing from being:

1 Unconscious incompetent to
2 Conscious incompetent to
3 Conscious competent to
4 Unconscious competent

In each instance the attitude of the student develops from one of total acceptance that facts are true, through the stage where uncertainty is beginning to creep in, until eventually everything is automatically questioned and alternatives are sought or created.

The psychomotor domain

For the *psychomotor* domain we can consider a spectrum of expertise for students. The range would be from:

1 Being unable to do something, through
2 Doing something with a set of instructions, to
3 Doing something without instructions, to
4 Devising new ways of doing something and giving instructions to others

Although Bloom et al. (1956) defined these categories and levels over 60 years ago, they are still regarded by many, myself included, as a useful tool with which the objectives of learning can be made clear for teachers, students and examiners. Always check what the learning outcomes are for each part of your course before you start. Since assessment will be linked to the learning outcomes, knowing the learning outcomes will help you to know what you are working towards during your studies.

Tutor comment

'I expect students to focus on the aims and learning outcomes and use these to guide their learning.'

2.6 Characteristics of distance learning

At first glance the characteristics listed in the subheadings in this section do not appear to be exclusive to distance learning, but will be present in all effective learning. However, as described in each paragraph, each characteristic takes on a greater significance, and is made possible in a distinct way, in distance learning.

Learning by doing

Good distance learning involves active learning, which is the main emphasis of what is called 'constructivist' learning theory. This 'stresses the need for learners to discover, explore and try out new ideas' (Clarke 2008: 8). You will be asked to complete activities or tasks that are built into the learning materials. These are the equivalent of activities or tasks completed in the classroom. Some of these activities will be for you to complete on your own, but for many, you will need to work with other people. You may also be asked to contribute to an online discussion group or forum. Given the ubiquity of digital technologies and the use of social media by staff and students in their everyday lives, it is not surprising that such technology is becoming increasingly prevalent within learning environments. You may be asked to contribute on *Facebook*; write part of a blog or a wiki (editable web page); or post regular *tweets* to a *Twitter* account set up for discussion of a specific topic. All of this is the equivalent of making a contribution to a group discussion in the classroom. It is by such means that you and your 'peers' begin to create or 'construct' new knowledge.

Tutor comment

'Students should try to develop the skills necessary for the online learning and distance learning formats, with the support of their tutor, their department and their company sponsor (where relevant).'

Learning by assessment

You may be asked to complete self-assessment questions (SAQs) (including multiple-choice questions – MCQs) either on paper or via the Internet. These are the equivalent of doing short, regular tests in the classroom. The results of the tests don't count towards your final mark for each module, the answers are usually provided for you and it is a way of checking on your own progress. Self-assessment questions can also be used by a group of students in a local study group to share issues about progress on particular topics with their peers (fellow students). With developments in technology, ever more sophisticated programs can provide high-quality specific feedback to such assessments.

By completing SAQs, checking your progress and reading feedback, you are likely to perform much better on those assignments that do count towards your final mark. It is a very pragmatic approach to learning.

Other forms of so-called 'formative' assessment may also be included. Formative assessment is assessment that occurs during learning to inform and direct learning. It provides feedback to you about progression towards a goal or standard. It may carry marks, but the principal purpose is development rather than judgement.

> 'Having assignments on a regular basis helps me in studying and it gives me an idea of how I should be studying and what things I should be focusing on. Moreover it's a great way of assessing how I am doing.'

Learning by reading and responding to feedback

Feedback may be incorporated into the original learning materials, written by the author of the module in anticipation of your responses to activities or SAQs, or it may be written by your tutor in response to assignments you have submitted in the course of studying the module. The assignments may or may not count towards your final mark for the module, but either way the feedback is provided to enhance your learning. Perhaps it will give you ideas about how you could have improved upon your answers, and perhaps it will give you pointers as to what you need to concentrate on before the final assignment is due. Good feedback will include not just the 'right' answers (indeed in many cases there is no such thing) but suggestions as to why certain responses would be appropriate and others would not. Feedback can also provide you with something very positive: what is good about your work and in what ways your work has improved.

Learning by attending study days

Some distance learning courses include compulsory days or weeks of attendance in person. In part, these will be to deliver those areas of the curriculum that are better suited to the face-to-face mode of teaching and learning, such as demonstrations or laboratory work (although even some of these are now provided online – see Sections 5.10 and 9.4). In addition, you may need to participate in person in group or individual tutorials either at your host institution or at a local study centre and/or attend to complete an assignment at the end of each module.

It is interesting that thousands of students who are studying on MOOCs are voluntarily attending a bricks and mortar centre to do their studying and to participate in practical sessions. Coughlan (2014) reports that

> *Coursera*, a major California-based provider of online courses, is creating an international network of 'learning hubs'. They are running in more than 30 cities, from Baghdad to Buenos Aires, Moscow to Mumbai and Shanghai to Santiago. The typical completion rate for a MOOC is about 5 per cent to 10 per cent, [whereas] for MOOC students attending learning hubs, the completion rates are between 30 per cent and 100 per cent.

This suggests that you would be well advised to attend any study days that are on offer for your course.

Tutor comment

'Students [should] be prepared (having gone through modular text material that is provided), when attending the workshops, tutorials and lecture sessions.'

Learner autonomy – taking control of and responsibility for your learning

One of the most significant differences between distance learning and conventional courses is that you have to take far more responsibility (although, as mentioned in the Introduction, with the changes taking place in the delivery of courses to on-campus students, this distinction is becoming less clear). Because distance learning is centred on you, the student, you have to make a lot more decisions. Although the course and module leaders will set targets (for example, assignments to complete or seminars to attend), you will be organizing your own study timetable in between those, and balancing your study with the rest of your life. You will, to a large degree, have control over the time, place and pace of studying and, to some extent, be able to choose the materials that you use to study. You may also have some say in the nature, frequency and timing of assessments and as to where the assessments are completed. But with this control comes responsibility. You will have to ensure that your work and assignments are completed according to the schedule you have set out. (See Section 3.6 for suggestions about a study schedule and a weekly planner.)

Learning by reflection

You are more likely to take control of your learning if you build in time to regularly reflect during your learning. Think about what you have read, what was discussed in a group tutorial, your own ideas as they develop, your achievement during a practical session and the progress (or lack of it) that you feel you are making.

'Keeping a reflective diary was a lifesaver too, it helped with keeping a focus on the tutorials and kept a perspective overall to refer to for support and contemplation. Reflecting on the contents [of the diary], a clear direction and sense of "moving on" emerged.'

In some courses, the reflective diary or 'log' that is written about the learning experience or the experience of completing an assignment is, itself, part of the assessment for the course and awarded marks. This is especially common where the course is directly related to work. The log may be written and submitted as one complete document, or you may be asked to regularly submit entries to an online learning log, possibly situated within the virtual learning environment. Alternatively you may be asked to create and regularly contribute to a web log or blog (see Chapter 5 for more on blogs). It is an opportunity for you to reflect in a critical manner on how you are coping with self-management, stress, motivation, time management, external obstacles, communication and interpersonal difficulties. At the end of the learning process you will be asked to identify what changes have taken place (for example, in your effectiveness, confidence, beliefs, attitudes and values) and reflect on these changes. (For useful 'Critical Reflection Forms' for a variety of situations, go to the *Learn-Higher* learning resources at www.learnhigher.ac.uk/ and use the search term 'reflection'.)

As you will read in Section 2.8, reflection is an important part of the Kolb (1984 and 2015) Experiential Learning Cycle. (The concept of reflection in professional practice had been developed in depth by Donald Schön in 1983.) Arguably (as in the learning cycle) you need to obtain feedback (from your tutors, peers or workplace mentor, for example) before the process of reflection can take place. We will look at the support available from each of these groups of people in Chapter 4.

2.7 Sources of learning

You will employ a number of strategies to help yourself learn, but I suggest that you pause to consider at this point the ways in which you will access information from which to learn. In the face-to-face taught situation your tutor is largely responsible for providing access to information, through lecturing or demonstrating, but most students following a course on campus are also likely to have to find sources for themselves at various stages in their studies. As a distance learner you are likely to have to take more of the responsibility for finding sources of information for yourself.

Activity Five

List the various ways in which you, as a distance learner, are likely to access information for learning. Two suggestions are:

- By reading the learning materials provided in workbooks, study packs, online, etc.
- By observing someone perform a task at work, on the television, on video, or via the Internet

Commentary

In addition to the two ways suggested above, you will probably have included some of the following:

- By reading books and articles found by searching library resources – these might be in paper format, or, as is now often the case, in electronic format, accessible via your PC, laptop or tablet
- By accessing information on CD-Rom/DVD or online (e-learning, online learning, or on mobile apps), including watching someone demonstrating something in a video clip (e.g. via *YouTube*)
- By accessing information from professional associations, including from their websites
- By discussing subjects with other students, either face-to-face or via the Internet through 'live' online discussion groups, using *Skype* or similar technologies
- By accessing relevant information on social media, including following *Twitter* feeds from experts in the field, joining *Facebook* pages for study groups and so on
- By discussing subjects with your tutors, either face-to-face or via email
- By examining a picture or diagram
- By examining a painting, drawing or sculpture in an art gallery or exhibition
- By listening to someone in person, on the radio or online explain various concepts or procedures, or speak a language you are learning
- By listening to music at a concert, on the TV/radio, on a CD or DVD, or in a podcast
- By going to a play or ballet at the theatre
- By thinking something through and considering all of the options based on your present knowledge and making an educated guess about what might be the result of certain actions
- By attempting problem-solving, that is, trying something out to see if it works and revising the method in the light of the results
- By reading recommended textbooks/e-books, details of which are provided by your course or module tutor(s)

Some of the above are clearly more relevant to some subjects than to others. As you will learn in Section 2.10, we all have preferences for the ways in which we like to learn, so you may not have included some of the above.

We will look in more detail at resources for studying in Chapter 6.

The Workplace as a Resource

As well as (hopefully) receiving support from your mentor and other colleagues at work (see Section 4.6), an increasing number of people are enrolling for distance learning courses that are directly related to their work. Whilst this might lead to a degree of conflict between the time allocated to study and time doing the actual job for which you are paid, there are many advantages to doing this, not least that your studies will have a very definite relevant and specific subject focus. Successful completion of the course can potentially lead to promotion and/or a pay rise, so such a course also provides the necessary motivation that is required to work hard and impose self-discipline. In addition, the workplace may be able to provide some of the resources that you will need for learning and for your assignments.

What About Your Own Experience?

As the above section makes clear and as has already been mentioned in Section 1.9, some students, especially more mature students, may begin their course of study with a great deal of knowledge and experience of their own, based on many years working in one or more professional contexts. Clearly this is valuable to both you and your fellow students. However, the traditional pattern in academia (and the one still very much in vogue in most universities) is that information can only be added to the accepted body of knowledge in a particular field after being reviewed by peers or acknowledged 'experts' in the field. This is usually done via the system of academic publishing (see Section 10.7 for more information on this) to ensure the accuracy and validity of the new contribution. Increasingly, though, as has already been mentioned, knowledge is being 'constructed' (especially at postgraduate level) within the context of group work, especially when using online discussion groups (see Sections 2.11 and 9.1), and it seems inevitable that greater value will in time be placed on knowledge that has its origins in this way.

> 'I found that a lot of the assumptions I make as a professional, self-employed person simply don't apply to academia. For example, personal experience counts for nothing – citing lots of authorities other than yourself counts for everything. Bit shocking that one, at first.'

2.8 The learning process

The Experiential Learning Cycle

What you do with information once you have accessed it is crucial. Learning is a continual process and it is *not* a passive one. We remember 10 per cent of all we hear, 50 per cent of all we see and 90 per cent of all we do. The figures seem

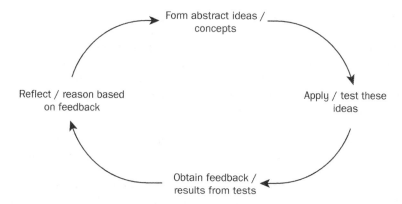

FIGURE 2.1 Continuous Learning Cycle
Source: loosely adapted from Kolb (1984 and 2015)

to vary in different versions of this brief maxim, but the message is always the same: we learn best by doing, by experience. Good distance learning materials will encourage active learning.

Nor does learning happen in straight lines, that is, it is not just a simple process of going through a few stages from beginning to end and finishing, and *hey presto* the learning is complete. Rather, it has been likened to a cycle or a spiral.

Kolb (1984 and 2015) combined these two concepts of experiential learning and cyclical learning in his four-stage Experiential Learning Cycle. The cycle moves through 'active experimentation', 'concrete experience', 'reflective observation' and 'abstract conceptualization' (Figure 3.1 in both editions, pages 42 and 68 respectively). This cycle has been adapted many times by many people. My own interpretation of it, which I have found to be useful in a higher education setting, is shown in Figure 2.1.

The stages are more clear-cut in a scientific experimental setting, but the process is equally applicable to the arts, humanities and social sciences. An *abstract idea* cannot be fully absorbed or internalized until it has been *applied* in some way and objective *feedback* received on its application. This will involve some sort of *activity*, even if only talking the idea through with a tutor or fellow student. Having obtained the feedback on your idea you are likely to *reflect* on it, refine that *idea* and *test* it out again. Any reflection will be affected by other learning experiences that are stored in your memory. The feedback will sometimes come via an internal process, for example, by your own reading – it doesn't always depend upon receiving feedback directly from others.

Learning may begin at any point in the cycle – you might have thought a lot before participating in an activity, or you might just launch yourself straight into something – and you are likely to go round the cycle many times before a particular concept or idea is fully learnt. Even then, you may return to that particular learning cycle at some point in the future and go round a few more times to refine or develop your learning. You may start at the reflection stage, having heard about someone else's activity and its outcomes, or you may observe or be part of someone else's test and draw your own conclusions from that learning experience. These conclusions may lead you to formulate your own ideas that you then test out. The movement round the cycle may not be smooth and the length of time it takes to move from one stage to the next will vary considerably from one person to another and for the same person in different learning situations. What is important is that you complete the full cycle and do not simply stick at one particular point, having completed only one or two stages in the cycle.

In 1971 Kolb created the Learning Style Inventory (LSI), by which it is possible to assess an individual's orientation towards learning (Kolb 1984: 67). The LSI was revised in 1999. Thirty years of research on individuality in learning have affirmed the value of the Experiential Learning Cycle and of the LSI, and in 2011 the new KLSI 4.0 was born (Kolb and Kolb 2011). This introduces nine learning style types (Kolb 2015: 143–51) and is regarded as better defining the unique patterns of individual learning styles (p. 143). It also includes an assessment of 'learning flexibility' by measuring how individuals change their learning style in response to different situational demands:

> Learning flexibility is the ability to use each of the four learning modes to move freely around the learning cycle and to modify one's approach to learning based on the learning situation. Experiencing, reflecting, thinking and acting each provide valuable perspectives on the learning task in a way that deepens and enriches knowledge. (p. 150)

Honey and Mumford (1992) adapted Kolb's cycle to use as the basis for their own Learning Styles Questionnaire, which we will look at in Section 2.10.

Reflection is an essential element of learning. If we make mistakes, or indeed if we succeed, we need to reflect on that experience so that we know either how to avoid making the same mistakes again (where we have been unsuccessful) or to ensure that we repeat the process (where we have succeeded). Even before learning begins, it is possible to reflect on the learning process itself (as outlined above), to consider what skills and attributes you already possess and can bring to the process and which ones you need to acquire. It is also worthwhile considering the potential problems you might face in learning at a distance. (You were encouraged to do both of these in Chapter 1.)

2.9 Approaches to learning

As well as recognizing that you need to complete the full learning cycle, it will be useful for you to recognize that students adopt various approaches to learning. Although it is beyond the scope of this short guide to include a comprehensive survey of the research in this area, you might find it useful to acknowledge the approach that you are inclined to take. You might want to attempt to adjust that approach if you consider that any change is necessary. It is important to recognize that we learn in many different ways, and that the most effective learners are those that are able to benefit from a wide range of learning opportunities. A bit of self-reflection at this point about your approaches to learning and preferred styles of learning might help you avoid focusing on one approach or style of learning to the exclusion of others.

Surface and deep learning

Two approaches to learning that have long been recognized are termed *surface* and *deep* learning (Marton and Saljö 1976). They represent the extremes of a continuum. At one end a student's learning is orientated to rote learning: the intention is memorization and the focus is upon trying to learn elements of content 'off-by-heart'. At the other extreme a student's learning is orientated to comprehension: the intention is understanding and the focus is on the content as a whole, its structure and meaning, and on connections between different elements.

The approach that you take will depend upon your concepts of learning, and the learning environment (the type of task, the workload, the intellectual demand, the quality and quantity of support from staff, and so on) that you are in. Clearly the approach that will lead to a better quality of learning is the deep approach. The danger of the surface approach is that you will not be able to use what you have learned because you have not really understood it; you will simply be able to restate it. Having a deeper approach to learning is more likely to make the subject more interesting and enjoyable and to make it of more use to you. That said, there might be times when you decide (knowingly) to take a surface approach to learning because it is more practical to do so. Such a decision could well be part of a third approach to learning.

Strategic learning

Entwistle and Ramsden (1983 and 2015) identified the *strategic* (achieving orientation) approach to learning. The student taking this approach aims to gain the highest grades and looks for ways to achieve this. This student is also balancing the demands of all of his/her courses (and/or work and family/social life) and making choices about best use of time and effort. It depends how one interprets the characteristics of this approach as to whether one admires or deplores it. (Most people, in order to get through their day, need to be strategic about their workload and prioritize those tasks that are going to be most productive/rewarding and/or that the boss is demanding!)

'The course team sent us a lot of distance learning material. I only read what I had to in order to find an essay title and complete the assignment. I did not have time to read it all. However, now I have finished the course, I have gone back to the material and used it at work.'

One area of learning where many people aim to be strategic is when preparing for examinations (see 'What to revise' in Section 8.2 and the warnings included there). It has been suggested by various researchers (for a summary, see Race 2014, Chapter 4) that those students who are 'cue conscious' (that is, want to learn, carefully read feedback on assignments, and listen out for and are aware of tips from their tutors about what might be important in an upcoming exam) perform better in those exams than those who are oblivious to those hints. Some students are 'cue seekers' and, as well as doing all that a 'cue conscious' student will do, make an even greater effort to perform well in exams. This might include seeking further clarification on feedback received on assignments or more feedback from their tutors, as well as positively seeking suggestions from their tutors about what might be included in an exam. Whether or not tutors are willing or allowed to give such suggestions is another matter!

The decision about *your* overall approach to learning (and the responsibility for that decision) has to be yours.

2.10 How do you prefer to learn?

Just as we differ in our *approach* to learning, we all have preferences about *how* we learn. There are several alternatives to analysing this: two that students have found helpful are detailed below.

Learning Styles Questionnaire

One is the Honey and Mumford (1992, 2006b) Learning Styles Questionnaire and the four learning styles the authors have identified: *activist, reflector, theorist* and *pragmatist.* Their analysis is loosely based on Kolb's learning cycle. They suggest that the four styles of learning are associated with particular stages in the learning cycle. If, for example, your preferred style is that of activist, you are more likely to feel comfortable at Kolb's stage of 'concrete experience'. In practice, most people show a preference for at least two of the styles. However, since the aim is to complete the full learning cycle, it follows that we should also aim to develop all four styles of learning if we are to fully benefit from all aspects of learning.

Activity Six

The Learning Styles Questionnaire and how to score it are available in Honey and Mumford's (1992) *The Manual of Learning Styles* and as the *The Learning Styles Questionnaire* (2006b). It is also available *for a small fee* (unless your institution has a licence) on Peter Honey's website (see 'Study guides on the web' in the Further Resources section at the end of this book for details). It is well worth completing it in order to get to know your preferred learning style. General descriptions of the four styles and suggestions for using the results to improve your learning are also included in the book and on the website. See also Honey and Mumford (2006a) *The Learning Styles Helper's Guide.*

Commentary

Very few people are all-round learners, so don't be surprised if you score high on one or other scale. The results will indicate those situations in which you will function best and those in which you are likely to perform less well. If you have any choice in the matter, you can select those learning experiences that suit you best, but there are also some suggestions included in Honey and Mumford (1995) as to how you might develop further those areas where you are less strong, so that you can benefit from all kinds of learning.

The VARK Questionnaire

The VARK Questionnaire developed by Neil Fleming, New Zealand, and Charles Bonwell, USA (2006), enables you to discover (or confirm) your learning preferences:

V = visual graphic, i.e. pictures

A = aural/auditory

R = visual text, i.e. reading

K = kinesthetic, i.e. using all of the senses of sight, touch, taste, smell and hearing

MM = multimodal

A website has been developed on which it is possible to complete the VARK Questionnaire interactively. (For more details see 'Study guides on the web' in the Further Resources section.)

2.11 The impact of technology on learning: a brief survey of the literature

Whatever the learning styles and preferences you have identified yourself as possessing, as a distance learner (along with on-campus learners) you will be faced with the practicalities of participating in many different types of learning activities, using a variety of methods and tools, and of learning in ways which may be significantly different from how you have learned previously. It is crucial, therefore, that you are very flexible in how you approach your learning, being sure to employ all of your learning skills to complete all forms of activities. Some of these tasks you will perform on your own, but increasingly you will be expected to cooperate with others on your course to achieve your learning outcomes. The technology that is now available to do this (especially mobile phones and other mobile devices) certainly makes group work and other activities for distance learners far more feasible than previously.

Bonk (2014: x) believes that,

> Online learning that was once quite suffocating, redundant and dreary and best described as shovelware or electronic page turning at the end of the last century is now highly collaborative, social and individually driven. Times have changed. Learners have markedly different roles when online. For instance, they do not just discuss, debate, or add comments to learning content made available for a class; instead, they often generate new content in the form of podcast shows, blog posts, videos, wiki-based glossaries and mobile applications others might use now or in the future. A culture of producers has arisen to augment – or at times, entirely replace – the browsing or consumption-based online learning common in the mid to late 1990s and early 2000s.

He goes on to propound that 'pre-packaged online content with limited learner choice or control is often replaced by "free-range learners" who have ample opportunities to self-select their learning content' (p. xiii). In particular, he believes that the ease with which online videos can be created enables greater use of multimedia in online learning (p. xi). He acknowledges that 'the "free-range learners"…need advice, mentoring and peer ratings from which to select the content that works best for them' and that as well as concerns about 'the quality, credentialing and usability of open educational contents', there are 'questions of why, how and when learners use such content' (p. xiii).

In other words, in the course of your studies, you can expect to use some of the technological tools mentioned above and throughout Section 2.11, and elsewhere in this book, and to receive advice on the appropriate use of such tools from your tutors. If the tools are not already familiar to you, or if you are unsure about some of the terminology used in the ever-expanding field of 'technology for learning', you will find Chapter 5 very useful.

Perhaps just as important as the technological tools themselves are the principles or theories of learning (or 'pedagogy' as they are sometimes called) that underpin their use: the things that essentially help the learner to learn. Some commentators in this field believe that the way we learn could, and probably will, undergo a 'transformation' (Laurillard 2013: xx), given the advances in electronic and mobile technologies for learning that have already been made in the twenty-first century. Others welcome the advent of so-called 'digital' learning tools as being able to facilitate better learning, whilst still using tried and tested educational approaches, such as being able to access lectures online, for example by using *Blackboard Collaborate*, submit an essay electronically (using a VLE), or access resources electronically. The reality at the time of writing (2015) is probably somewhere along the spectrum, with the transition from paper to web-based PC technology to mobile technology taking place slowly and incrementally. But with user access to the Internet using a mobile phone having increased so significantly (for example, it has more than doubled between 2010 and 2014 in the UK), such developments cannot be ignored. See the Introduction to Chapter 5 for more statistical information.

Whichever generation of technology is being used, the use of group work in learning is certainly on the increase. As well as being seen, quite rightly, as an opportunity to develop essential skills that are needed in the workplace, it provides the means for you to demonstrate what you have learned from your own reading, observations and experience (in the workplace and elsewhere). It is regarded by many educators as providing the ideal opportunity for students to collaborate to actually 'construct' knowledge, so demonstrating learning outcomes at Bloom Levels 4, 5 and 6, rather than relying solely on input from their course providers and tutors. As well as constructing knowledge by interacting with other people, you may also do so through interaction with your own 'context' or 'environment', that is using experiences in your everyday life, including your workplace, to help you assimilate the principles you are covering in your studies.

Mobile learning will certainly facilitate this approach. Berge and Muilenburg (2013) reinforce the view that 'M-learning is all about what learners do with mobile devices, rather than how educators want learners to use mobile devices' (p. xxxii). However, there are many educators who are concerned about this, emphasizing the need for the additional input of teachers for effective learning.

Clearly tutors, increasingly referred to as 'e-moderators' (Salmon 2011), will need to monitor the process and to intervene and give a clear steer, should the contributions of individual students reach the stage of leading others in the wrong direction. Some form of discussion board within a VLE (such as *Blackboard*) or a closed group on *Facebook* (or one of the growing number of mobile apps for groups) are ideal ways for such work to take place for distance and on-campus students alike, although on-campus students will obviously have the opportunity to meet face-to-face as well.

Some would mourn the lack of face-to-face contact that group work using digital technologies implies, although others believe that it provides a much more equitable environment, and facilitates a far more democratic learning process to take place. Salmon (2013) believes that 'The lack of face-to-face and visual clues in online participation is a key ingredient of equity and success rather than a barrier. If the remoteness and virtuality are handled appropriately, they can increase the comfort level of e-moderators and participants alike' (p. 23). She goes on to say that e-learning activities provide 'an excellent opportunity...to establish amazing and real opportunities for cross-cultural, cross-disciplinary learning' (p. 25). This can only be a positive thing for you as a student, and you are encouraged to engage fully with the process when such opportunities arise in your studies.

As Khaddage and Lattemann (2013: 125) propose 'Today's society needs critical thinkers, inventors, creators, and not just ordinary students who acquire one-way, static education, and mobile apps could provide this dynamic, collaborative method of learning.' They believe that, 'Mobile apps, along with cloud-based computing for teaching and learning, will soon become the future of higher education' (p. 127). Bonk (2014: xiv) continues this theme, believing that 'there will be greater opportunities for experiential learning, game-based learning, inquiry-based learning, learner-learner connectivity and still other novel learning formats.'

As well as enabling group work and other learning activities, the new digital technologies can provide a much improved 'safe' support system for you (as in support from other students and from tutors), with text messaging, blogs and tweets providing the ideal media through which to encourage those students who are feeling especially isolated or struggling to cope with a particular concept. Further, such ways of working enable the learning to be more tailored to your needs (including those related to the workplace), so improving motivation and encouraging you to develop a self-directed and independent approach to learning.

Wonderful though the developments in technology for communication have been in the twenty-first century, it mustn't be forgotten that the role of the human in harnessing the technology to improve and increase the experience of teaching and learning is still the key to success. Without the necessary focus on the learning process, the wonders of technology are explored in vain. I agree with Beetham and Sharpe (2013: 2) that 'Learners are no longer seen as passive recipients of knowledge and skills but as active participants in the learning process.' But, as Laurillard (2013: xvii) points out, whilst 'online access to opportunities for inquiry, discussion, production, collaboration and acquisition...does enable informal, self-directed, independent learning activities...it is not education'.

Similarly, knowing how to use digital technologies in everyday life doesn't mean that you can use them to learn – you need help from teachers to do so. You will find a great deal more about guidance for participating in group work, including multicultural group work, in Section 9.1, and in the remainder of the book there are examples of using digital technologies for learning that are likely to form part of your distance learning course.

2.12 The future of distance learning

It is becoming increasingly impossible to separate ideas about the future of distance learning from the future of *all* learning, which is already being transformed by the ubiquity of mobile technology in most people's everyday lives. Since we live in a mobile world, where mobile technology plays a key role in a mobile society, people naturally expect to communicate when 'on the move'. It is obvious, therefore, that they are also going to want to learn when they are away from their desktop PC at home or at work.

Overall a picture is emerging of new and imaginative solutions to the challenge of providing quality, accessible distance learning experiences in all subject areas at relatively low costs. No doubt in the future such learning will become a normal part of all levels and modes of education, and distance learners will be familiar with a variety of methods. Who knows what those of you reading this book a few years after its publication will be using – so-called 'wearable' information and communication technology such as wrist watches and contact lenses or spectacles connected to the Internet? For the moment, those of you encountering current approaches for the first time may well seem overawed by the variety of learning with which you are presented. Whatever the methods, your tutors will provide appropriate guidance. Always read instructions carefully and remember to check the assessment criteria for any assignments so that you focus your efforts (and your answers) appropriately. As an increasing number of educators and educational institutions make this paradigm shift, you as students will need to be ready – and willing – to shift also, in order to embrace an ever-increasing and exciting range of learning opportunities.

However, the future of distance learning may not be about ever more sophisticated forms of technology, but rather about increased access to technology that is currently available. As Fisher et al. (2014: 196), in their chapter on 'Future developments', believe, such developments will be about 'power egalitarianism . . . enabling conditions that arise from the democratisation of and access to the latest technology', rather than 'new' developments in technology. They highlight the learning theory of 'connectivism', according to which 'education is about preparing people to be social: to be resilient and flexible in an ever-changing world' (p. 6). They believe that access to technology leads to 'benefits such as individuality, creativity and the centrality of students' (p. 7).

It is perhaps inevitable that there will be such a shift in thinking within education. According to Cochrane (2013) too, the main shift in pedagogy that m-learning has promoted seems to be from teacher-directed content to student-generated content and student-generated learning contexts (pp. 254–5). Whilst many will agree with this, I think it is important to remember that (for the time being at least) your learning still needs to be done within a defined framework of learning, with clearly stated aims, and to include specific learning outcomes, and that it needs to be monitored by your tutors.

In the future, there may well be a move away from pre-written courses with a pre-determined set of learning outcomes for all students, to learning with customized (that is 'individually-oriented') outcomes (Cairns and Alshahrani 2014: 29). However, whilst m-learning can provide a unique learning pathway for you, the student, often determined by yourself as you discover new resources, sometimes that pathway will need to be, at least in part, pre-determined in negotiation between yourself and your tutor, dependent upon the nature of the learning activity and its desired learning outcomes.

There may even be a shift away from accredited learning (where learners are awarded certificates after proving that they have demonstrated a prescribed set of learning outcomes) to learning for immediate use within your personal context or for where the benefit to society is paramount, and recognition by an approved institution is secondary or even irrelevant. Such is the case with many students who are participating in the increasing number of MOOCs that are on offer from mainstream universities. However, employers for the foreseeable future are going to be impressed by your gaining official recognition from an approved educational institution for successfully completing a fully accredited course, and hopefully by reading the rest of this book you will be better prepared to achieve that.

Chapter summary

In this chapter you have:

- Considered what learning is, what and how you will learn, and how some aspects of learning are particularly significant in distance education
- Created your own list of sources of learning
- Looked at learning as a cyclical and experiential process
- Been introduced to different approaches to learning and to different learning styles
- Reflected upon your own learning preferences
- Considered the impact of technology on learning now and in the future

3 Practicalities of studying

Introduction • Place of study • Getting organized • Pace of study • Time of study • Periods of study • Time management • How will you use your time? • Course-specific information • A note on rules, regulations and complaints procedures • A note on registration and payment of fees • And finally... • Chapter summary

Introduction

Thinking about the following practicalities at an early stage will help you begin to address some of the issues that are of concern to all students but are particularly important for you as a distance learner, as you are likely to do most of your studying at home. The chapter deals with the *where*, the *when* and the *how* of your studying. As you read through each of the following elements, make notes of the conclusions you come to about *yourself*. The chapter also provides a checklist of the information you need about your programme of study and looks at the expectations that you might have about others and that others might have about you.

3.1 Place of study

'Having two children and demands from the household I found that studying at home was a frustrating experience with constant interruption, unless it could be done early in the morning or late in the evening. The solution for me is simply to block out all day Saturday and go to my office to study and don't leave until the study I want to accomplish is completed...also during the week, sometimes I will stay late at work...to complete the assignments.'

Finding the right place (and time) to study is crucial and preferences vary with the individual. Some people can pick up their materials anywhere (on the train or bus, in a busy staff room, in the lounge) and instantly start to concentrate. Most people, however, need a special space for study – one where, when you sit down, you immediately move into study mode and where you are not distracted. Apart from anything else, it is helpful if you can leave your books undisturbed from one period of study to the next and you are then ready to start again straight away, rather than spending the first 15 minutes sorting out where you were up to last time. However, the ability to access e-books on mobile devices does to a degree make this process easier. The choice of working with or without music in the background is obviously yours, but there are some simple pointers to what will aid concentration and promote good health:

- A warm, comfortable room (or part of a room)
- A working area with a good supply of natural light
- A desk/table at a height within the range 66–73 cm
- A comfortable (preferably swivel) chair at the right height for the table
- A computer screen (if using a PC) to which you drop your eyes (rather than straining your neck to look up to it) and which is ideally 50 cm in front of you and at a right angle to the window
- Room to spread out the books currently in use
- Room to store hard copy materials not currently in use in an organized way, such as in labelled ring-binders or files
- Voicemail or an answerphone so that you are not distracted when studying
- Set times of day for reading and answering emails and text messages and checking *Facebook*
- A boring view from the window, so that you don't spend your time watching the world go by!

Difficulty: 'Identifying a study place outside the home [so] that as soon as I entered my mind was in a set to study.'

Strategy: 'I booked a room in a university library for lengths of time.'

Activity Seven

Make a note of the ideal place available to *you* to study. If such a place does not yet exist, note down any things you may need to do to find/create somewhere approaching your ideal.

3.2 Getting organized

As well as sorting out where you are going to study, there are various other things to plan in advance. Your familiarity with technology will influence how you approach some of the admin tasks of study. Some people now use only online tools for note-making and organizing information. There are many good applications that exist for this, such as *Evernote* for example, which enable you to make notes and task lists on your mobile devices. You may instead prefer just to keep notes on your laptop in a *Word* document or similar. Similarly, there are many useful pieces of software such as *Endnote* which can help you to save and record academic references. It is worth researching these tools independently or enlisting help from peers, or your institution's library service, who may be able to give you advice on some user-friendly applications.

Many will still adopt a paper-based approach, and indeed most people will probably use a combination of both digital and 'traditional' study tools. When studying at a distance, things that you take for granted when you are a full-time student on campus are not always available at your local shop. A supply of stationery items that you may not have bought for a while, such as printer paper, file paper and loose leaf binders, a hole punch and a stapler, might come in handy. Post-it notes are invaluable and you may want to buy index cards for noting details of references. If you are not already using a calendar in Microsoft Outlook or on your mobile phone, you might find a wall planner helpful with time management, and a highlighter pen may prove an invaluable tool when reading through your learning materials and photocopied articles. Remember to order plenty of ink cartridges for your printer so that you are able to print out useful materials that you access online.

You may have received a reading list when you registered for the course. You might need to order some of these items in advance, especially if you don't have a local bookshop or library with a large stock. As discussed earlier, it is now common to access your university library collection online which can vastly speed up your ability to access course materials. If you do need to obtain something in print form, or if it is not available to you electronically, remember that it can easily take six weeks for a new book or hard copy of a journal article to arrive from your university library. You may find it quicker or more convenient to buy a book using an online bookshop (see Section 6.4 for details) or it may be possible to organize a reciprocal arrangement between a local university library and the library of the educational provider where you are registered (see Section 6.2 for details of how to do this).

Activity Eight

Make a shopping/borrowing list. Don't forget to include a new dictionary if you haven't bought one in recent years. It is crucial that you look up words you haven't encountered before. This will improve your understanding of the course materials and increase your vocabulary. A thesaurus is also useful when it comes to written assignments. Of course, many people can now access both a thesaurus and a dictionary via their computer.

Consider all the practical things you think you will need to study at home, including a good reading lamp for hard copy materials. Something you may have overlooked is having good access to the Internet in your chosen place of study. If you don't have this already, ensure you set up good broadband access so that you can study online, or check out a local study centre or library with computers available. You will almost certainly need a computer to access university materials.

3.3 Pace of study

'Timing is everything. Make sure that you are aware of submission dates and do what it takes to meet them. The pressure of the course mounts up considerably if work is rushed and late. You have to feel that you are in control of the course. Extensions for one module just leave less time for the next.'

The pace of study might be imposed on you by the course tutor, in so far as particular assignments are due in on specific days, or you have to prepare for a group seminar by a certain date. Alternatively, you may be able to choose your own pace at which to work through the programme of study. Either way you need to plan your study time (see Section 3.6). Some people do very little for weeks and then cram towards the end of a module; others work more evenly throughout the module. Clearly the second is the safer option and generally helps you to produce work of a higher quality. Either way, effective study requires a significant amount of time.

Activity Nine

Make a note of *your* intended study pattern – just your general approach, not the detail at this stage.

'I found writing [the] title of [an] assignment and [the] objectives and submitting these by a deadline prior to commencing written work extremely valuable in that: i) you had to really focus your thoughts and get on with the literature search instead of leaving things to the last minute; and ii) once agreed with [my] supervisor it prevented me from changing my mind.'

'You...need to identify topics and start literature searching early so that you can get the information and complete the assignment.'

3.4 Time of study

'It is important to set aside time every day, or nearly every day for study. A lot of little bits spread over a week is much better than the whole day every Saturday.'

Whether the pace of study is decided by you or imposed externally, you still have the choice about *when* you study – morning, afternoon or night. Some people are able to set aside full days or half days in which to study, others manage with evenings or snatched hours here and there. For some it is their choice, for others it is a case of using whatever time is available, when it is available. Ideally you should build into your week specific times in good-sized chunks when you intend to work, and stick to them.

'Block out certain days for study only.'

'Get into a routine.'

'Allocate time specifically at the same time each week for (a) allocated reading time (b) allocated writing time.'

As the above comments from students show, there is no *right* way for everyone – you have to discover what suits you.

Activity Ten

Make a quick note of those days of the week/times of the day when you think you are regularly going to be able to study. (You will be asked to look at this issue in more detail in Activity Fourteen.)

3.5 Periods of study

Most of us benefit from short frequent breaks in the course of our studies: every 30 to 40 minutes seems to be the norm. Pushing yourself beyond this can lead to your concentration lapsing and recall of what you have studied being much reduced. You don't have to have a cup of coffee *every* time of course: a bit of a stretch, a very short walk or a short meditation would be just as effective and much healthier! Others find that a fairly long period of study followed by a long break suits them best. Only you can decide which suits you. Once you have decided honestly which is best for you, try to stick to this and take breaks at the right time for the right reasons.

Activity Eleven

Make a note of the period of study that you know or think will suit you best.

If you are using a computer for a lot of your study activities it is advisable to take frequent short breaks rather than less frequent longer breaks. This helps prevent headaches, eyestrain and aches and pains in the hands, wrists, arms, neck, shoulders and back. Either formally build in other study activities at regular intervals or take informal breaks to stretch your arms and legs.

3.6 Time management

'I consider the most important aspect to be time management, whether in finding time to do the work or in keeping up with the studies at an even rate of progress. All other considerations pale into insignificance and tend to fall into place if you can manage the time.'

Having considered each of the issues in Sections 3.3 to 3.5 above, you are now in a strong position to get down to some serious consideration of how you are going to manage your time. Managing your time effectively and efficiently is one of the most difficult things to achieve – you need to become an expert at *creating* time. At the beginning of your studies the months may seem to stretch endlessly ahead of you but unless you make a plan and work to it, you will find that time goes by very fast.

Activity Twelve

Take a few minutes now to reflect upon *your* attitude towards time and on how well you use time. Note down a sentence or two that encapsulates these thoughts.

Tutor comment

'Students need to be aware of time management and of putting the whole study programme in a balance that includes family life and other factors.'

'Whilst time management would seem to be a good plan, I found I had to be "in the mood". However, when I was, I didn't want to take a break if things were going well (i.e. absorbing written material or working on assignments).'

'The conflicting demands of studying, work and home life must be known to all. It is far harder than being a full-time student on campus and in my mind should always be recognized as such.'

Commentary

Some people know that they are well organized and use their time effectively every day. Others will acknowledge that they are 'hopeless' at planning the use of their time – things 'just happen' and they react as best they can, as soon as they can. Most of us are somewhere between these two points.

Even when we try to discipline our use of time, other factors such as physical or mental tiredness or illness (our own or that of a member of our family) may come into play and we are thrown off course. This is inevitable and we need to build a degree of flexibility into any plan of study that we make. If we get too anxious about not being on schedule, that anxiety will be counterproductive. Our minds need to be capable of concentration and creativity. You are likely to need to modify your plan as the work progresses. Indeed, a key component of time management is regularly reviewing and amending schedules.

Most people would welcome the opportunity to have long periods of time to devote to their studies but that is a luxury enjoyed by the few. While it can be quite difficult to switch to study-related activities from doing other things, that is often the reality. Some people can combine the two, such as having ideas about your studies while doing household tasks or taking physical exercise. However, it is important to sometimes have a complete break from studying as well. You will be more productive if you're feeling mentally and physically refreshed. Digging in the garden for an hour or going for a brisk walk can work wonders.

'I found one of the problems...was reduced concentration after a busy working day. The coping strategies which I employed were to take exercise (to clear my head!), to have a break if ideas were not forthcoming and finally allowing myself *not* to study if I was over-tired.'

There are many aspects to time management, but there are two that we need to look at in detail here. The first is planning, as far as possible, the whole period of your study (one semester or one, two or three years or more?), dividing the years/semesters into parts (months?) and setting a timetable for yourself. The second is looking at a typical week within this period of time, and working out how you are to find a specified number of hours per week in which to study.

Study schedule

Taking the above commentary and your own inclinations into account, you need to draw up a realistic schedule for the whole of your study period. Remember that you must allow plenty of time for seminar preparation (if these are included) and for completing your assignments. The deadline for these will usually be imposed by external factors, such as the submission date of your assignment or a schedule for seminars – these should be stated in the student handbook. (You might, at a later stage, have to build in dates agreed with a group of your fellow students for informal support groups as well.) Using these dates you can calculate how many months/weeks you have between now and your deadlines and design a study schedule. This might simply be a list of tasks with proposed completion dates against them, but in order to see the relationship between different tasks it is better to draw up some form of table or chart which is divided up into monthly, weekly or even daily sections on one axis and by a series of tasks on the other (this is known as a *Gantt* chart).

Strategy: 'Planning a timetable for study and stick[ing] to it – easier said than done.'

'Put built-in emergency time near to [the] assignment date – there are always untoward situations which disrupt plans.'

One example of what a study schedule might look like is given in Figure 3.1. This example is of a typical UK two-year part-time master's programme schedule but, of course, you can adapt it to the particular programme and time schedule you are working with. You will see that it includes several months for writing a research dissertation. In fact the planning of your research project (where one is included in your course) and the literature search and preparatory reading for it should ideally start as soon as possible after the start of your course, and certainly no later than the start of the second year of a two-year part-time course. Once you have decided on your research topic, you will need to devise a more detailed study schedule specifically for your research project. Suggestions for what to include in that more detailed schedule, and a great deal more information about doing your research project, are provided in Chapter 10.

Tutor comment

'Students should think ahead in the planning of major events. Thus, [they] have to plan study time prior to assessments, assignments and examinations, planning in preparation for project activity, planning for library and other information acquisition time and so on.'

Year: Month	1:1	1:2	1:3	1:4	1:5	1:6	1:7	1:8	1:9	1:10	1:11	1:12	2:1	2:2	2:3	2:4	2:5	2:6	2:7	2:8	2:9	2:10	2:11	2:12
Introductory reading	→	→	→																					
Residential		→																						
Module 1				→	→	→																		
Assignment 1						→	→																	
Module 2								→	→	→														
Assignment 2										→	→													
Module 3												→	→	→										
Assignment 3														→	→									
Module 4																→	→	→						
Assignment 4																		→	→					
Dissertation																→	→	→	→	→	→	→	→	
Revision for finals																						→	→	→
Final written examinations																								→

FIGURE 3.1 Course study schedule
See Appendix two for a larger format of Figure 3.1.

Activity Thirteen

Now create a first draft of your own study schedule. You might want to add specific months or weeks (that is, dates) to your schedule or you may simply use the consecutive numbering as in the example in Figure 3.1. Although you will not be able to fill in the tasks in detail until you have finished working through this guide and perhaps received more information from your course tutor or fellow students, make a start on drafting your schedule now. You could even include the study of this guide as one of the tasks. You could also make an entry for talking to other students about how they are feeling about starting to study in this way, or a few months on, how they are coping. You could certainly include time for reading any recommended introductory texts and, of course, time for actually working through the learning materials.

Clearly many of the tasks will overlap and will therefore appear in the same week or month of the schedule. Some tasks will have to be completed consecutively rather than concurrently, since you won't be able to start one until you have completed the other. Following up relevant readings for each module, including time for reflection on what you have read, needs to be scheduled before beginning to write the assignments. You also need to build in some allowance for unexpected circumstances that slow you down.

Don't forget to allow for holidays (yours and other people's) and for any significant holy days and national holidays when people you wish to contact may not be available or facilities you might wish to use may not be accessible.

'Trying to schedule myself and assign time for studying and planning ahead helped me a lot in both studying and doing my assignments. Planning ahead makes me feel secure and that I have things under control.'

'Leave time for things to go wrong. Books may not be available, the computer might not work, a family problem may occur.'

Commentary

You need to be flexible within broad limits that are fixed externally (such as the dates for a tutor-marked assignment or the final examination) and regularly review your progress and amend your timetable. Once you start to add a lot of detail, you might be better buying a large, wall year planner so that you can fit everything in. You may prefer to have a planning document on your laptop or PC that you can update; you may find a simple *Excel* or *Word* document works well or there are low cost tools online such as *SmartSheet* or similar (www.smartsheet.com).

Remember, don't let this activity/process become a substitute for real work!

Weekly planner

Although some weeks will vary from others (especially if your work involves different shifts in different weeks), most of us have some sort of pattern to each week. It is usually possible, therefore, to build in study time at the same time or times each week. If you are on a mixed-mode course of study you will, of course, have certain fixed times when you need to attend your college or university for the face-to-face sessions.

'No such thing as balancing time demands, some weeks do more of one [activity] than [an]other.'

Activity Fourteen

You will probably find it helpful to sketch out a grid as in Figure 3.2 showing a typical week in your life, including first the things that you *have* to do each week, then those regular commitments that you would prefer not to have to drop while you are studying. Then try to add in time for studying in those places where you have free time. Sometimes it will be useful to have an extended period in which to study, but you could also make use of other shorter periods of time for doing a fairly short activity or going to the library on a regular basis, if one is within easy reach, to keep up to date by reading a journal in your subject area, for example. (Increasingly journals are available online, so you may not need to physically go to the library.)

In practice you may find your weeks turn out to be far from typical and you need to be flexible in the number of hours you spend each week on your study. Sometimes study activity will be more intensive than others, especially as a deadline for an assignment approaches. It is difficult to suggest how long you will need to spend studying each week as the amount varies tremendously from one student to another and from one course to another. The particular type and level of course on which you are enrolled will affect the time you need to study (anything from, say, six hours for a level one short course up to, perhaps, 20 hours a week for an intensive master's level programme). Even where your course handbook suggests an amount of time per week, some students will need to spend longer than others studying for the same course, as we all study at different paces and it will, perhaps, vary from one part of the course to another.

Student handbook

'...you will normally complete a module every 3 months, which involves approximately 150 hours of study time. It is suggested that students should spend 10–13 hours per week (or approximately 50 hours per month) studying in order to fulfil course requirements of completing one 15-credit module every 3 months. Modules will normally run for 10 weeks and be followed by a 2-week gap (rest period) between each module. On occasion, modules may run for longer periods or have a slightly longer gap between the next module if there are public holidays.'

Hour of the day	Monday	Tuesday	Wednesday	Thursday	Friday	Saturday	Sunday

FIGURE 3.2 Weekly planner

Note: Since people begin and end their days at different times no details have been included in the Hour boxes. A 16-hour day has been assumed, but if you sleep for considerably more or less than 8 hours you could always add or delete rows/hours accordingly in your own version of this planner. Half-hours could be created by dividing the boxes.

See Appendix three for a larger format of Figure 3.2, suitable for photocopying.

'I have found it best to plan to spend half to one hour a night regularly, with extra when possible. Most people can find half an hour during the day/evening, even when the kids are screaming. It is absolutely essential to be disciplined about spending the time, and spreading [it] out in this way makes it much easier to keep up. For commuters like myself, the time on the train/bus/tube can be very usefully spent – instead of reading the paper or the latest novel or sleeping!! If it's too chaotic at home, stay at work for an extra half hour. Spending regular time is probably the most important thing you can do.'

Commentary

It has to be said that what happens in reality often bears little resemblance to the neat timetable you have created. Many people have to learn to do more than one thing at a time. But when it comes to studying, most of us need to give it our undivided attention if we are going to do it well.

Clearly, if it looks as though you are not going to find enough time to study within your current lifestyle, something has got to change. It may be that you need to delegate more of your work tasks to colleagues, or domestic tasks to other members of your family (assuming that they are willing to take on more responsibility!). Or it may be a question of having to prioritize your tasks and ensure that those at the top of the list (that you really *have* to do) are definitely done at the beginning of the day or week, with the less essential ones dropping off the bottom of the list if necessary. Sometimes it may be necessary to make more radical changes if you are going to find time for study. A favourite pastime might have to be given up for a while, or you may have to renegotiate your working hours temporarily if there is no other way to find the time. (If you are completing your course to improve your skills in the workplace, your employer might be more sympathetic to this idea.) Whatever you decide to do, you have to be sure that this is the right thing and be firm in your efforts to find the necessary time to devote to your studies.

A useful aspect of the whole process is to reflect from time to time upon the plan that you made and compare what you actually did with what you had planned to do. This review can then be used to inform a revised plan, building in more realistic time allocations for different activities. Don't worry about having to change your plans sometimes – the important part of the whole activity is to help you to think strategically.

Keeping the balance

If you are following a mixed-mode course that includes some modules by distance learning alongside other modules by traditional face-to-face methods, you will need to take care that the distance learning elements don't get squeezed out by the pressure put upon you by your face-to-face tutors. You may find it helpful to request an occasional face-to-face tutorial with your distance learning module tutors (if they are available) even if this isn't actually required as part of your course attendance. You could also try to arrange an informal get-together from time to time with your fellow distance learning students. These two strategies can help keep alive the reality of your distance learning modules and serve as a reminder of the work that needs to be done for them. If you cannot meet up in person, use texting, tweets, *FaceTime*, *Skype* or emails to keep in touch with your tutors and your fellow students.

'Time: huge factor, not to be underestimated. To keep on a full-time job and study is very stressful. Hobbies and social life will have to be put on hold.'

3.7 How will you use your time?

Tutor comment
'Students need to manage their study time between reading learning materials, participating in online interactions and completing formative and summative assignments.'

It's all very well having decided exactly when you are going to have your times for study, but the really important part is using that time in the most effective way. Once you have decided when you are going to study in a particular week you will find it useful to set yourself specific tasks for that week. If an assignment is due at the beginning of the following week, there is little room for negotiation, but you could still set times for specific aspects of preparing for and writing up that assignment, such as: read Chapter 3 of...and make notes; write the first draft; edit the first draft; complete the bibliography; and so on. Don't forget to leave time for thinking and reflection too.

> 'Sometimes the task, e.g. [an] essay seemed overwhelming, therefore [it was] better to break down [the] task [in]to small achievable outcomes within...small study slots.'

If an assignment is not imminent it is all too easy to relax and think that you have all the time in the world for your studying, but it's amazing how quickly the weeks fly by. By setting yourself goals for each week/day or even by the hour (and meeting them!), you give your studying purpose and meaning and you will get a sense of achievement on completion of each task that will feed your motivation (especially if you give yourself little rewards). It is important to distinguish between those tasks that are essential, those that are desirable, and those that are neither but are nevertheless worthwhile.

> 'The most helpful practice I found for me in being a part-time student with a full-time job has been setting up a study routine and goals for each day/week. At the beginning of each [module] I look at the deadlines and chapter dates and decide when I need to have completed each section/project. At the end of each day of studying, I determine what I intend to do and accomplish at the end of the next one. That way, when I sit down to study, there is little transition time needed; I can start right up and I know if I'm on track.'

You need to be quite self-disciplined in this whole process, not just when it comes to starting on a particular task, but knowing when to stop as well. It is easy to stretch out a task you are thoroughly enjoying for several hours, knowing that you have a more difficult one to start next. In other words, you have to manage tasks as well as time. Sometimes you also have to accept that the work you produce is *good enough* for the purpose, even though it is not the *best* that you could have achieved given unlimited time and energy. This last point is reiterated by Simpson (private communication, 2015) who believes that sometimes 'Perfectionism can be the enemy of progress.' And for those occasions when you do find that you are beginning to fall behind in your schedule of reading your learning materials or writing assignments, Simpson (2013: 126) recommends 'the 3S model': what he calls 'the world's shortest guide on how to catch up'. It is only a 'stop gap' solution, to take away the pressure that builds up when it looks like you are going to miss a deadline; once you have caught up, you need to return to studying more carefully.

- S = Skim. Sometimes when you need to catch up, it's OK to skim what you're reading and just get a feel for it without reading it word for word.

- S = Skip. Sometimes it's OK to skip some materials altogether if you need to, and if it's not vital for the next bit of study.
- S = Scrape. If you're behind doing an assignment, then occasionally it's OK to aim to just scrape through. You don't have to do everything perfectly.

> 'Time planning is the most important aspect. Not to say "I've got a free day" and sit down after breakfast to plough through it till you drop. Be realistic. Set a study period of, say, two hours which will include a plan of what you hope to achieve in that time.'

There may be times when you genuinely need to revise your plans – studying is quite an unpredictable activity – but a regular review of what you plan and what you actually achieve is likely to be quite revealing. The occasional amendment is to be expected – but under-achievement of set goals every week may be cause for concern, and you may need to discuss this with your module or personal tutor.

For more detailed advice on time management there are some excellent online materials on the *LearnHigher* website at www.learnhigher.ac.uk/learning-at-university/time-management/. They include suggestions for working more effectively and a 24-hour time-use grid entitled 'How do you use your time?' if you want to get a proper (and honest!) idea of what really takes up your time. (Go to http://new.learnhigher.ac.uk/blog/wp-content/uploads/time_use_diary.pdf to download or print this useful one-sided document.)

3.8 Course-specific information

You will not be able to realistically make your plans until you know more about expectations. All students have them – of themselves and others – and others will have expectations of you. It is as well to identify them at an early stage and a good starting point is the course handbook or student guide. Such information will provide you with a better understanding of what you should expect from your educational institution and what might be expected of you. It should include details of when and how you can expect support from administrators, tutors and fellow students and of what your tutors' expectations will be of you. It should also include details of assignments and when these are due to be submitted and to whom.

Most of the information that is specific to your course should be sent to you by the course administrator in the school or department of the college or university where you are registered for your course. Details may be included in various letters that are sent out to students or in a course handbook or student guide that is distributed by the course administrator at the start of your studies or is available online. If you have received this guide to studying at a distance from the course administrator as part of an initial pack of materials, the chances are that you have already received other information as well. This section of the guide is provided to act as a checklist for you, so that you can identify if there is any information that you still need from the school/department. It is written in note form only. The notes are grouped together under various headings.

Activity Fifteen

It is recommended that you look through the checklist (below) at this point. Check the information you have previously received about your course and institution against these details, which provide an outline of what you should expect to receive. You can then make a note of information that you still need to obtain from your institution. I have also included real examples (in boxes) from various student handbooks, as well as some comments from tutors (in both this section, and elsewhere in the guide). Remember that these are examples from specific universities; your own course guide is likely to contain different information.

Programme/course information

- Programme website address
- Philosophy of the programme, including general aims and outcomes
- Programme outline/structure/content, including module dates, and how the programme will be delivered (teaching and learning methods)
- Module outlines, including learning outcomes
- Course materials you can expect to receive, and how and when you will receive them (detailed information about each module and resources specific to each module should be distributed a couple of weeks before the start of that module)
- General resources available to support the programme, such as textbooks/journals/websites/mailing lists/study skills materials
- Details of any costs that you will have to meet, such as for specialist equipment, summer school activities, field work, and so on

---

Difficulty: 'No space between modules.'

'Course moves too quickly without any breathing space between modules.'

Student handbook

'For each module a comprehensive set of learning materials is provided, divided into manageable learning units. For each learning unit a page is provided describing the learning objectives, the practical exercises and any other activities associated with the section. References are included for each section and a link provided to the University library's Distance Learning Services.

'A comprehensive set of learning materials is provided for each unit. Participants draw on this material during the learning activities, which are designed to build on the existing knowledge of participants. Tutor-directed, peer-directed and self-directed learning activities are used as appropriate.

'Tutor-directed activities include synchronous online tutorials for clarification and elaboration and asynchronous discussions via bulletin boards and email. Peer-directed activities are used to develop breadth of understanding, together with problem-solving and team-working skills. Generic study skills are developed through self-directed activities, such as additional reading and the posing of follow-up questions using email.'

Contacts for support

Difficulty: 'Clarification re. role of individual tutor and how much to access this support.'

Student handbook

Module tutor

'The module tutor will be responsible for the provision of technical support for the module, module tuition, the provision of feedback on assessments and the monitoring of student progression.'

Personal tutor

'The personal tutor will be responsible for the provision of continuity of support for the duration of the programme.'

Student

'The student is responsible for: her own computer equipment; returning assessments by the set deadlines; providing the module tutor with information on any factors, such as illness, that are affecting her progress.'

- Role of and support you can expect from academic tutors/'local' tutors/mentors/other students/course administrator/IT technicians/subject librarian/distance learning librarian
- Contact details (name/phone and fax numbers/email address) of each of the above (note that the details of students should not be given out to other students unless express permission has been sought from the students to do this)

Tutor comment

'Tutors expect students to try and work through the materials as much as they can before asking for help.'

- Office location and times of availability
- How quickly can you expect a reply to a phone message, text or email? Is there a limit to the number of emails you can send or the number of minutes of phone calls you can make per module?

Student handbook

'You can expect us to reply to your email communications within a reasonable period of time. Generally we aim to respond within 24 hours, or by the next working day, but this may not always be possible (e.g. during University closures). Similarly, we expect you to generally respond to email messages from the ODL Team within 24 hours or by the next working day, although we fully appreciate that this may not always be possible.'

'Another very helpful thing was to be in touch with another international student already enrolled in the program and studying from abroad. In September, prior to the start, Britain is on bank holiday which they take very seriously! It is not a custom here for people to be gone in mass any more than a day or two so I wasn't sure what the delays in response were due to. It made me nervous about the program (which it turns out is very well run). Communicating with this international veteran student eased my concerns. Also, I could hear from him some genuine experiences with the program which I also found helpful.'

'Email: essential for keeping in touch with tutors and other students. Email lists should be exchanged on 1st Study Day.'

Tutor comment

'Tutors expect students to help each other via discussion rooms and email.'

Tutorial details

- Face-to-face/electronic?
- How many and when?
- Record of meetings?

'As a distance learner, I missed having a peer group to share ideas with, exchange information and motivate one another. My institution, however, provided some residential events and conferences, and attending these when possible enabled me to make contacts and links and reduce the feeling of isolation.'

Attendance requirements

- What are they? When are they?
- Residential/day schools/summer schools/field trips? Are they compulsory and are there penalties for non-attendance?
- Do you have to attend face-to-face laboratory sessions or workshops as part of your course assessment?
- Information on what to do if you are likely to miss teaching sessions due to religious holidays, illness and so on.

'Distance learning served me well – the day at the university once a month was a useful focus and made the best of our time there.'

Don't forget to inform the course administrator in advance if you know you will be absent from a face-to-face session because of a religious holiday or for any other reason. Similarly, if you find that you cannot attend a session or keep to any externally imposed schedule of work or submission of assignments because of illness (yours or that of a member of your family), make sure you contact the course administrator. In some circumstances you will need an official sickness certificate from your doctor.

Hardware/software requirements

These should be specified if there are elements of e-learning/m-learning in your course (see Chapter 5 for more details on e-learning/m-learning).

- Computer, mobile device and Internet hardware, platform and specifications
- Software type and version, including of multimedia players and so on

Electronic learner support systems

- Are course materials available via the course website or virtual learning environment (VLE)?
- How do you obtain a username and password to access online materials?
- Are there any online learning materials provided by your university to help with general study skills?

Assessment specifications

Types of assessment

- Self, peer, tutor, formative, summative?
- Forms of assessment – essays/posters/oral presentations/reports/group work/lab work/MCQs?
- What are the assignments?
- Is there any choice in form of assessment or in exact subject of essays, projects and so on?

Student handbook

'This programme involves no formal examinations. Instead you will complete assessments associated with each module. These are designed to check your understanding, breadth and synthesis of knowledge while at the same time being intellectual, stimulating and challenging. A range of different assessment methods will be used including: essays, reports, projects, practical exercises, workbooks, *PowerPoint* slides and contribution to discussion threads.'

Submitting your work

> **Student handbook**
>
> 'It is important to remember to always keep copies of any work that you have submitted. If you are sending your assignments to the University . . . from your place of work or home obtain a certificate of posting from the post office (this is free) as proof of submission on time. However, we recommend that you send work by recorded delivery.'

- To whom? Where? When?
- How? Paper – in person/by post? Electronically – email attachments, web forms?
- Details of how work should be presented – margin sizes/fonts/style of references
- Is it possible to submit draft assignments for tutor comments before the final submission date?
- Will you be sent a reminder that your assignment is due?
- Penalties for late submission? These can be severe, even to the extent that no marks at all will be awarded, or there may be a sliding scale, where you lose more marks the later it is. (See quotes from Student Handbooks later in this chapter.)
- What should you do if you know that you are likely to miss a deadline due to illness or other extenuating circumstances?
- Are there any 'mitigating circumstances' that would be taken into account if you were late submitting your assignment?
- What is your institution's policy on plagiarism?

> **Student handbook**
>
> 'Plagiarism is the theft or expropriation of someone else's work without proper acknowledgement, presenting the material as if it were one's own. Plagiarism is a serious offence and the consequences are severe.'

> **Tutor comment**
>
> '. . . plagiarism, by far the biggest problem in an online course. Despite plain warnings and instruction as to the precise nature of plagiarism, some students will compose an assignment by unattributed concatenation of Internet material. Assignments should wherever possible be uniquely personalized to the student.'

Marking/assessment criteria

- What are they?
- Is poor spelling or grammar penalized?

- Are there extra marks for good presentation?
- What percentage of the marks is awarded for each assignment within each module?
- Is it possible to see examples of assignments submitted by previous students?
- Information about classifications of qualifications and marks/grades required to achieve them, for example, 'first class honours degree'

Student handbook

'All coursework will be assessed using the following Grading Scale:
Distinction – 70% and more
Pass with Merit – 60–69%
Pass – 50–59%
Fail – Less than 50%'

Student handbook

Types of assessment used for different modules

i. One seminar presentation (20%); two 4000-word fully referenced essays (80%)
ii. A one-hour written examination (20%); four assignments of 2000 words each (4 × 20%)
iii. 1500-word written assignment (20%); a presentation (20% plus 10% by peer review); four web-based worksheets (4 × 5%); and end of module two-hour examination (choice of essay plus MCQ test) (30%)

Difficulty: 'Uncertainty over standard required.'

'Essay writing: a help would be to see samples of style expected (from previous groups).'

Feedback on assessments

- What form will the feedback take?
- How soon will that feedback be given?

Student handbook

'Feedback on formative and summative assessments will be provided by using the bulletin board or email as appropriate. All students are invited to discuss the feedback on their assessments.'

Progress

- When/how often will my progress be monitored?
- Will review meetings be held?
- Are there SAQs to monitor my own progress?

Student handbook

'The monitoring of progression through a module will be the responsibility of the module tutor. This will include the monitoring of contributions to the bulletin boards to assess group participation. In cases where illness or pressures of work have led to lack of progress, the student may be allowed to withdraw from the module and to re-enrol at a later date. Assessments are structured, requiring students to provide regular reports on their progress.'

University/college information

- Information about university/college facilities and services, such as careers, welfare, library, study skills unit, language centre, equality unit, students' union, and so on
- Map of the university or college campus and of the department where you will go if you do have to attend face-to-face sessions

---

'If you're eligible to join the Student Union, you can take up their offers on discounts on study materials, books, IT equipment etc. If you manage this well, it can save quite a bit of money over the period of study.'

Your feedback/module evaluation

- How and when should you submit this?

Student handbook

'We value student feedback very highly. After completion of each module you will be provided with a module evaluation form. Students will not be permitted to access learning materials for the next module without first completing and returning these forms to us.'

Student handbook

'All students will be invited to anonymously complete a feedback form. The results will be reviewed by the Programme Committee and appropriate action will be taken.'

A note on rules, regulations and complaints procedures

Student handbook

'If you do not inform us of problems with meeting deadlines, we are required by the University to deduct marks for work submitted after an agreed deadline. For each late item of work, University rules require 5 full marks to be deducted for each calendar day that the work is late, up to a maximum of two calendar weeks (or 50 full marks). If a piece of coursework is not handed in by the end of two calendar weeks, a zero mark will be awarded for this work.'

Each institution has its own rules and regulations about attendance, missed deadlines for submission of assignments, non-attendance at examinations, plagiarism and so on. Make sure that you are familiar with these at the start of your course. They should be available in your institution's student handbook, which may be available in paper and/or web format. Also available should be details of the procedure to follow if you have a complaint about any aspect of your programme or institution. However, my advice would be that you always take your complaint to the course leader (possibly via the course administrator) in the first instance. Very often misunderstandings, actions, omissions and so on can be rectified far more easily and effectively by informal means, and with less stress for all concerned. It is, nevertheless, your right to take the formal route, should you wish to do so.

Student handbook

'Students are reminded that late submission will only be permissible in exceptional circumstances. The deadlines for coursework to be handed in are stated in the module calendar. Coursework should be handed in to the Module Co-ordinator by using the coursework submission system. A failure to submit coursework on the date stipulated, and in the absence of an extension agreed by the member of staff concerned, will result in a fixed penalty of 10% reduction of the coursework marks. If the coursework is more than one week late the penalty will be increased to 25% and this increases by 25% for each week (or part thereof) overdue.'

Student handbook

Complaints procedure: informal procedure

'Complaints should be made as soon as possible, and in any case within one month, after the event or actions (or lack of actions) which prompted the complaint. The complaint should be made in the first instance to the Programme Director, who will look into the matter and shall give a response to the complainant normally within 10 working days following receipt of the complaint.'

A note on registration and payment of fees

If you have registered for your course you will have already found your way through the maze that is your institution's registration procedure. If you have not yet registered, or are in the process of doing so, take heart – you will get there in the end.

Many traditional colleges and universities are still in a transitional period regarding the introduction of flexible procedures for the registration of distance learners and for the payment of fees, and the procedures at many institutions are still rather cumbersome. However, online systems are now more often the norm and should make registration easier. If you experience any difficulties in this area, my advice is always to contact the administrator of your specific course and they will intervene on your behalf.

And finally...

'Remember that you are a student of the university. You are entitled to use university and student union facilities. I found it important that the course staff sent us details of university activities.'

'Go to the graduation ceremony. You earn that day.'

While the above suggestion about using the facilities at the university or college is clearly more relevant to students with fairly regular attendance at their institution, a lot of useful information for all students, including distance learners, is usually provided via the institution's website. In addition there are a number of other ways of being in touch with and obtaining support from various people. These are explored in the next chapter.

Chapter summary

In this chapter you have:

- Considered various study patterns that people use
- Made decisions about where and when you would prefer to study
- Prepared a draft study schedule for the whole course
- Sketched out a plan of your weekly study pattern
- Checked the information you have previously received about your course and institution against the checklist provided
- Identified information you still need to obtain
- Learned more about what you can expect from your educational institution and about what your tutors and others will expect from you

4 Getting support

Introduction • Coping strategies • Support from your tutor(s) • Support from other students • Support from the course administrator • Support from family and friends • Support from those at work • Support from other agencies • Taking a break • Chapter summary

Introduction

You may feel that you are quite happy to get on with your studying totally on your own and don't need any support or input from anyone. Some people do manage to be fully independent learners for the duration of their course and simply turn up at the set time to take a formal examination and pass with flying colours. However, these are certainly the exception. Most of us need support from someone at some stage in our studies (and I speak from the experience of being a distance learner as well as a tutor of distance learners).

Feelings of confidence and enthusiasm are likely to be mixed with some feelings of doubt and apprehension when embarking upon any new project, and starting a distance learning course is likely to create a similar mix too. If in the course of your studies the negative feelings begin to dominate, however, it is important to do something about it, as they could reduce your self-confidence and lead to a downward spiralling in your studies. That's when you need to know who to turn to for support. Talking about your feelings will help to give you some sort of perspective about them and hopefully provide ideas for overcoming the problems leading to the negativity. Try to remind yourself that this period of studying will not last forever. Try too to build in some time for rest and relaxation alongside your working and studying life.

'My leisure time was reduced while distance learning but I accepted this, as it was only for a comparatively short span of my life.'

4.1 Coping strategies

In spite of our best efforts to remain positive, we all have times in our lives when we feel that we can't cope. The pressure of studying on top of everything else that life throws at us can sometimes be in danger of tipping the balance. Strategies for coping with (and even for enjoying!) studying are suggested throughout this guide, and the practical suggestions in Chapter 3 should help you to feel more in control. But, however organized we are, we sometimes need someone else to help us to see our way through a difficult patch.

'At the beginning of the course I was terrified, but now I can manage my stress. The help of the other students is enormous.'

Many distance learning students have found that their fellow students can provide the encouragement and advice that are needed (even when communicating only by email or text messaging). At other times you may need the help of your tutors. Very often there is a practical solution that will help release the pressure of the moment, perhaps by being directed towards some relevant source materials for your essay or by being allowed a short extension when an assignment is due in (although this can sometimes simply prolong the stress). Also, don't underestimate the help that the course administrator can give you. Sometimes, however, the only solution to relieve the pressure is to simply get on and complete the task that is hanging over you.

Student handbook

'Deadlines are designed to help you plan your course workload. It is essential that you try to keep to the published deadlines for each module. If you do not keep to these deadlines you will create a backlog and are likely to experience problems in catching up. It will also make it difficult to manage the rest of your course workload.'

'It is possible that at some stage you may experience difficulties in meeting a deadline due to exceptional work or household pressures. If you do experience problems please contact us as soon as possible. If necessary, we can arrange to discuss workload planning with you. We are happy to discuss workload problems, help you develop a revised work plan, and discuss extensions if appropriate and in exceptional circumstances (i.e. illness, bereavement, and unexpected work commitments).'

The first, very important, step to finding a solution to a problem is that you have to acknowledge that there is a problem and identify as precisely as possible what the problem is. Expressing a general feeling of being overwhelmed or too busy or too tired will not help anyone to help you – you need to try to be specific. If you can do this, you may even recognize for yourself what you need to do to address the problem. Very often in the process of 'talking something through' with another person we can find our own solutions.

There are many people within and outwith your own educational institution who can provide much of the support that you will need to successfully complete your programme of study.

4.2 Support from your tutor(s)

'You can't have enough contact with staff – it keeps you sane and on the right track...students who are in distance learning need much more contact with tutors etc. than regular university students.'

Keeping in touch with your tutors will provide your link with the people who can speak with authority on any aspect of the academic content of your course. (You may have several tutors if your course consists of several modules.) Although the benefits of getting support from other students are many, it is your tutors who are experts in their fields and who will often (but not always) be the ones who have written the learning materials. It is also your tutors who will interpret your own ideas on all aspects of the course, marking your assignments and ultimately deciding on a grade for your work: it is as well to seek feedback from them at various stages throughout each module rather than leaving it to the formal assessments.

Tutor comment

'Students [should] look to their self-interest when needing advice and help. This is done by regular contact with the tutor. This contact needs to be student driven with supervisor co-operation.'

The opportunities provided to contact your tutors will vary from course to course: they may include or exclude particular methods of communication, such as phone or email, and may have a time limit imposed. You need to establish at a very early stage what your opportunities are (see Section 3.8). Whatever means of communication are available you need to do some preparation before any substantial contact with tutors (or indeed with anyone else from whom you need help – such as your workplace mentor or the course administrator). You need to be clear yourself about the points you wish to discuss – you may find it helpful to write them down beforehand. This will help to ensure that neither your time, nor that of your tutor, is wasted.

Tutor comment

'I also ask students to make sure that they have provided enough information in a plea for assistance so that a proper response can be formulated. (For instance, you tend to get "I loaded the program onto my PC and it won't run. What am I doing wrong?")'

Your tutor is the key person to provide information about new resources available in a specific subject field (journal articles, websites and so on). They are also best placed to give their views on new developments in the field or to help you discover your views on certain issues. This will help you develop your own ideas further. The feedback you receive from your tutors to your formal and informal assessments is crucial. Assessment is not just about a process of making judgements and allocating grades: it is another opportunity to learn, if you carefully consider the feedback provided.

'I found the programme very interesting and learned a lot. I never thought distance learning could be so rewarding. I am particularly impressed by the attention and guidance given by the course tutors.'

Tutor comment

'As a distance learning tutor you need to be aware of distance learners' needs and provide appropriate support and guidance.'

'Thinking back [over] the past four years, I could not imagine without your great help [being] able to finish the degree programme. You are my mentor. It was a long four years and I have gone through big changes in my life, but I finally did it with your kind guidance and instructions.'

Tutor comment

'As a distance learning tutor I have learned a great deal about different working practices and cultures. This has been a really fulfilling experience.'

4.3 Support from other students

Some course tutors organize formal learning groups or sets for their students' mutual support, but even where this is not the case, you will find it is well worth the effort to set up something on an informal basis.

'Peer support was the greatest asset.'

'...the key issue...is the lack of contact with both students and tutors/lecturers. Of course email is a great invention, and it helps. But there's no substitute for actually meeting other people and discussing things generally – whether it's course related or simply the price of coffee in Starbucks.'

The benefits of being in touch with other students are several. The benefits of meeting together face-to-face, if at all possible, will usually outweigh the difficulties of making all of the arrangements to be away from home for a couple of days for a short residential session and the hassle and cost of the travelling. However, you can still be supported by and support other students whom you will never meet face-to-face.

'...a...programme via distance learning draws people together through adversity. Fellow students are a strong support.'

Why do you need other students?

Strategy: 'Being able to talk through issues, concerns, ideas with another student on a regular basis.'

Others can help you to learn

As referred to in Section 2.8, talking things through with others can constitute the 'apply' part of the learning cycle. Having to express the ideas that have been swimming around in your own head for some time is an excellent way of refining those ideas, especially when others are prepared to listen carefully and give constructive feedback. It also provides the opportunity for you to become familiar with using academic language specific to your course or subject discipline.

'Keeping in contact with other students in the same course and discussing our studying problems together gives me a feeling that I am not alone.'

It is still generally regarded in most cultures that the academic tutor is *the* expert in his or her field. It is, however, becoming increasingly accepted that they are not necessarily the sole authority on a subject, and that fellow students or peers on a course can also make a significant contribution to the construction of knowledge. This is especially true where the students involved have a wide and varied experience of the workplace and of life in general.

'At times there were feelings of isolation and lack of contact with others. This is when a list of willing fellow students' telephone numbers and emails can be so helpful. My closest friend was not usually feeling low when I was, and vice versa. The mutual support was invaluable.'

You might have informal discussions or you may agree in advance that all members of the group will read a particular journal article or section of the learning materials that will form the basis of your discussion. Group members may be willing to discuss an assignment topic before you each start to write it, or to read each other's draft assignments before submission. Increasingly some form of group work is becoming part of the formal assessment requirement for a course. You will, therefore, no longer have the option of choosing whether or not to participate in this form of activity, as it will become a necessity, even if your natural inclination might be to work on your own. We will look in more detail at strategies for working with others in Section 9.1.

> **Tutor comment**
>
> '[There is the opportunity for] interaction with fellow students through the website facilities provided for the programme participants, cooperation in joint project activities and in social gatherings during workshop and other university attendance periods. Enjoy the experience. It is worthwhile.'

Others can lift your spirits and boost your confidence

Isolation can be very destructive. The general support that is available from other students on the same course can give a great boost to your flagging morale, especially when you find that others have found a particular unit of the course materials just as difficult as you have. And even if you are the only one not to have grasped a particular concept, you are very likely to learn by listening to others discussing it. Conversely you can help your fellow students by making an input to group discussion.

> 'Study days gave me useful information but also allowed me contact with other students to discuss problems and let off steam.'

Others can motivate you

If you know you have a group meeting (virtual or face-to-face) scheduled for a couple of weeks' time this may give you the push that you need to get through the next unit of materials. You can then talk things through with others with the same study interests as yourself before you have to express your own ideas on paper in the form of a written assignment for your tutor. Enthusiasm is infectious.

> 'I befriended a fellow student and we supported each other over the telephone. We both had times of self-doubt, but negative thoughts were soon dispersed, as we listened to each other's concerns and offered encouragement to one another.'

Meeting others can be fun

Making friends with others on your course can be one of the most rewarding aspects of studying. Meeting others can be an important social occasion as well as an intellectual one.

How can you keep in touch?

> 'It is of course possible to contact other students – but it is not like having informal discussion with a larger group round coffee etc.'

Since communication with others in a group is more effective if you can actually meet face-to-face, organizing an informal study group in your geographical area, even if one isn't organized officially by your university or college, is likely to prove very worthwhile. Several courses have an occasional face-to-face meeting, often at the start of each module; it is then much easier to contact others subsequently by various other means. Where students on your course are so dispersed that it just isn't possible to meet, try to exchange phone numbers or email addresses, or, if not already an expected part of your coursework, ask the course tutor to organize telephone conferencing, computer conferencing or a forum or discussion group via the course website. Very often someone poses a question via such a forum that you really wanted to ask, but didn't like to, for fear of appearing ignorant. Remember that we can only learn what we acknowledge that we don't already know.

> **Tutor comment**
>
> 'Students should be aware that studying at a distance can be quite lonely. However, online discussion rooms can greatly alleviate these feelings of loneliness.'

As mobile technology becomes far more prevalent in society in general and in education in particular and adds to the convenience of using social media, there is ample opportunity to keep in touch with other students by both formal and informal means. In addition to the 'official' discussion rooms, *Facebook* and *Google Groups* are becoming increasingly popular means of communication between students, helping to reduce the feelings of isolation. The use of *tweets*, *texts* and *Facetime* are also increasing in popularity in an educational as well as a social context. (See Section 5.6 for more details of the use of mobile technology in learning.)

> 'One of the most useful things I have found is developing a group of friends on the same course, with whom you can share problems. With most people being on email at home or work, this is very easy.'

4.4 Support from the course administrator

'...the administrator was indefatigable in advising, answering queries, seeing we got material, putting us in touch with...and other personnel.'

Your first point of contact with your college or university is probably with the course administrator for the course on which you enrol (they may be called something other than this, such as course secretary or admissions officer). She or he will very likely be able to deal with most of your queries about the course: dates of attendance at the institution for short courses, submission dates for assignments, the format in which assignments must be submitted, how you can contact your tutors or other students, and so on.

A friendly face (or voice) can make all the difference when you're feeling as if you don't belong or are a bit swamped with the many aspects of your studies with which you have to cope. A quick email or short phone call will usually be enough to get things sorted. Details of who to contact and how and when to contact them should be included in the course handbook. (The friendly face of one particular course administrator at the University of Leeds was mentioned more than once in the comments collected from students for this guide.)

4.5 Support from family and friends

'I feel it is important to enlist the help and co-operation of other family members and friends.'

'Good family support was available to me and without this I don't think I would have coped.'

Included in the comments received from students are many that emphasize the importance of support from those closest to you. It may be tempting to try to keep everything to do with studying totally separate from the rest of your life, but (as was mentioned earlier) your studying will affect and place demands on others. The wise student is the one who cultivates mutual understanding about their studies with those with whom they live and socialize. If you are fortunate enough to have people who take an interest in what you are doing, don't shut them out. They may not be able to empathize with you at a subject-specific level but they will be able to give emotional and practical support. That said, you also need to ensure that they know when you want to be left alone to study. But having someone cook you an evening meal at the end of a full day at work followed by a couple of hours study is wonderful!

'Be amazingly organized. Sit the family down and realistically look at the essential household jobs, who is going to do them and when. Be realistic, they may not get done as you would do them, but they will get done. Little and often. Obtain all the local takeaway menus, and buy iron-free clothes. I paid my older children to Hoover, empty the dishwasher, use the washing machine and make the tea. I was broke, but these things did get done.'

4.6 Support from those at work

This may be of a formal nature through some form of mentoring scheme or it may simply be a colleague or line manager taking a helpful interest in what you are doing. A growing number of organizations operate a system of workplace mentors who are responsible for supporting the development of one or more colleagues. If you already have such a mentor they may regard supporting you in your studies as an extension of this role. Such a role will complement that of your academic tutor. He or she will help you make connections between your academic course and your workplace.

'Mentorship was new to me, but as a distance learner I identified a senior [colleague] in my organization [who] provided a mentor role throughout the study. This added support from a different angle, and was constructive in enabling correct action to be taken in times of stress. It also helped me to identify the key people to speak to regarding work-based difficulties and study, and was supportive in negotiating for time to undertake the research part of the [degree].'

A mentoring scheme will usually include the following characteristics:

- Mentors exist to help you to explore your options. They are there to facilitate that exploration, not to tell you what to do. As such, a mentor is more likely to be a colleague (preferably with some years of experience) rather than a line manager.
- Mentors are there to give practical guidance, including helping you (the mentee) to access resources and identify opportunities for promotion or even for a change of career direction.
- A mentor's role is to understand you and help you to make choices, but they are not there to judge.
- They are, however, there to help you to identify your strengths and weaknesses, to formulate goals (perhaps to address those weaknesses) and to monitor your progress towards those goals.
- Potentially, mentoring will lead to changes in your life and to you taking action. Your mentor is there to support you whilst those changes are taking place.
- Learning will be at the centre of that change.

Whether or not such a formal mentoring scheme exists in your organization, if your studies are related to your work, the importance of forging a good relationship with those from whom you will need information or co-operation cannot be overemphasized. They could be crucial in helping you to gain access to information and people within your organization that are needed to help you complete your assignments. They may also be willing to give comments on your assignments before you hand them to your tutor, give you ideas of topics for discussion or group work, or supervise you while you practise skills that you are learning. You may even find that you are entitled to a limited amount of study leave.

'It may be appropriate to suggest that students negotiate more than the set study days off from work for the course. Perhaps applying for funding to enable "backfill", etc.'

Even if your studies are not directly related to your work, it would be as well to talk to your line manager about what you are intending to do before you begin. You may need her or his understanding and support at some stage, such as when you need to take a day's leave in order to meet a looming deadline for an assignment. You need to be clear about whether or not it is acceptable to use IT or photocopying facilities at work for study-related tasks, and if these can be done in working hours or only after the end of the working day.

Strategy: 'Having helpful colleagues.'

Activity Sixteen

Make enquiries about any mentoring schemes that are in place at work, and find out if these will specifically support you in your studies. Even if a formal scheme does not exist, fix up a time to talk to work colleagues and/or your line manager about your studies. Make a note of those areas where there was agreement about what assistance/support you might expect.

4.7 Support from other agencies

If you identify that you have problems with your study skills, it may be possible that one or more of the resource books or websites listed at the end of this guide can provide the help that you need. Check out the library website of your own education provider for study skills (especially information literacy) support too. Many institutions have study skills support centres or units. Although it might be harder to access help from people there when you are a distance learner, many institutions recognize this and most offer some skills resources and tips online.

If you need more study skills support, many universities offer study skills workshops on a particular aspect of study (writing a dissertation, using the library, or other research skills); you may decide you would benefit from making time to attend these, if you can practically do so.

If you feel that you need more in-depth support, it may be possible to obtain help from the guidance or counselling service at your institution or students' union (if there is one), though again it will be more difficult to do so when you are not attending face-to-face. Nevertheless, do contact the agency that you feel is most appropriate (information should be available on the institution's website if it is not in the student handbook). As a student of the institution where you are registered you are entitled to services equivalent to (if sometimes different from) services to other students.

Disabled students

Legislation in the UK and elsewhere makes it illegal to refuse to serve, offer a lower standard of service or offer a service on worse terms to a disabled student. This means that if a disabled student finds it unreasonably difficult to use a service, an educational institution has to make reasonable changes to that service. This should result in all physical places/buildings being made accessible, as well as departmental, faculty and institutional websites, intranets, virtual learning environments (such as *Blackboard*) and all other resources – not just electronic/ digital. In other words, learning materials in whatever form must also be provided in a suitable format to be accessible to all students. In the first instance, you should contact your programme leader or course administrator if you need any of the course materials in a different format from that provided as standard.

Some education providers have a special service unit where disabled students can receive information and support for their studies from a Disability Officer or Learning Support Adviser. (Information on such a service should be included in the student handbook.) Staff in those units will sometimes liaise with individual departments on behalf of students if they have not been able to obtain materials in a suitable format or at an appropriate time (such as reading lists well in advance of the start of a module) or help you to obtain funding for a diagnostic assessment (for example, for dyslexia).

In addition to or instead of such in-house support, there are a number of organizations and resources that are available to students (and prospective students). SKILL (the National Bureau for Students with Disabilities, www.skill. org.uk) used to provide free information and advice for individual disabled students (and for people contacting them on behalf of disabled students) and for professionals in education who work with disabled students. Although there is still information available on the SKILL website, the organization itself closed in 2011. However, DisabilityRightsUK is now providing some of the services that SKILL used to provide. Their website can be found at www.disabilityrights.org. They offer a disabled students helpline on 0800 328 5050, which is free to use from most phones, for students studying in England. You can also email them on students@disabilityrights.org. They also offer education-related fact sheets. If you live outside of England, it is definitely worth searching online for details of a disabled students' service in your country or region.

See also Sections 5.18 and 5.19 for information and help with technology for blind and partially sighted people, and on accessibility of electronic learning materials.

Dyslexia

Some adults when returning to study discover that difficulties they have had with learning for many years can be attributed to dyslexia. Dyslexia is a specific learning difficulty that can cause problems with reading and spelling. It can also cause problems with some skills in mathematics. It is estimated that approximately 10 per cent of the population may be dyslexic. Dyslexia is not linked with lesser intelligence, but rather with poor performance of physical connections between some areas of the brain, that is, it is neurological. 'People with dyslexia often have strengths in reasoning, in visual and creative fields...' (Dyslexia Action website: www.dyslexiaaction.org.uk). Dyslexia was recognized under the Disability Discrimination Act in 1995 and specifically mentioned in the Equality Act in 2010. Educational organizations have a duty to make reasonable adjustments to ensure that those affected by dyslexia are not disadvantaged compared to their peers.

Both the British Dyslexia Association (BDA) and Dyslexia Action provide information and support for people with dyslexia and literacy difficulties. Dyslexia Action can help you to arrange a formal face-to-face assessment with one of their own assessors (specialist teachers) or with a Chartered Psychologist. You can also arrange your own assessment by contacting your local independent Dyslexia Association (see www.bdadyslexia.org.uk/membership/local-dyslexia-associations/lda-directory). There will be a fee for this assessment, but some students may be entitled to a free assessment. (You would need to inform your education provider of your assessment beforehand to get any financial help that might be available.) If you think you might be dyslexic there is a very brief 'Adult Dyslexia Checklist' on the British Dyslexia Association website at www.bdadyslexia.org.uk/common/ckeditor/filemanager/userfiles/Adult-Checklist.pdf, plus more information for adults at www.bdadyslexia.org.uk/dyslexic/dyslexia-and-specific-learning-difficulties-in-adults.

It is also possible to take online dyslexia screening tests that are endorsed by the BDA. One is called 'Spot Your Potential' and is available for a fee at www.lucid-research.com/p/145/spot-your-potential/?affiliateid=4. This 'will help you discover your personal strengths as well as indicating if you have dyslexia' (from the website). Another is Screening+ Profiler, available (also for a fee) at http://doitprofiler.com/screeningplus-profiler.aspx. This uses a suite of tools which 'not only identifies dyslexia-type traits and difficulties' but also seeks 'to maximise your skills and understand the challenges relating to many aspects of life'. A screening test will provide an indication of the possibility of dyslexia but a proper diagnosis can only be obtained by undergoing a full assessment by a qualified practitioner. Such tests can be used therefore to determine whether or not a full psychological or diagnostic assessment would be warranted. If a screening test indicates that you are not in fact showing signs of being dyslexic, this could save you the much greater cost of getting a full diagnostic assessment. However, if the screening test suggests that you may be dyslexic, you would be well advised to get a full assessment so that you receive a detailed report, containing practical advice.

The report might enable you to get help in some of the following ways:

- Give you suggestions for improving some or all of the following skills: spelling, report writing, study skills, revision and exam techniques, time management and general organization
- Highlight your strengths and help you to achieve your full potential
- Help you to be able to explain to others about your dyslexia, which might stop people criticizing your poor spelling or maths
- Help you to get reading lists well in advance for your modules (although this would be helpful for all students, not just those with dyslexia)
- Help you to get more time for your written assignments and in your examinations
- Help you be able to make special arrangements for submitting assignments and sitting examinations, such as using a computer with a spell checker
- Help you to get someone to help you take notes if you have to attend any lectures as part of your course
- To get funding and help from your education provider, including funding to buy a computer that will support special software to help dyslexic students to read on screen more easily. (Such support is sometimes only available for full-time students. In the UK you can apply for a Disabled Students Allowance from your Local Education Authority (LEA) if you are studying at least 50 per cent of a full-time degree course. Postgraduate students and Distance Learners are also eligible for this allowance.)

(Information for the above checklist came from the British Dyslexia Association and Dyslexia Action web pages and from SKILL.)

You would need to show your assessment report to your course director and/or LEA officer if you wish to obtain specific support to help with your learning as a dyslexic student. Some students prefer to implement coping mechanisms themselves and choose not to disclose their disability to anyone else. For details of other study resources available for dyslexic and other disabled people, see the 'Guides for disabled students' in the Further Resources section at the end of the book.

4.8 Taking a break

If, in spite of all the support available to you, your personal circumstances mean that it is just too difficult to continue with your studies, it is a good idea to try to negotiate a break and to return to studying when things improve. There is no guarantee that this flexibility will be available on your particular programme of study, but it is definitely worth exploring the possibility. It is much better both for you and for your institution that you complete your studies eventually, rather than 'dropping out' all together, even if it takes you a little longer than originally expected.

Student handbook

'You can choose to withdraw permanently or temporarily for a designated period of time. In the case of the latter, you must indicate a firm intention to resume study and continue your course when your personal circumstances change. Temporary withdrawal will generally be granted on either medical or personal grounds.'

Be aware, however, that as the following example shows, there may still be an overall time limit for completing the whole programme.

Student handbook

Temporary leaver status

'If you are experiencing problems, you may apply for temporary leaver status. If this is granted then your studies are suspended for an agreed period of time. Registration with the [institution] is temporarily withdrawn and you could lose access to the library and other resources. You may then, with the permission of the Programme Director, resume your studies at a later date. However, you should be aware that programme awards will only be made if you complete within 5 years of the initial registration notwithstanding any period of temporary leave.'

Chapter summary

In this chapter you have:

- Considered which coping strategies might be most appropriate for your particular situation
- Learned how previous students have benefited from the support of others (tutors, students, work colleagues, family and friends)
- Investigated what support might be available to you during your studies, including specialist support for disabled students

5 Technology for learning

Introduction • What do we mean by e-learning and m-learning? • What skills are needed for e-learning and m-learning? • Glossary of terms • Online learning • Email and mailing lists • Mobile learning (m-learning) • Virtual learning environments (VLEs) • Discussion rooms/conference boards/bulletin boards • Self-assessment questions (SAQs) • Lectures, demonstrations and podcasts • Videoconferencing • Blogs and vlogs • Wikis • RSS feeds or news feeds • Other forms of e-learning • Viruses, security and backing up work • Health and safety issues of technology use • Help with technology for blind and partially sighted people • Accessibility of electronic learning materials • A cautionary tale • Conclusion • Chapter summary

'The most important factor – get a computer and learn how to email and use [the] Internet.'

Introduction

The advent of the Internet and associated technologies in recent years has had a major impact on learning. The growth of the Internet can be gauged by looking at the statistics. The United Nations' telecommunications agency, the International Telecommunication Union (ITU), in its 'The World in 2014: ICT Facts and Figures' (2014) states:

> The new figures show that, by the end of 2014, there will be almost 3 billion Internet users, two-thirds of them coming from the developing world, and that the number of mobile-broadband subscriptions will reach 2.3 billion globally. Fifty-five per cent of these subscriptions are expected to be in the developing world.

> Internet [use] has reached 40% globally, 78% in developed countries and 32% in developing countries.

Globally, there are 4 billion people not yet using the Internet and more than 90% of them are from the developing world.

This international picture reminds us that the Internet is not yet ubiquitous. Nevertheless in the more developed parts of the world (see, for example, the statistics for Great Britain below) rapidly expanding use of the Internet means that you are likely to encounter some elements of learning technology in your studies if you are registered with an educational institution in those parts of the world.

- In Great Britain, 22 million households (84%) had Internet access in 2014, up from 57% in 2006.
- Access to the Internet using a mobile phone more than doubled between 2010 and 2014, from 24% to 58%.
- In 2014, 38 million adults (76%) in Great Britain accessed the Internet every day, 21 million more than in 2006, when directly comparable records began.

(Office for National Statistics (ONS) for the UK 2014)

However, even in the more developed world where access to the Internet via a fixed broadband connection or using a mobile phone or other mobile device is rapidly increasing, still not everyone makes regular use of a computer. For study purposes, many valuable learning resources continue to be distributed as printed materials or as radio or television broadcasts (although these are often made available via the Internet as well). There are increasingly, however, elements of e-learning (learning electronically), or m-learning (learning electronically via a mobile phone or other mobile device), in most programmes of study in higher education. In this chapter you will explore the implications of that for your studies.

Whilst I acknowledge that ownership of, or regular access to, a desktop personal computer (PC) or laptop may still be a luxury that not every distance learner can afford, it is becoming increasing likely that you will either already or soon possess a mobile device that could be used to access the Internet. Even if you don't yet have a smartphone or have access to a PC at home, it is possible that you could arrange to use one at a local learning centre or library or at your place of work. It should be made clear in the information you receive from your course provider exactly what elements (if any) of learning technology you will be required to use.

Many of you using this book prior to or at the start of a return to learning after a gap of some years may well be what Baroudi and Marksbury call 'digital immigrants' (2013: 373) when it comes to using technology for learning. However, as the years go on, the ubiquity of mobile technology in other aspects of your life will probably mean that this becomes no longer true. For others that very ubiquity of mobile phones (smartphones) and other mobile devices, such as tablets and laptops, already means that inevitably you are expecting to use them for learning purposes, in order to benefit from the portability, flexibility, accessibility and immediacy that they facilitate. As LaMaster and Ferries-Rowe emphasize, each of these devices is 'in each student's personal control', which for them is key to m-learning, in that it 'empowers students' by giving them choice (2013: xiv and 395). This is especially true when mobile phones are used, not only to receive information immediately that it is made available by a course provider, tutor or fellow student, but to enable you to make a contribution to online discussions from anywhere at any time. Of course, these developments have the potential to change the nature of learning for all learners, not just those studying at a distance.

For those of you who are not yet familiar with such developments, this chapter is essentially an introductory guide to some of the many forms of technology for learning being used in education today. It also explores briefly some of the issues raised for students using this technology. We will start with a brief look at the distinction between e-learning and m-learning, then move on to look in more detail at exactly what we mean by the terms in practice.

As indicated by the very brief definitions I have used above in brackets after the terms e-learning and m-learning, there is an argument to be made that m-learning is simply another form of electronic learning, but using a physically different device, usually using touch-screen technology rather than keyboard technology. This is true to some extent, but some see m-learning as something quite distinct from e-learning and some proponents are of the view that the increasing use of mobile technology may bring about a significant shift in learning; the jury is still out on this issue. Much of current provision would still be called e-learning, meaning that various elements of a course are being delivered electronically. Some educational providers are using m-learning to deliver a traditional 'course' by converting it to a format suitable for a mobile interface. Quinn (2013: 84) argues that this is simply e-learning on a mobile device, and that m-learning is potentially a lot more than this. (For a more detailed discussion on how the use of mobile devices is affecting approaches to learning, see Section 2.11.) As we will see below, learning using technology doesn't all have to be networked, but the very essence of most m-learning is that students are very definitely connected, either to one another or to the 'cloud' from where apps and data can be retrieved and where data can be stored. Consequently, m-learning can potentially run into difficulties if that connection is lost, or if there is incompatibility between different interfaces. This highlights the need for backing up your data locally for those occasions when the technology fails you.

5.1 What do we mean by e-learning and m-learning?

Activity Seventeen

List those things that you consider come under the headings of e-learning and m-learning.

Commentary

You may well have included some of the following:
- Using computers and mobile phones and other mobile devices for learning
- Online learning
- Learning on the Internet
- Web-based learning
- Learning using web pages

- www (the World Wide Web, or the web)
- The virtual (not physical) classroom
- Learning via a virtual learning environment (VLE)
- CD-ROM or DVD learning
- Computer-based learning
- Emailing
- Using electronic mailing lists
- Conferencing boards
- Discussion rooms
- One-to-one chat
- Podcasting
- Facebook Groups
- Tweeting

All of the above (and many more!) are elements of learning using technology. You will see from the list that *online* learning is one type of learning using technology. However, not all learning using technology is *online* learning, that is, you do not need to be connected live to the Internet for all learning that uses technology – you may receive CD-ROMs, DVDs or data pens with files or programs on them, which you can use on your own PC, tablet or laptop.

You are increasingly likely to be expected to engage in some aspect of e-learning or m-learning during your distance learning course, if only to communicate with your tutor by email or text message occasionally. The information provided by your department before you registered as a student should have indicated if there would be any elements of e-learning or m-learning on your course. More detailed information is likely to be provided as the course progresses. You should also receive information about the specification for *hardware* (that is, mobile device/ computer/printer/modem and so on) required, and about which versions of *software* (that is, computer programs/version of Windows and so on) you will need to install on your computer to enable you to access the materials provided.

Activity Eighteen

It is very frustrating once the course has started to find that you do not have the required hardware or software to use files sent to you on disc or data pen or made available to download, or to access information on the web when asked to do so. It is recommended that at this point you find any documentation already received about this and check that your hardware and software are up to the required standards. A university or college helpdesk is usually available to provide advice on how to access required software, much of which is free to download from the Internet (e.g. Adobe Reader). If a helpdesk is not available, you will need to contact your course leader or administrator.

Commentary

Some universities provide students with the hardware that they need for their course of study. One university (Long Island University, New York) bought 12,000 *iPads* for its new undergraduates, in part in a bid to increase recruitment, but also to provide the uniformity of access that this enabled, by all of the students having the same interface (Baroudi and Marksbury 2013). Lancaster Medical School (UK) issues laptops, which are fully supported by the University, to its undergraduates, and have also recently started to issue *iPads* when the students are going on work placement, as they are easy to wipe clean in a hospital environment. Increasingly, however, students begin their courses in universities, with (at least) their own laptop and smartphone. If you are already registered on a distance learning course, you will hopefully already have been given information about what type/make/model of mobile device (if any) it is preferable or even compulsory for you to use, so that you can access the necessary apps. Other education providers have used the solution to there being different apps for different mobile devices by delivering apps via cloud-based computing, enabling them to be used via a variety of devices. A growing number of universities now also provide a software service for laptops by using *Application Jukebox* to deliver software to students to run on their *Windows* laptops, anywhere that they have an Internet connection. The applications run on demand and take very little time to load. This is particularly good news for distance learners who otherwise would have to wait for downloads, or who may have no access to some of the software titles that campus-based students can find on computers in university PC labs.

5.2 What skills are needed for e-learning and m-learning?

In many ways e-learning uses the same methods of learning as traditional forms of learning; it is the tools that are used that are very different. The key difference about e-learning is that you, the student, have far more control over the resources that can be accessed and the order in which those materials are used. This is generally a positive thing, but it can also lead to feelings of being lost out there in cyberspace and in need of some form of guidance. This guidance is provided, in part, on the course website by your module tutor, particularly through the use of navigation aids. Increasingly though, the responsibility for learning is being shifted towards the learner *learning*, rather than the teacher *teaching*. Online learning is playing a significant part in this shift and many learners are now expected to work with others online to learn collaboratively via discussion rooms and other electronic means (see Sections 5.8, 5.12 and 5.13).

The skills that you will need for e-learning (in addition to IT skills needed to use your particular computer and the software installed on it) are essentially those needed for conventional learning – reading, note-making and writing – but they have to be used in different contexts. Perhaps one of the most obvious additional skills (but one that is often overlooked) is the ability to touch-type, since so much work is done via the computer keyboard, so you may want to investigate one of the free online typing tutors that are available. (Such a program may be provided via your institution's student skills webpage.) The other significant area where care is needed is communication (one-to-one and in a group) with other students and your tutors. You will look in more detail at email and group discussion in Sections 5.5 and 5.8 and in Chapter 9, where you will also explore working with others, together with other forms of learning and assessment that are likely to become increasingly common in distance education. Increasingly, students are asked to submit (or are given the option of submitting) assignments written as a series of web pages, rather than in a word-processed document. Clearly not all of you will possess the skills needed to do this at the start of your course and you will need to familiarize yourself with the appropriate software well in advance of the time for the assignment (Macdonald 2008: 154–5).

I cannot emphasize enough how important it is to familiarize yourself with your own computer (or one in a learning centre that you will be using for your studies) before the start of your course. In particular, time spent using your web browser to explore university (especially library and learning support) and course websites will be time well spent (see Activity 19).

For those of you wanting to know more about e-learning skills, especially if the course you are following is being delivered entirely online, I would recommend more specialist books such as Alan Clarke's *e-Learning Skills* (2008) and *IT Skills for Successful Study* (2005) or *Study Skills Connected: Using Technology to Support Your Studies* by Stella Cottrell and Neil Morris (2012). (See the Further Resources section at the end of this book for details.)

Clearly, whilst many of the above skills are also relevant when using a mobile device, there is a different sort of 'digital literacy' required for m-learning than for e-learning, with the basic need for touch-screen technology being perhaps a very strong forefinger and thumb! Whilst touch-typing becomes something of a redundant skill when using a mobile device (because of the small size of the keyboard, unless an external keyboard is attached to the device), knowledge of the layout of a QWERTY keyboard is not wasted, since you are still going to need to navigate one, even on a touch screen. Swiping (or 'swyping' as *Google* call it) certainly speeds up the use of a touch-screen keyboard, and the speed with which some people use tapping or pinching on their touch-screens can be quite staggering. You may be really familiar already with using these devices socially but if you are unfamiliar, it is important to be open to learning how to use them.

In addition, you are likely to be encouraged to embed photographs, audio or video clips into some of your assignments, which may be submitted into a blog or a wiki, so, if this is not something you have encountered before, preparing data in such formats may be yet another new skill you will need to acquire. (See also Section 5.6 for further information on the 'dos' and 'don'ts' of m-learning.)

5.3 Glossary of terms

Many of you will already be very familiar with much of the terminology used when working with technology for learning but, if you're not, it would be worth reading through the terms in Figure 5.1 to ensure that you are clear about their meanings. No doubt within the next year or two there will be several more terms in common use. Some of the types of technology will be explored in more detail in the pages following the glossary.

FIGURE 5.1 Glossary of terms used in e-learning and m-learning

3D MUVEs – Three-D Multi-User Virtual Environments, such as *Second Life* – a 3D social software application – 'provide virtual three-dimensional spaces, tailored by their designers, which can accommodate more than one participant at a time... The participants each have at least one avatar (a virtual representation of themselves), able to move around in the 3D environment and interact with other avatars.' (Salmon 2011: 65)

Apps – a shorthand term for 'applications' used on mobile phones and other mobile devices; another term for what was previously known as 'software' or 'program'

Asynchronous voice board – a conference board or discussion room where participants can post audio messages (instead of text-based messages) at any time that can be listened to by other participants in their own time (Salmon 2011: 87)

BlackBerry – the brand name of a Smartphone

Blended learning – a mixture of e-learning and face-to-face learning

Blog – a web log or diary of an individual on a website (can be on open access or password-protected)

Broadband – a fast and powerful channel by which to connect your computer to the Internet. A faster version known as **fibre optic broadband** is increasingly becoming available

CBL – Computer-based learning – learning that uses computers, forerunner of e-learning

CD-ROM learning – learning from data files, audio or video on a compact disc-read only memory, which has a reasonably high storage capacity

Chat – one-to-one (or more) synchronous conversations by text, audio or video that take place in real-time by being online at the same time as one or more other people – for example *NetMeeting*, *iChat* – often used as part of 'Help' facilities for IT support and for real-time discussion of academic subjects

Cloud-based computing – a means of accessing apps and data on remote servers using different types of electronic devices, without having to store the data on any one device

Conferencing boards or discussion rooms (asynchronous) – e.g. *FirstClass* or within a VLE. Places where discussions can be held by threads or themes. People can respond in their own time to questions/comments posted by others

Data pen (also known as a **digital, electronic, USB** or **flash pen**) – a file-storing device on which to store backups – plugs into the USB (universal serial bus) port of your computer

DVD learning – learning from audio or video training programmes or films on a digital versatile disc or digital video disc, which has a larger storage capacity than a CD-ROM

E-book – the whole of the content of a book is made available electronically. (It is increasingly becoming the case that some academic libraries are making some books available in electronic format only.)

Email attachments – electronic files attached to email messages

Emailing – sending messages electronically via a computer or mobile phone. This can be used for communicating (asynchronously – not at the same time as others) one-to-one or, via mailing lists, to groups of people

E-moderators – 'the new generation of teachers and trainers who work with learners online' (Salmon 2011: ix)

E-text – a book, report or journal article (or any other text-based document) that is made available electronically by a publisher, bookseller or library

Facebook – a social networking service

(Continued)

FIGURE 5.1 (*Continued*)

Facetime – an app that is available on an *iPhone* to enable one-to-one videoconferencing for two people using the same make of mobile device

Google Docs – a software program by which you can create and edit documents whilst working with other users online

Google Groups – a software program by which you can form and use a discussion group with others online

GPS (Global Positioning System) device – uses satellites to determine its location

Hypertext mark-up language (HTML) – the core language used to create web pages

Internet/net – networks of computers linked together around the world

Intranet – an internal network within an institution/organization/company

iPad – the brand name of a very popular (and relatively expensive) tablet

iPhone – the brand name of a very popular (and relatively expensive) smartphone (produced by US technology giant 'Apple')

iPod/MP3 player – iPod is the brand name often used as the generic name for a portable media player – a hand-held digital music and audio book player (some also store and display photographs and videos) (The popularity of the *iPod* has diminished considerably with the advent of the *iPhone*, although a new *iPod Touch* was launched in 2012.)

LANs – Local area networks, many are available at no charge, such as in airports, railway stations and coffee shops

Microblog – another name for a very short message (maximum 140 characters)

M-learning – learning via mobile technology, such as mobile phones, **PDAs** and **MP3 players**

MMS – Multimedia Messaging Service – the term used in some parts of the world for the service through which short messages using text or other media (for example video, sound or images) are sent and received using a mobile phone (maximum 160 characters in Latin alphabet or 70 characters in other alphabets, such as Chinese)

Modem – a device by which a computer is connected to the telephone line

MOOCs – Massive Open Online Courses – many of which are offered for free by some universities (and by some for a fee), for which there are no pre-requisites regarding entry qualifications or prior knowledge – often lead on to students studying on longer and fee-paying courses. They are offered by universities such as MIT and Harvard in the US (*edX*), Stanford's *Coursera*, and the OU UK's *FutureLearn* (that carries courses produced by over 50 other universities too). Between them these MOOCs are attracting millions of students. (At the time of writing *FutureLearn* has 370,000 students enrolled for a British Council course preparing for an English language test. The six-week course, Understanding IELTS: Techniques for English Language Tests, has students from 153 countries, with the biggest number from the Middle East, Asia and Latin America.)

Myspace – a social networking service

Online learning – learning by going 'online', i.e. connecting to information via the Internet, often via a telephone line

OpenCourseWare (OCW) – online educational materials provided for free, often as part of MOOCs

Open Educational Resources (OERs) – free learning materials offered by organizations such as the Open University

PDA – Personal digital assistant, an independent hand-held electronic organizer and file-storing device

FIGURE 5.1 (*Continued*)

PDF – Portable Document Format, a file format used to embed text and images. You need to have Adobe Reader software on your computer to read files in this format.

Pencast – the digital broadcast of a demonstration or lecture using a 'pen' on a whiteboard to show text, mathematical calculations, drawings, and so on, using software such as *Livescribe*

Podcasting – the delivery of multimedia files via the Internet to a PC or mobile device

Portal – a single entry point or gateway on an institution's website through which students can access all areas relevant to their studies. It is likely to include the way into enrolling on a course, reading email, accessing the library catalogue, accessing online learning materials, joining social and study groups, submitting assignments and evaluating courses. It may be linked to a **VLE**

RSS feed – (RSS – really simple syndication) – an automated system of receiving notifications of when web pages are updated

Server – a powerful computer that is used to store collections of web pages that can be accessed via the Internet

Service provider – an organization or company that hosts a server and provides both access to web pages via the Internet and launches web pages to the Internet on behalf of its staff/clients

Skype – software that enables users in different places to communicate live by video or audio via the Internet – useful for participating in tutorials and chatting to grandchildren

Smartphone – a mobile phone with advanced facilities such as a touch screen, a miniature QWERTY keyboard, email capability, camera, music and video players, and apps, for example GPS, group work software, and your university portal.

SMS – Short Message Service – the term used in many parts of the world for the service through which short messages are sent and received using a mobile phone

Social Networking Service – a website used to build an online community, members of which can keep in touch by posting messages or blogs in their 'space' and updating their personal profiles.

Tablet – a mobile computer with a touch screen display, for example a *Kindle* or an *iPad*

Text messaging or **texting** – a way to send and receive messages using a mobile phone on a phone network (maximum 160 characters)

Tweet – a very short message or microblog (maximum 140 characters) posted on *Twitter* that can be read by multiple recipients simultaneously

Twitter – a social networking service where account holders use the Internet to send and receive' tweets'

URL – Uniform resource locator or address of a website, usually beginning with 'http:// www....'

Virtual Learning Environment (VLE) – a powerful computer environment that is used to provide students with access to a variety of electronic learning resources in-house

Vlog – a video blog

Web-based learning – learning using web pages

Web browser – software used to access websites, e.g. *Internet Explorer* and *Mozilla Firefox*

Web page – an electronic 'page' on which information is held and displayed on screen

Web 2.0 – The term commonly used to describe the more interactive features of the World Wide Web, such as social networking services, blogs and wikis.

(Continued)

FIGURE 5.1 (*Continued*)

Website – a collection of related web pages

Weibo – a Chinese social networking service through which microblogs or 'tweets' can be sent and received

Wiki – a place on an editable website where several people can collaborate in creating factual content

World Wide Web (commonly abbreviated to www or simply the web) – the vast collection of information available around the world on web pages 'invented' by Tim Berners-Lee with Robert Cailliau in 1989 whilst working at CERN, [the European Organisation for Nuclear Research] the European Particle Physics Laboratory in Switzerland. (www.w3.org/People/Berners-Lee/ accessed 9 February 2015)

World Wide Web Consortium (W3C) – for setting international standards for the WWW, founded and directed by Tim Berners-Lee

---

5.4 Online learning

An increasing number of course leaders are providing information and learning materials online, in the form of course websites. Access to these is likely to be restricted and you will need a username and password from your course leader to use them. Materials are often available within the VLE for the course. These sites provide a 'portal' to relevant material and will typically have some or all of the following information/features:

- Programme and module information
- Learning outcomes for each unit of study
- Assessment details, including dates for submission of assignments
- The facility to submit assignments for marking
- Schedule of learning
- Interactive e-learning materials
- Opportunities for self-assessment questions (SAQs) and feedback (see Section 5.9)
- University/college staff information and contact details
- Access to recorded lectures, which, although provided for students attending the university, can also be made available to those studying remotely (see Section 5.10 for more details)
- Links to lots of other resources, both internal and external to your college/university, including electronic library resources (see Chapter 6 for more details)

Some of the above may be an additional version of information provided in paper-based format, but some elements may well be available in the online version only. In some instances e-learning will be used to *supplement* traditional forms of face-to-face learning or paper-based distance learning, in other cases e-learning *replaces* other forms of learning. This means that a student with access to the Internet can enrol on some courses from anywhere in the world without attending their university in person.

> **Tutor comment**
>
> 'The most satisfying conclusion is that the online learning is being successful. Many students tell me that they are taking what they have learned and are applying this to their in-house projects.'

5.5 Email and mailing lists

Email is still perhaps the most common form of online learning used (although it may soon be superseded by text messaging for shorter messages). It provides a very fast and relatively cheap way in which students can receive support and information both from their tutors and from other students on their course – their peers. It is the electronic equivalent of calling in to see your tutor in their office or chatting to a fellow student before, after or even during class. In order to use email you will need, as well as having the necessary hardware and software, to register with an email provider, many of whom provide their service at no charge. Emails can usually be downloaded from the service provider very quickly via the Internet. Many people can also access their email by going to the website maintained by the service provider. This means that emails can be accessed from any networked computer or mobile device around the world – very convenient if you are travelling as part of your job. Of course email is unable to transmit the verbal and non-verbal signals from one person to another that are present in, respectively, telephone and face-to-face communication and this can be detrimental to the process. It is likely you are accustomed to using email socially or professionally. However, as a refresher of best practice, below are a few guidelines for using email:

- Use a meaningful subject heading in emails.
- Keep your message relatively short. Some people suggest only one screenful, including anything longer in an attached file.
- Include the purpose of the message at the start, then provide more detail thereafter. People can then make a quick judgement about their interest in the message and if it is relevant to them they will not close it before you get to the point.
- It is very difficult to get 'tone of voice' into an email and sometimes the meaning of a message can be misunderstood. Try to check that your message is not going to cause offence. Some people like to use the symbol ☺ to reassure the recipient of an email that the message is meant to be friendly. Other people find the practice immensely irritating.
- Read through your email message before posting it and check for ambiguity and spelling mistakes. Although email can be quite ephemeral, many people file their mail into folders for future reference, and meaning can be later misunderstood because of errors.

- It is good practice to regularly review messages received; check that you have responded where necessary; delete those no longer required; and archive those that you don't want to delete into appropriately named folders.
- Always delete without opening any messages that are flagged up by your service provider as 'junk' or anything that has a strange subject heading or has been sent from an unfamiliar address. The message may contain a virus or may trigger a virus if you respond to it or open an attachment.

> 'Email is a great invention. As [an international] distance learning student I found Internet and email a helpful tool. It is the only way to communicate with the other students and professors.'

Mailing lists can be used to share information via email with people who have a common interest. An electronic mailing list is quite similar to a postal mailing list in that it is a method of distributing the same information to lots of different people. Mailing lists are typically used to discuss work with colleagues/students at other institutions, share news, collaborate on projects and publications, announce jobs and conferences, and keep in touch with current developments in your subject area. In order to get information from a mailing list you need to subscribe – that is, you need to ask that your name and email address be added to the list. Other people can then send information to you and others on the mailing list simply by posting a message to a single email address. These messages are then forwarded to all members of the list. To a large extent mailing lists are now being superseded by posting messages to a group using *Facebook* or *Twitter* on mobile devices. However, in the academic community, mailing lists are still popular.

There are a number of different services you can use for finding out about what mailing lists exist and how to join them. The National Academic Mailing list service known as *JiscMail* hosts a wide number of different mailing lists for the academic community in the UK. You can search their website (www.jiscmail.ac.uk) for mailing lists on a subject of interest to you, but you will need to keep your search term fairly broad, for example, 'literature', rather than 'Dickens'. You will find instructions for joining and leaving lists. You can access the email lists via your email account or via a web browser.

5.6 Mobile learning (m-learning)

Given the increasing popularity of mobile phones and other mobile devices, it is not surprising that a growing number of students are using these to access online learning, including the course website, VLE and discussion boards. Many universities and colleges and VLEs are developing mobile apps to make this access more flexible and convenient for students. Such apps typically provide a single point of access into central university services, such as the library and timetabling, (and even, in at least one case, whether the washers in the launderette on campus are busy or nearing the end of their spin cycle!) as well as specific course resources, such as a discussion room. These apps provide what Khaddage and Lattemann (2013: 121–2) describe as the three 'Ss' – 'speed, security [and] simplicity'.

However, as was discussed in Section 2.11 mobile devices are changing the very nature of the learning that is taking place, and often involve the individual student capturing data from a variety of sources for inclusion in their assignments or combining them with the resources of others in collaborative group work. Such a shift in the form of learning raises various issues about how students use their mobile devices and what they do with the data that they collect. It is therefore perhaps appropriate at this point to flag up some of those issues that I will call 'the 'dos' and 'don'ts' of mobile learning'.

Just as there are right ways and wrong ways of doing things when using email and group conferencing (see Sections 5.5 and 9.1 respectively), there are various what might be called 'ethical' things that should be considered when becoming engaged with mobile learning.

There is no feasible (or desirable, perhaps?) way for academic staff to monitor what a mobile device is being used for by distance learners during 'learning'. It is crucial, therefore, that each student takes personal responsibility to use technology appropriately and ethically.

Protecting others

Dyson et al (2013: 406) list a number of ethical concerns about using m-learning. Since their work was primarily intended for those introducing m-learning into schools, some of the issues would hopefully not be relevant to readers of this book. However, others are worth highlighting here.

Given the very mobility or portability of mobile devices and the ease with which built-in still and video cameras can be used, it may be tempting to record people/places/things to refer to and even incorporate/embed later in an assignment. Care should be taken to check that you obtain any permissions needed to make such recordings. Further, you should not share publicly any data that is meant for use by only a limited group of people, for example posting multi-media clips on *YouTube*. What one person might consider 'fair game' or acceptable to post in a public place might cause great pain and offence to another.

In particular, for members of a variety of cultural groups (be it those defined by age, ethnicity or religion) there are issues related to using mobile phones and other mobile devices, and these may require you to be sensitive to different ethical considerations. Certainly some members of some ethnic or religious groups may be unhappy about having a video or photograph of family members posted on social media.

Some education providers have a written Acceptable Use Policy (AUP) (Dyson et al. 2013: 410) about how and when it is acceptable to use technology, though clearly it is very difficult to enforce this (or indeed make it relevant) in relation to mobile devices, especially when being used away from the institution concerned. Others prefer to call them RMUPs or Responsible Mobile-Use Policies in order to make it clear that the policy deals with mobile technology use rather than desktop computers and that all users need to take personal responsibility for the use of mobile devices (p. 412). You may want to check the website of your education institution to find out if it has an AUP or RMUP and make sure that you become familiar with its contents.

Protecting yourself

Conversely you need to take measures to help protect your own privacy and dignity by minimizing the chance of someone else intercepting data transmitted to or from your device. This might become a particularly sensitive issue for those of you engaged in work-based learning or sensitive research work, such as in the medical field. When you are using cloud-based computing, such as *Google Drive* or *MS One-Drive*, it is especially important to pay attention to data security, since there is always the risk of your cloud account being hacked or even your provider's server coming under attack. How you provide this security will be device dependent, but it is likely that, in addition to passwording your account, you will be able to use some sort of encryption of files before transferring them to a server. This could become cumbersome, with an extra layer of passwords, so you may decide to differentiate between those files for which you are happy to rely on the built-in encryption of data by your provider (such as for less sensitive data), and those for which you are happier building in the double protection of encrypting them yourself as well before transfer. It is important that you also make backups locally of data files for those occasional times when your provider is not available and your data is temporarily inaccessible.

There is also the potential that your mobile device and therefore your location could be tracked via GPS, so you may want to think carefully about when and where you have GPS/location services switched on.

Finally, at the time of writing there is a lot of publicity about the horrendous practice of 'trolling' on social media sites, such as *Twitter*, and the lack of effective action by the service providers to deal with it. Trolling (or so-called cyber-bullying) is when people post abusive messages to people's account pages about them or their families causing, at best, minor irritation and, at worst, significant distress. In other words, using a mobile device is not risk-free: you need to balance what you see as the benefit of having an account such as *Twitter* for learning or social reasons against the potential of receiving such abuse.

5.7 Virtual learning environments (VLEs)

> **Student handbook**
>
> 'The programme is delivered within a password-protected Virtual Learning Environment (VLE). Support for students is provided through the use of email, bulletin boards and text-based computer conferencing within the VLE. Deadlines are posted to the course calendar, also within the VLE.'

There are various VLEs available, such as the commercial *Blackboard* and the Open Source application *Moodle*. Some universities have developed their own individual in-house VLEs. To use a metaphor, VLEs are electronic equivalents of the resources available in real physical university or college buildings. You are likely to be asked to access information and/or study materials and to contribute to discussions within one. Most VLEs can be accessed from anywhere in the world via the Internet, using a web browser such as *Mozilla Firefox* or *Internet Explorer*, or via the appropriate app for your mobile device.

Most VLEs, including *Blackboard*, have the following facilities:

- Access to web-based learning materials
- Structured gateways to other internal and external electronic resources

- Discussion rooms of defined membership
- Self-assessment multiple-choice questions with feedback
- Short answer tests
- Secure delivery of essay material
- Satisfaction (evaluation) questionnaires

You will need a username and password to access specific materials for your course. As a registered student at your institution you may well have already received information on how to obtain your username and password for this resource. When submitting essays and other forms of assignments to your tutor via the VLE, you need to do so well before the stated deadline to allow for any problems with the Internet. Technical difficulties will not be accepted as 'mitigating circumstances' for late submission: it is your responsibility to allow plenty of time.

5.8 Discussion rooms/conference boards/bulletin boards

These are a useful way of holding discussions with tutors and other students when regular face-to-face tutorials or seminars are not feasible. There are facilities for some form of electronic discussion within the virtual learning environments mentioned above. They provide a variety of synchronous and asynchronous systems. In addition, *WebEx* and *FirstClass* are conferencing systems used by some course providers. *WebEx* incorporates a 'web meeting' facility that is used by some educational providers for online seminars, and *FirstClass* integrates email and social networking with group conferencing, online submission of work and much more. It also supports synchronous real-time 'chat' with other users. You can connect to *FirstClass* via a mobile device. Others use a mobile app such as *Google Groups* to facilitate discussions.

> **Student handbook**
>
> 'The synchronous tutorials take place at times posted in the course calendar and last for one hour. Two sessions are normally offered during a week to allow participants in different time zones to log-in at the time most convenient to them. The tutorial logs are saved and added to the course as additional web pages, thus allowing those unable to join at the specified time to catch up on the discussion.'

Electronic discussions can provide a very valuable and stimulating forum for intellectual debate, as well as providing much needed support to otherwise isolated students. Sometimes a large cohort of students on one course is subdivided into groups of six or eight students/learners/participants who co-operate electronically in some form of group task. Some tutors provide two types of electronic rooms for a particular cohort of students – one for the academic work and a second one for more social/informal chat. The tutor is likely to act as a moderator of the discussion in the academic room, but may not necessarily intervene or make any contribution to the discussion. In some cases the tutors do not have access to the second, informal room, and these rooms become very much the electronic equivalent of the common room or bar (students have to provide their own beverages!). However, the university or college will reserve the right to monitor all electronic communication to ensure that the regulations are not being broken. You are likely to find some sort of conditions for use of computer systems in your student handbook.

Tutor comment

'Our virtual seminar discussions...are best characterized as an exchange among equals and do not resemble the traditional lecturer–student hierarchy. I have learnt a lot from the online debates with my students.'

All systems use some form of threading for particular themes in the discussion so that users and moderators can keep track of different elements or themes that arise. Many systems enable tutors and students to upload documents, for example *Word* or *PowerPoint* files that are appropriate to share with other members of the group. It is possible to read the contributions of others to such a discussion without actually making a contribution yourself – commonly known as being a 'lurker' (but also as a browser or vicarious learner/participant). However, the manager or moderator of a group (and sometimes all members of the group) will be able to see who has been reading the messages but not contributing.

Tutor comment

'The tutor's role is to encourage, facilitate and support online interactions between students to create an online community, which we feel is an essential component to a successful distance learning cohort.'

Sometimes an element of your course may be assessed by your contribution to a discussion room. If this is the case at some stage in your course, you need to check what the criteria for assessment are and ensure that you meet them. It is not usually simply a case of making a contribution, but rather you are assessed by the quality of that contribution. In some higher level courses everyone in the group may be provided with questions for discussion that are based on readings that you have been given earlier. Your contribution may well be judged, not just on what you post to the discussion room, but on how effective you are in prompting contributions from others. (See also guidance on group discussions in Section 9.1.)

'At the start of the course I wondered what it would be like to not only not be in a classroom with other students, but not all be in the same time zone, so not be able to exchange back and forth concurrently. I found that the time zone differences were not a problem. The amount of participation by each student in the discussion rooms was a bigger factor. If students provide input to the discussion rooms, then the class is so much richer and the timing isn't an issue.'

5.9 Self-assessment questions (SAQs)

SAQs (referred to in Section 2.6) that are regularly used as a type of assessment are often provided by electronic means. They may be found either within the VLE or on a web page linked from within the VLE or from another website provided for your course. They can also be made available on a CD-ROM, so that you don't always have to work online. SAQs can also be provided via an app on your mobile learning device.

Online assessments are quick and easy to complete and they provide you with virtually instant feedback about your progress. They are not intended primarily to judge you, but rather to provide you with the opportunity to recognize where more help or work is needed and with ideas for appropriate further study. Such assessments are known as formative assessments, which will help you to reflect on your past work and improve your future performance, although SAQs are also sometimes used as a form of summative assessment, when they will count towards your final mark.

5.10 Lectures, demonstrations and podcasts

Even though most of you will rarely or never attend your educational institution in person, it is becoming increasingly likely that you will be able to virtually 'attend' lectures and demonstrations produced there. Many universities now routinely record the lectures given in the main lecture theatres, using a single video camera connected to the Internet (a webcam) focused on the lecturer. Both on-campus students and distance learners can watch these so-called 'talking heads' at a later time or date, via the course website, *YouTube* or a mobile app, either by 'streaming' them whilst connected online to the Internet, or downloading the file from the Internet and watching it offline. More sophisticated materials may be created with software that has the facility for you to see the video with sound of the lecturer, plus accompanying text of the sound script on screen at the same time, using software such as *Blackboard Collaborate*, so accommodating the needs of any students who are deaf or hard of hearing. Some materials also include accompanying *PowerPoint* slides, such as might be used during a face-to-face lecture, making for a more interesting and hopefully more effective learning experience.

Other software can be used by your tutors to create teaching demonstrations or simulations by capturing what happens on the screen of their own PC, for example, working out a mathematical calculation or showing how to use a database or other software, and providing an accompanying audio commentary. Such demonstrations might also be provided using pencasts, using software such as *Livescribe*, for example working through an explanation of a complex subject using text and drawings on a 'whiteboard' or working through an equation. In order to access any of these materials your computer needs to be equipped with the appropriate additional hardware and software, that is speakers, video and sound cards, and some form of media player software. Such learning materials are rapidly increasing in popularity: if your module includes them your module leader should give you detailed information on how to set up your computer.

Some course providers are beginning to use podcasts to deliver course content, in line with the increasing availability of podcasts that can be downloaded from the large news and media organizations. However, good quality podcasts are still very time-consuming and expensive for educational institutions to produce. They are more likely to be created for use by lots of students, for example an induction tour of library services, rather than for specific subject learning materials for a small number of students. However, they are likely to become more prevalent as organizations create MOOCs which will potentially be accessed by many thousands, if not millions, of students. (See Glossary of terms in Figure 5.1 for more details.)

5.11 Videoconferencing

Each of the above methods is used for 'one-way' communication, with no facility for feedback. Videoconferencing enables you to have a more interactive learning experience, by facilitating two-way communication with your tutor and collaboration with your fellow students in small groups. The increasing use of 'monitor-top' webcams by individuals, and the built-in videos in laptops, tablets and smartphones, now makes the use of this method of delivery, using a 'live' video connection more likely at some point in your course. You will need to use software such as *Skype, Tango, Fring* or the recently introduced *Firefox Hello*. This method provides the opportunity to seek instant clarification on something that isn't clear and to put forward your own point of view.

5.12 Blogs and vlogs

Blogs (web logs) have been shown to help prevent feelings of alienation and isolation that are often experienced by distance learners (Dickey 2004). Essentially, they are the record of an individual's thoughts/ideas/comments written on the web on a regular basis, rather like a journal or diary, with the latest entries appearing at the top of the blog. Initially they were mainly made up of text, but increasingly people are adding audio or video files to their blogs (hence 'vlogs') and many people also include a photograph of themselves or other images. Some people's blogs can be read by anyone and everyone who locates them (that is, they are in the public domain), while others are limited to those people to whom the writer gives a password. Although a blog is owned by one person, there is the facility for others to add comments on the content of the blog.

For study purposes, you may be asked to keep a log of your learning experience (see 'Learning by reflection' in Section 2.6), which is marked as part of the assessment for the course, or you may be asked to contribute to your log on a regular basis about a particular topic that you are researching, as a contribution to a group work exercise (see 'Working with others' in Section 9.1), or to comment on the blog of someone else in your group. Your tutor may keep a blog that you are expected to access on a regular basis, so that they can keep you up-to-date with announcements about the course or about developments in your subject area. There is an RSS feed (see Section 5.14) on most blogs, so you can get a message on your PC screen when someone else updates their blog and others will get a message when you update yours. For a personal blog or one that is to be accessed by a relatively small number of people (for example, your study group) it is probably better to password-protect it to ensure privacy.

As a blog is arranged in reverse chronological order, it is not always easy to follow a particular thread in the development of the writer's ideas, especially if a blog is wide-ranging in its subject matter. For some purposes, it might be more appropriate to produce a wiki (see Section 5.13) or contribute to an online (threaded) discussion group (see Section 5.8).

If you find information on someone's blog that you wish to refer to or even quote in one of your assignments, you need to reference it as you would any other source, including the author and title of the blog, the date of entry of the particular excerpt, and the date you accessed it on the web. You should only cite other people's blogs if you can be sure of the authenticity of the authorship. As with any other website, you need to evaluate a blog for quality (see Section 6.7). Many blogs are not suitable for academic work as they are simply the personal views of an individual. Be aware that it can be very time consuming to read through the blogs of other people, and the value of doing so in many cases might be questionable, in terms of the volume and quality of information you might retrieve (other than in the blogs of those in your study groups).

Your institution may provide a blogging tool with which to set up your blog, or you may need to use one of the free blogging tools available, such as *LiveJournal* (www.livejournal.com), *Myspace* (www.myspace.com) or *Blogger* (www.blogger.com) (now part of *Google*), or one of the many proprietary brands of software. You can use *Google* (or one of the many other blog search engines) to search for blogs written by other people in particular subject areas. Increasingly people post their blogs/vlogs to their *Facebook* accounts. Once again, care needs to be taken to carefully control access to the materials in your account.

5.13 Wikis

Whereas a blog facilitates the adding of thoughts and comments in chronological order by one person, a wiki enables collaborative authoring of factual content arranged by subject or topic. It is a useful tool for group work (see 'Working with others' in Section 9.1), especially for thought-storming at the beginning of group work and for the group to produce a joint report or web content at the end of a project. It is also useful if members of a study group want to jointly create agendas for, and then record what happens at, face-to-face meetings. Your module tutor may set a piece of coursework where all members of the group have to contribute to a wiki on a particular topic. With some software you can create private wikis. There are potential problems when wikis are on open access, as anyone from outside of the group could access and edit them (including deleting content) inappropriately. It is advisable for one individual to take responsibility for regularly checking and re-editing content where necessary.

As with blogs, you may find useful information in other people's wikis that you might want to cite, but once again you need to be careful about the validity of the content. Wikis should only contain verifiable information, but some people may add content that is mainly their own opinion on a topic, rather than fact. It is possible that there is misinformation in more recently added articles, until the moderator has had a chance to check content. (Always look to see if the writer of an article has included references to validate the content.) However, wikis are potentially an extremely useful source of up-to-date information on a wide range of subjects. Because of the arrangement of wikis it should be easier to search and use them as source material than it is with blogs. For an example of a major wiki project, see *Wikipedia*, a free online encyclopedia maintained by the Wikipedia Foundation, a non-profit-making organization. It was started in 2001 and currently (February 2015) has over 4.7 million articles in English, plus millions more articles in over 200 language versions. There is an app available to use *Wikipedia* on your mobile device.

Complementary to *Wikipedia* is *Scholarpedia* – a free wiki begun in 2006 that consists of articles written by and peer-reviewed by members of the academic community worldwide. It is more likely than *Wikipedia* to contain accurate and reliable information, since each article has a curator (usually its author) who is responsible for its content. Any modification to the article has to be approved by the curator before the article appears in its final version. It is much less wide ranging than *Wikipedia*, containing just a few hundred articles in the scientific field, but is useful if your studies are within this area.

Your institution may provide a wiki tool with which to set up your own wiki or you can set up your wiki using one of the free software packages, such as *MediaWiki* (www.mediawiki.org) or a proprietary brand of software. You can search for content in wikis using a search engine such as *Qwika* (www.qwika. com), which searches millions of articles in wikis in a dozen different languages.

5.14 RSS feeds or news feeds

RSS is a method of being kept informed when a web page is updated. Using software for the purpose (a feed or news reader) you can receive notification about updates on lots of different web pages to one place on your computer. While you are working in any program on your PC, a brief message alert pops up on screen when an update on any of your chosen web pages is received. You can then go to the reader at a time of your choice and read all of the new web pages from within the reader. You have to download the software to be able to receive RSS feeds. You need to subscribe to some software, but there is some free software available, for example *FeedReader* and *FeedReader Connect* for mobiles at www. feedreader.com.You have to add into the reader the URL for each web page about which you wish to receive notification of updates. This can usually be done by dragging and dropping the RSS icon from the relevant web page into the reader.

You need to be sure that it is important to your studies to be kept up to date about each of the web pages that you flag up in the reader, otherwise you can waste a lot of time reading irrelevant information. That said, using RSS feeds can save a lot of time rather than having to go to each of your 'favourite' web pages on a very regular basis, only to find that most of them have not been updated since the last time that you visited.

5.15 Other forms of e-learning

In addition to the above generic forms of e-learning, many courses now include access to specific, very sophisticated forms of interactive e-learning packages. Some of these are highlighted as examples in Section 9.4. In Sections 9.2 and 9.3 there are also pointers to interactive e-learning study skills materials in the areas of report writing, mathematics and data collection and analysis.

Activity Nineteen

Although you are unlikely to encounter all of the above elements of e-learning on your course, you will probably be expected to use some of them. If you have already received the course documentation, use this to make a list of e-learning methods due to be used on each of your modules and, if possible, try to familiarize yourself with them at this stage.

If you already have the necessary hardware and software to access the Internet, go to your course website and explore. There may be a link from that website into the VLE that you will be using.

5.16 Viruses, security and backing up work

With increased access to electronic resources comes the increased risk of receiving a computer virus, especially if you are downloading files from other people. Some of these can be devastating, destroying your work in seconds. Other less serious ones can still be really annoying and difficult to eliminate.

You need to ensure that you have anti-virus software on the computer(s) you are using – at home, work or the study centre. The software will warn you if you do receive a virus and give instructions on how to deal with it. You need to regularly update the software. Although *iOS* (the operating system that powers the *iPad, iPhone* and *iPod*) and *Android* (the operation system that powers most other smartphones and tablets) are less susceptible to virus attack than the *Windows* operating system used on many PCs, you may nevertheless want to consider installing some sort of anti-virus software on those too.

You are at much greater risk with mobile devices of having them stolen, in which case your personal data, credit card details and saved passwords for accounts and various databanks are at risk of being stolen. It is advisable to make it harder for others to access such information by protecting your device with a password, passcode or PIN. (See also the earlier discussion on 'protecting yourself' in relation to mobiles in Section 5.6.)

It is important for each of the above and many other reasons to keep a backup of all of your work. Hours of work can be lost in seconds if something goes wrong with your software and your computer 'hangs' on you. Experts might be able to help you retrieve lost data files, but most of us don't have such sophisticated skills – best to use a data pen, a writable CD-ROM, an external hard-drive or cloud storage to make copies of all your files at very frequent intervals. Citing a lost or damaged file containing your assignment as a 'mitigating circumstance' for non-submission by a specified deadline is unlikely to be accepted as a valid reason by your tutor or an examiner.

'A computer with Internet [connection] or access to one easily is vital. It will become your best friend and your worst enemy. Keep backup discs of all work. This sounds so obvious and yet several people lost whole assignments and I "lost" three transcripts which took me three further days to retranscribe.'

5.17 Health and safety issues of technology use

In an item on the BBC News website in December 2014 it was reported that US doctors had carried out a study showing that reading e-books could be adversely affecting your sleep and potentially damaging your health (www.bbc.co.uk/news/health-30574260). They found that people took longer to fall asleep, had less deep sleep and were more tired the next morning, when they had been reading an e-book at bedtime. This is because the blue light, the wavelength common in smartphones, tablets and LED lighting, is able to disrupt the body clock because it can slow or prevent the production of the sleep hormone melatonin. In turn, sleep deficiency has been shown to increase the risk of cardiovascular disease, metabolic diseases like obesity and diabetes, and cancer.

Similarly there are concerns amongst doctors that the light emitted from some computer screens can affect the cells in the eyes' retinas, leading to severe sight problems. People with developing cataracts or age-related macular-degeneration (AMD) can be particularly vulnerable to the adverse effects of bright lights, and are advised to wear sunglasses on 'bright' days, as UV from sunlight may contribute to their development. It is similarly unwise to expose their eyes to long periods of 'blue' light from computers and mobile devices. A new lens called the *Blu-Tech* or *Blue* lens, which contains a pigment that filters blue light without impacting colour perception, has been developed and spectacles incorporating such lenses may help to mitigate against the effects of such light. Whilst the full effects of such technology on our eyes and general health will probably not be known for a generation, it is perhaps wise for all of us to limit use of screens of all kinds in the late evenings, and to take regular breaks from using mobile devices and computers throughout the day. Some people suggest the 20:20:20 rule, where every 20 minutes we take a break from looking at the screen for 20 seconds and focus on something that is 20 feet away (www.news-medical.net/health/Does-looking-at-a-computer-damage-your-eyes.aspx). In addition, for the sake of the whole of our bodies, it is a good idea to take a longer break from your computer every couple of hours or so and have a walk around.

5.18 Help with technology for blind and partially sighted people

Whilst all of us need to take care with our use of technology for the sake of our eyes and general health, blind or partially sighted people will have particular concerns. The Royal National Institute of Blind People (RNIB) provides a lot of information about the positive help that technology can give, once your computer is correctly set up. Settings built into your PC or laptop will enable you to change the size of content and select colours that suit you. In addition you can download free 'assistive technology' software to your computer quite easily. This will enable you to magnify the content and even let you speak to the computer and the computer speak to you, so that there is much reduced need to use the screen. If that is not sufficient, you can pay for more sophisticated software, which has more features and better support than some of the free software. If you are registered with an educational institution, you can contact their disability support centre: staff there will be able to advise you on the most appropriate software for your particular needs. See: www.rnib.org.uk/information-everyday-living-using-technology/computers-and-tablets for more information.

If you are in the UK and studying without being registered with a college or university, RNIB also has an 800+ strong body of volunteers known as the 'Technology Support Squad', who will help you to set up your computer, Internet link or mobile telephone, visiting you in your home if necessary. There is also a telephone support service available from the volunteers.

5.19 Accessibility of electronic learning materials

As mentioned in Section 4.7, learning materials (in whatever form) must be provided in a suitable format to be accessible to all students, including disabled students. This is especially important in the case of materials on the web. In particular, dyslexic students may find some websites difficult to read because of the background colours or because of the font used for text.

Many institutions now use the Web Accessibility Initiative (WAI) Web Content Accessibility Guidelines (WCAG) for help in making e-learning materials accessible. WAI is run by the World Wide Web Consortium (W3C) and works with people around the world to help make the web accessible to everyone, irrespective of any disabilities they might have.

If you find that any of the materials you need to use do not conform to these standards and you are unable to access them without difficulty, you should contact the course leader without delay.

5.20 A cautionary tale

Whilst the use of learning technology is clearly becoming increasingly popular, it does not necessarily have universal approval from all educators and students. E-texts are certainly a very convenient way of accessing lots of information, with a tablet device being able to store thousands of e-books. They also have the function of increasing the size of fonts, enabling those who are visually impaired to read text that would otherwise be too small for them. But, whilst they seem to be good for reading 'consecutive' text, it is less easy to navigate around an e-book or to make notes whilst reading (although it is possible to do both, and the search facility for specific words or phrases is a real bonus).

Various studies cited by Simpson (2013: 114 and 120) have suggested that, where students have a choice, they often prefer to read paper text rather than reading on screen (for example at the Open Polytechnic of New Zealand), that learning is more effective when students are using conventional text books than using e-books, and that sometimes using a computer can become a barrier to learning rather than an aid. However, more studies will be needed on students' reading preferences as digital technology becomes more prevalent and mobile devices for reading become the norm before any definite conclusions can be drawn. If your personal preference is for reading text on paper, at least some of the time, then there is always the valid (though costly) alternative of printing out materials.

Where technology *is* widely accepted as being a very positive development is in the field of student support, in both an academic and a non-academic capacity. Communication between students, and between students and their tutors or non-academic support staff, is highly motivational, and such communication is certainly enhanced by the technology. A positive and encouraging text message, tweet or email to a struggling fellow student might make all the difference between persevering through a difficult patch and abandoning their studies all together. Whilst posting a message in a group discussion forum is another possibility, a more personal message that addresses their particular needs or situation is likely to be more effective, and appreciated.

Conclusion

The overall message of this chapter must be to be prepared for anything and to try to use the full range of learning technologies to greatest effect in your studies. What you are likely to encounter during your course is a mixture of what is included in this chapter, as well as many other as yet unknown media, as both the technology and educational practice develop.

Chapter summary

In this chapter you have:

- Considered the various types of e-learning and m-learning that you are likely to encounter while registered as a student
- Considered issues that using e-learning and m-learning may raise for you, such as the skills that you need to make the most of the experience, and some of the potential challenges that you might encounter with accessing materials online
- Had the opportunity to familiarize yourself with some of the methods of learning you will need to use on your course
- Had the opportunity to explore what hardware and software you may need to obtain before starting you course
- Had the opportunity to explore your course website and possibly your VLE

6 Resources for studying

Introduction • Course materials • Library resources • Library catalogues • Bookshops • Periodicals/journals in various subject disciplines • Abstracts and indexes • Electronic resources • Managing references • IT support • Chapter summary

Introduction

As well as receiving a set of learning materials from your college or university you will probably receive various lists containing details of supplementary readings, some of which you may need to read before the course starts. You need to make a decision about how many books you need to buy (if any) and find out how many you might be able to borrow or access online through the library. You will also need to search for and retrieve information from many other sources when it comes to preparing for your assignments. It is a good idea to find out now what your sources are, and if necessary to make arrangements in advance for accessing resources.

6.1 Course materials

You will either have already received or will shortly receive a set of materials related to your course – they may be paper-based, on a CD-ROM, DVD or data pen, or available on and downloadable from the web. If you are following a full programme of study you will probably receive material for each module a couple of weeks before it starts. As well as learning materials, you may receive a copy of one or two set textbooks (in paper or e-book format) which are integral to your studies, and/or possibly some photocopied articles or links to articles online. Video or audio files might also be included for some modules.

Difficulty: 'Panic when course materials received – new language not work-based topics.'

Strategy: 'Start at the back!! Read the references and recommended reading list. Select a recent comprehensive reference which covers the topic in a broad way. Reading this first may give an overview of where the module fits with current practice/application to your work.'

> **Case studies**
>
> Case studies provide ideal student-centred activities. They are being used increasingly as course materials in higher education to bring to life, in an interesting and relevant way, those ideas and concepts included in your course. The degree to which case studies are included on a course clearly will vary according to their relevance to a particular subject area, and within that area from one module to another.

Typically they are used in subjects with a practical application, such as business, management or technical studies. Case studies provide description and analysis of real-life situations or scenarios from which learning can take place. (Three brief case studies are included in Chapter 9 of this book to demonstrate instances where online learning has been used effectively in the areas of group work, labs, and fieldwork.) They might also be used as the basis for assessments, with you having to suggest solutions or strategies to solve the problems presented within case studies. Conversely you may have to write case studies after observing colleagues or processes in your own workplace or during work placements to demonstrate particular issues or practices (Davis and Wilcock 2008). (Case studies are also used as an approach to doing research – see Sections 10.1 and 10.7.)

You will find examples of case studies in a variety of subject areas on the website of a National Teaching Fellowship project (conducted at the University of Gloucestershire) at http://insight.glos.ac.uk/TLI/ACTIVITIES/NTF/CREATIVE HOPS/EXAMPLES/Pages/BriefCaseStudyExamples.aspx.

6.2 Library resources

Students are increasingly turning to electronic resources available via the web to find information for completing their assignments. Thousands of electronic journals are now available and these provide far more up-to-date material than books can. If you have access to the web you are likely to go there first when you begin to search for resources. In this sense you are not disadvantaged by being a distance learner. The best starting point for any student looking for resources will be the library website of the educational institution where you are registered. This is especially important for distance learners as you will need usernames and passwords from the website to access electronic resources off campus. (We will look in a lot more detail at electronic resources in Section 6.7.)

> 'Library access is a significant issue. Many books [at my] university [library] which are popular text[s] are [on] one week loan and therefore no use to us as we are...80 miles away.'

However, many resources are still only available within a conventional (not electronic) library. A number of different library resources are probably available to you. It is possible (especially if you are employed by a large organization) that you will find some of the materials you need at your place of work. Even if there is no formal library it is worth asking around various people – you may find the text you need sitting on someone's shelf. Your local public library (where available) may have some of the materials you need, or can get them for you via the document supply service (for a fee). It is unlikely, however, to have the more specialist journals that you will require. Even if it does not have a lot of the resources you need, it is possible that your local library could provide the quiet, well-lit, warm study space that you need and give you access to a PC. Some people find that the local branch of their professional association has a small specialist library.

> Difficulty: 'Being a long way away from the uni library.'
>
> 'When only in [my university] about one day per month, getting books out is impossible. I found using a local university library where I live the best option for access any day I want.'

If you do not regularly visit the institution where you are registered, it may be more convenient to use the library in your local college or university. More than 170 higher education institutions in the UK and Ireland participate in the *SCONUL* Access scheme. This enables students (and staff) to use and borrow materials from other libraries. If you visit the *SCONUL* Access website at www.sconul.ac.uk/sconul-access you will be able to check the list of participating libraries. Your 'home' library will need to participate in the scheme. If the library you want to use is also a member of the scheme, you will have to complete an online application form and have it approved by the library of the institution at which you are registered as a student. Your home library will issue an email confirming their approval. You need to print this email and take it with you, together with your ID/library card from your home institution, and this will allow other libraries to identify you as a bona fide member of the scheme. You will then need to register with the local or host library and obtain a library card that entitles you to use the host library and borrow books for the duration of your course. Some libraries will give reference only or restricted borrowing rights and you may not have access to electronic journals and databases to which the host library subscribes. Once your application has been approved, you can use any of the libraries on the list of participating institutions. You need not reapply for each library.

If you need to use a library not included in the *SCONUL* Access scheme, please contact the member of library staff who is responsible for services to distance learners at the university or college where you are a registered student. They may be able to arrange reading or even borrowing rights for you at your local library on an ad hoc basis. Other academic libraries, at their discretion, may allow you temporary membership (including borrowing rights) upon payment of a fee, which is likely to be considerably cheaper than the travelling expenses needed to visit your own institution, if you live some distance away.

Strategy: 'Ensuring that you have access to good library facilities prior to commencing your studies if accessing [your university] is difficult.'

'Visit other university libraries which have related courses and ask if you can join.'

'Local postgraduate library facility [was] very helpful and on [my] doorstep.'

As a registered student at your college or university you are, of course, entitled to use all of its own library facilities. In practice it may not be that easy to do so, especially if you live and work some distance away and never or rarely attend your study institution. If you can attend in person, then the usual reference, lending, photocopying and document supply services are obviously available to you.

Various paper library guides may be available to help you with your studies. These could include a guide to services that are available for off-campus users and a guide to referencing bibliographic and electronic resources in your assignments. Ask your course administrator or course leader for copies of these or contact the library direct. Most guides are now likely to be available online as well.

Some specific services may be in place to assist students on distance learning courses, such as:

- A specific point of contact (phone number, email address or text number) for assisting distance learners in using library resources
- Photocopy delivery service for distance learners only
- Postal loan service for distance learners only

Other services that are useful for distance learners may in fact be available for *all* students, for example:

- Off-campus access to electronic library resources (with appropriate username and password)
- Telephone renewals
- Online renewals/reservations

'Access through the Internet to the university library is wonderful, and apart from physically collecting or returning books you can do almost every other library activity, which is so helpful at distance.'

Activity Twenty

It is probably advisable to make an initial visit at a very early stage to the library that will be your main or sole resource centre. You might do this in person or you may be able to do it just as well by visiting the website of the library to discover what information sources are available.

Make a note of the most obvious sources of information likely to be relevant to your field of study. Some will be printed materials, and others will only be available online. It may be that those in the latter category can be accessed from your desktop computer without having to go to the library. However, you may need to register at the library in order to be able to access them in this way. Others may only be available using the library's own computers or from a computer on a university or college campus.

Increasingly, electronic resources are being made available to all students off-campus. However, each institution will have its own licensing arrangements with publishers. In many cases it is still more expensive for libraries to pay for a licence for off-campus access to resources. Even where electronic resources are provided to off-campus users by the library at the study institution where you are registered, you may need to make arrangements well in advance to receive usernames and passwords electronically or by post to access them, if a personal visit to that library is unrealistic.

6.3 Library catalogues

The catalogue of your 'home' or your 'local' academic library (whichever is most convenient) is likely to be the starting point in any search for resources, but remember that not all host libraries in the *SCONUL* Access scheme in the UK and Ireland (see above) will give you full access to all of its resources. In most libraries the catalogue will now be computerized, but in some libraries you may find that the catalogue is still only available on cardboard catalogue cards in drawers. Some may well have a combination of the two systems, where details of the older bookstock have not yet been transferred to the computerized system. Computerized systems vary and you may be advised to seek an introductory leaflet, verbal explanation or online guide of how to use it on your first visit to a new library (or its website). Usually an online library catalogue will have a subject index, so you can focus a search on a specific subject area. Most also have a keyword search facility, so you can enter your own topic area to get a list of holdings. (This will be in addition to being able to search by author or title of a book or journal title.) If the catalogue is computerized, you will be able to use it to search for electronic books, journals and databases in the stock of the library, as well as printed books, and to check your own library record and search for other web resources in your subject area. (You cannot use the catalogue itself to search for specific articles in journals or specific chapters in books, although increasingly libraries are using powerful search tools such as *NORA* alongside their catalogues, and these will enable you to locate full text electronic items as well as print books that can be borrowed.)

You may also have access to the catalogues of other libraries via the computers in your local library or via the Internet using your own PC, laptop or tablet, for example via *COPAC*, which 'brings together the catalogues of about 90 major UK and Irish libraries' (http://copac.ac.uk/about/).

COPAC is formed by merging the online catalogues of major UK research libraries:

- Members of the Research Libraries UK (RLUK), including the British Library, the National Library of Scotland, and the National Library of Wales/Llyfrgell Genedlaethol Cymru

- Specialist research libraries, such as the National Art Library at the V&A
- Museum libraries, such as the library of the Natural History Museum
- Specialist databases, such as the Register of Preservation Surrogates
- Nationally important research collections held in academic libraries, such as the Russian and East European Studies collection at the University of Essex.

(http://copac.ac.uk/about/libraries/)

Although such catalogues will provide you with bibliographical information, it may take some time to borrow the books themselves via your library's document supply service.

You can also go to the website of the British Library and search its main catalogue at http://blpc.bl.uk. The website provides the following information:

- We receive a copy of every publication produced in the UK and Ireland
- The collection includes well over 150 million items, in most known languages
- 3 million new items are added every year
- We have manuscripts, maps, newspapers, magazines, prints and drawings, music scores, and patents
- The Sound Archive keeps sound recordings from 19th-century cylinders to CD, DVD and MD recordings [listen, for example, to a 1909 recording of 'The Banks of Green Willow' at http://sounds.bl.uk/World-and-traditional-music/Ethnographic-wax-cylinders/025M-C0037X1631XX-0100V0]
- We house 8 million stamps and other philatelic items.

(www.bl.uk/aboutus/quickinfo/facts/)

You can order loan items or downloads of journal articles, conference papers or sections of a book direct, either as an account holder using a customer code and password (for regular customers), as a non-registered 'pay-as-you-go' customer using a credit or debit card through the British Library Document Supply Service (BLDSS), or via your university library service. If you are studying at a university outside the UK and Ireland, your library may be able to order licensed copies (paper or electronic) of individual articles from journals and individual chapters from books from the British Library, via the International Non-Commercial Document Supply (INCD) Service.

Many items in the British Library's collections can only be accessed in person at one of their Reading Rooms, for which you will need to register for a Reader Pass (www.bl.uk/reshelp/inrrooms/stp/register/stpregister.html). Anyone can apply for a Reader Pass, but due to pressure on their services the British Library cannot guarantee admission. You are encouraged to pre-register online, the benefits of which are that you can order items in advance of your first visit.

You can also access other major catalogues and several specialist catalogues from the British Library website.

You can search the contents of European national libraries at the website of the European Library, which is a free service that offers access to the resources of the 48 national libraries of Europe and leading European Research Libraries in 35 languages. Users can cross-search and re-use over 26 million digital items (books, posters, maps, sound recordings, videos, and so on) and 153 million bibliographic records. To facilitate further research, links are also provided to other websites in the Europeana group of Europe's leading galleries, libraries, archives and museums (www.theeuropeanlibrary.org).

Many other countries also have national libraries. As the International Federation of Library Associations and Institutions (IFLA) explains:

National libraries have special responsibilities, often defined in law, within a nation's library and information system. These responsibilities vary from country to country but are likely to include: the collection via legal deposit of the national imprint (both print and electronic) and its cataloguing and preservation; the provision of central services (e.g., reference, bibliography, preservation, lending) to users both directly and through other library and information centres; the preservation and promotion of the national cultural heritage; acquisition of at least a representative collection of foreign publications; the promotion of national cultural policy; and leadership in national literacy campaigns.

(www.ifla.org/national-libraries)

Wikipedia (http://en.wikipedia.org/wiki/List_of_national_and_state_libraries) maintains a list of national libraries (alphabetical by country), which is, in part, edited by IFLA members.

6.4 Bookshops

If a book is not easily available from your local library or via the document supply service or any other library, you may have to consider the option of buying your own copy, especially if you consider it as potentially a key text. If you are looking for a bookshop in the UK or Ireland, the Booksellers Association maintains a comprehensive database of bookshops.

You can search by bookshop name, town, county, postcode and the display will show bookshop details and Google map locations and streetview for all shops. You can search for all BA members, only independents, or independents and chain bookshops. Where the shop has a website, you can click straight through. (www.booksellers.org.uk/bookshopsearch)

You may be fortunate enough to have easy access to a good academic bookshop but even where this is the case, you may find it quicker, cheaper and/or more convenient to search for a book yourself using one of an increasing number of online bookshops available on the web. Some such bookshops, for example *WHSmith online* (www.whsmith.co.uk), *Waterstones* (www.waterstones.com), *Amazon.com* (www.amazon.com), and *Amazon.co.uk* (the UK branch of the US online bookshop, www.amazon.co.uk) will email you about new books which meet your specifications or relate to your previous buying or browsing habits.

You may simply use such services to get bibliographical information on new titles in your subject area or by a particular author with no obligation to buy from them. (There are other similar 'current awareness services' for books and journals – see Section 6.7 for details.) If you decide to purchase books from such sources, remember that you might have to pay postage and package costs on top of the price of the books themselves. In the UK it is possible to order books online from some suppliers (for example, WH Smith or Waterstones) and have them delivered postage free to a local branch of the store. You could also try websites that specialize in offering discounted textbooks for sale. The *GetTextbook* website at www.gettextbooks.co.uk/ compares the prices of textbooks from online bookshops around the world, saving you a lot of time. Increasingly, independent dealers in used books are using the *Amazon* website to sell their stock, so it is relatively easy to purchase from there. However, you need to take care that you are purchasing the latest edition of a book, otherwise some of the content may be out of date. Once you've finished with your textbooks you could even get some money back by selling them through a secondhand bookshop.

6.5 Periodicals/journals in various subject disciplines

Lists of journals, to which your university or college library subscribes, may be available for various subject areas as printed leaflets as well as on the computerized catalogue. Once you (perhaps with the help of your tutor) have identified relevant titles that are held by the library, it is as well to regularly check new issues as they are published for appropriate articles, as there is always a delay before they are included in published abstracts or indexes. It may be possible regularly to receive the contents pages of the most appropriate journals by email (again see Current awareness services for resources in Section 6.7).

6.6 Abstracts and indexes

Abstracts (brief summaries of articles) and indexes (lists arranged alphabetically) to journal articles may be available in paper or electronic format (in databases). Clearly electronic ones are much quicker to search (see Section 6.7 for more details). Author, title or subject searches will reveal relevant articles. While indexes are useful, an abstract of an article will be a great deal more help in enabling you to decide whether or not to get hold of the full article, since the abstract should give you a clear indication of the contents.

6.7 Electronic resources

Although academic libraries continue to stock thousands of books and hundreds of journals in paper format, many of the resources that you will need for your studies are now available in electronic format. These are likely to include e-books, e-journals, bibliographic (including full-text) databases and other databases that the library subscribes to itself, plus numerous library web pages containing links to external resources and tools available on the web.

Remember that, as with any other resources, you must provide references of any electronic resources that you use in your assignments, so as not to be accused of plagiarism. This is especially important if you quote word for word some of the information that you find. Many academic institutions now use plagiarism detection software (such as *Turnitin*), so they will be able to discover if you have simply copied things from the web, rather than written about a topic in your own words. You will need to record as much information as possible about websites you consult and from which you save information, including the full URL (web address) and the date when you visited the site. (See Section 6.8 for more on managing references and Section 7.3 for more on plagiarism.)

Information literacy

In seeking information relevant to your field, you are searching for very specific data from a huge amount of data. It is vitally important that, if you do not already possess them, you quickly acquire a set of 'information literacy' skills that will help you to extract, from the millions of resources available, those that will be most relevant to your studies and assignments. But being information literate means being able not only to find resources, but to manage, evaluate and use effectively the information that you obtain. The best people to help you acquire these skills are those who are familiar with the literature in your subject area – your tutor or a subject librarian or information officer.

As stated earlier, the best starting point for any student looking for resources will be the library website. You will need to use usernames and passwords to access resources to which the library subscribes, so you must go via the university or college network to be able to do so. Most academic library websites will also include links to workbooks or online tutorials to teach you how to use a range of library resources and how to search for other information on the web. The library materials are likely to include general tutorials, such as how to use the *Endnote* bibliographic management software, for example, and subject-specific tutorials for your own subject area. The *FAME* (Financial Analysis Made Easy) database, for example, provides information on companies, including financial data. The library website is also likely to include contact details for the librarian(s) for your subject area, so that you can liaise with them and get help with, for example, accessing electronic journals off-campus.

There is a comprehensive collection of information literacy web pages, workbooks and online tutorials linked from the skills web pages of Leeds University Library at http://library.leeds.ac.uk/skills. The materials are on open access, although some are only relevant to University of Leeds students (such as those about the University of Leeds Library itself). Remember that you will only be able to access the resource materials themselves (databases, e-journals, and so on) using a username and password provided by your own study institution and via your own library's website.

If you feel that you need a fairly in-depth guide to accessing and using information (in addition to the remainder of this chapter), you will probably benefit from going to Northumbria University's *SkillsPlus* materials at http://nuweb2. northumbria.ac.uk/library/skillsplus/, where you will find a variety of video guides, interactive tutorials and printable help guides on information literacy.

Author's note

Although I have attempted in the following paragraphs to include examples available around the world, I appreciate that some of the resources listed are relevant only to students who are registered with a study institution in the UK (and Ireland in some instances). My apologies to those of you who are registered with institutions outside of the UK. Hopefully your institution's library website will lead you to equivalent national resources.

Overseas students registered on courses run by UK education providers should be able to access the same electronic resources as UK students via the institution's library website. Occasionally licensing agreements of some libraries with the publishers might mean there are some access restrictions. In this case you would need to contact the person in your library with specific responsibility for services to distances learners (see Section 6.2) to make special arrangements to access these resources.

Databases – bibliographic and full-text

Bibliographic databases, giving references to the published literature in a specific subject area, are a good way of identifying respected work in your subject or by a particular author. They provide the facility for you to type in authors' names or words and short phrases that describe your area of interest so that you can precisely locate relevant published information. Your search will generate a list of references, mainly to journal articles, but also to newspaper articles, conference proceedings and some theses and official publications. From the list of references you need to decide which items look most relevant and locate these. Many databases include a short summary or abstract for each item to help you assess its value and relevance to your search topic. You may well find that some of the journals containing the articles which you have selected from databases will not be held in the library where you are a registered member. In this case you need to be sure of their relevance since you will probably have to pay something towards the cost of each item obtained by the library via the document supply service or you will have the cost and inconvenience of having to travel some distance yourself to obtain access to the articles.

Full-text databases are similar to bibliographic databases, except that they go a step further and provide links to whole articles (and other items) online, rather than just the references to the articles. This means that you can access resources in one operation, rather than finding references and then having to locate the resources themselves via the library catalogue or the web.

It is impossible to provide extensive details here of databases in lots of subject areas, since they are constantly changing and being updated. It is much better to consult your library's website. However, I will outline, below, details of some of the more generic services available together with a few subject-specific examples.

Some databases are multidisciplinary, and 'help you find peer-reviewed academic articles from all over the world, from many different publishers, over a long time period' (http://library.leeds.ac.uk/researcher-literature-search-databases).

One example of such a database is *Web of Science* (previously *Web of Knowledge*), which includes information that is carefully selected and evaluated. It consists of the 'core collection' of the *Science Citation Index*, the *Social Science Citation Index*, the *Arts and Humanities Citation Index* and the *Conference Proceedings Citation Index*. Some material on *Web of Science* provides the full text of an article, but for other articles just a reference and an abstract are given. An extremely useful feature of *Web of Science* is the ability to do a citations search; that is, you can search for articles that make reference to a particular author. This is very useful for finding out who has built on a seminal piece of research. *SciVerse Scopus* is a large abstract and citation database of peer-reviewed literature and quality web sources (19,500 journal titles from 5,000 publishers worldwide and over 4.6 million conference papers). It covers research in the scientific, technical, medical and social sciences fields and, more recently, also in the arts and humanities.

A relatively new 'meta' database tool, *ProQuest Central* – described by its producers as 'the ultimate cross-disciplinary research tool' – brings together 30 of their most highly used databases to create the largest single academic research resource available today. It covers 60 subject areas, and 21,000 periodical titles. Researchers can choose to search individual databases for targeted research or search all at once to find relevant results and information from other disciplines.

ABI/Inform Global (part of *ProQuest Databases*) for scholarly business information covers management, finance, marketing and business journals and other publications, providing abstracting and indexing services, together with full-text articles for 1923 onwards from more than 3,000 sources. There are several abstracting and indexing services for scientific literature, for example the *Inspec* database, produced by the Institution of Engineering and Technology, which contains bibliographic and indexed records to physics and engineering global research literature. Its key features are:

- Comprehensive coverage – 15 million records in the fields of electronics, computer science, physics, electrical, control, production and mechanical engineering.
- Content – indexing and abstracts of articles selected from nearly 5000 scientific and technical journals (1600 of which are indexed from cover to cover), some 2500 conference proceedings, as well as numerous books, reports, dissertations and scientific videos.
- Specialised subject indexing by experts that retrieves accurate and extensive results.
- Web links to the original article (where available) – currently nearly 7.5 million links.

(www.theiet.org/resources/inspec/about/)

The *Australian Education Index* (also part of *ProQuest*) is a comprehensive collection of educational research documents relating to educational trends, policy and practices. The database is produced by the Cunningham Library at the Australian Council for Educational Research and is Australia's largest source of education information. Coverage includes trends and practices in teaching, learning and educational management. It covers reports, conferences, symposia, meetings, journal articles, books and online resources (http://media2.proquest.com/documents/australian_education_index.pdf).

You can use a database such as *MEDLINE* (*EBSCO*) for biomedical bibliographical data (containing over 6 million citations and abstracts) and *UKOP Online* for information on UK official publications, 'containing 450,000 records from over 2000 public bodies, it is the most comprehensive source of information on official publications available' (www.ukop.co.uk/ukop).

The *International Bibliography of the Social Sciences* (*IBSS*) (*ProQuest*) 'is an essential online resource for social science and interdisciplinary research. IBSS includes over two million bibliographic references to journal articles and to books, reviews and selected chapters dating back to 1951. It is unique in its broad coverage of international material and incorporates over 100 languages and countries. Over 2,800 journals are regularly indexed and some 7,000 books are included each year. Abstracts are provided for half of all current journal articles and full text availability is continually increasing' (www.proquest.com/products-services/ibss-set-c.html).

CABI (www.cabi.org) is 'an international not-for-profit organization that improves people's lives by providing information and applying scientific expertise to solve problems in agriculture and the environment'. They produce *CAB Abstracts,*

the most comprehensive database of its kind, [that] gives researchers instant access to over 7.9 million records from 1973 onwards, with over 360,000 abstracts added each year. Its coverage of the applied life sciences includes agriculture, environment, veterinary sciences, applied economics, food science and nutrition.

It is available via its own platform at www.cabi.org/cab-direct/, or via various other platforms such as *EBSCO*. *CABI Full Text* is also available, 'which gives users automatic access to over 290,000 journal articles, conference papers and reports – 80% of which are not available electronically anywhere else'.

It should be possible to access some or all of the above (and many others) via your study institution's library website. Remember, though, that the databases are not in-house catalogues and that, if the database is not a full-text service, you will need to check the library catalogue to find out whether or not the journal or newspaper in which the article is to be found is held in your library.

Although there are some similarities to searching in various databases you will need specific instructions on how to search a particular database. Many libraries will have these instructions both in printed format and available on their web pages. You will sometimes need a username and password to gain access to the database; these will be provided by your library. In some cases they will appear on screen, in others you will need to request them from the library staff. An *Athens* (or possibly *Shibboleth*) username and password are needed to access several databases. For details of how to obtain your username and password, go to your university *Athens* information page. Off-campus you need to use a personal *Athens* account. This should be generated automatically for all students. *Athens* and *Shibboleth* are both Access Management sign-in systems for accessing electronic resources. Access Management provides the facility to have a single login system to access all of the resources to which your institution subscribes, instead of using a different username and password for each resource.

You will need to use the username and password given to you at the time of registration as a student to log into the library's web pages in the first place in order to gain access to further usernames and passwords (including *Athens*) to access some resources. This can be a very cumbersome process. Increasingly institutions are addressing this issue and are developing new systems to make access to all resources available via a single login. This will often be via a portal (see Figure 5.1 – Glossary of terms in Section 5.3).

Activity Twenty-One

Explore (briefly) the list of bibliographical databases that are available from your library's website. Bookmark, that is add to your 'Favourites' list, those that are likely to be most useful when conducting a full-scale literature search in your subject area.

'There is a confusing mass of online resources available to the student via the university library. While it is easy to ignore these as being too much, in fact a little time spent exploring them and finding ones relevant to the area of study can open the way to wonderful new information completely accessible from home.'

E-journals

A rapidly increasing number of academic journals are available on the web. Not all of these will be available to users of all libraries, since the individual library must pay a subscription before their users are allowed access. The library will provide a listing of the journals to which it subscribes, and links from its own website to those journals. E-journals should be listed in the library catalogue. Under the Developing Countries Initiative (DCI), some academic journal publishers such as Edinburgh University Press (EUP) and Oxford University Press (OUP) support the dissemination of high-quality research and academic knowledge worldwide. They provide journals either free of charge (online) to individuals, or at much reduced subscription rates (print) to academic organizations in countries classified as 'low income' in the World Bank Country Classification. The list of eligible countries is provided on the EUP website at www.euppublishing. com/page/infoZone/librarians/developingcountries. If you are studying in one of those countries, you do not need to sign up for the free service as EUP's website detects the country you are connecting from and grants free online access automatically via EUP Journals Online.

In addition to a library's own list of journals, there are various other listings of e-journals, for example, *Science Direct* (a database of more than 2,500 peer-reviewed electronic journals, including some on open access) at www.elsevier.com/online-tools/sciencedirect/journals#journal-title-lists. It is often possible to obtain articles via such listings even when your own library does not have a subscription to the journal, but you will have to pay a fee yourself to access them, for example, *Ingenta-Connect*, which currently has 5 million full-text electronic articles available from an expanding range of more than 10,000 leading academic journals.

As with most of the web-based databases, electronic journals require a password for access. These passwords are kept on secure library web pages that cannot normally be viewed off-campus. However, there should be a way of remotely accessing the computer network of the institution at which you are registered as a student and find the password that is needed for access to the resources.

A growing number of open access journals are appearing on the web, largely as a result of the Open Access Movement, a worldwide movement that aims to make peer-reviewed research literature in all subjects and all languages freely available via the Internet. The *Directory of Open Access Journals* (www.doaj.org) (set up in 2003 by Lund University in Sweden) is a useful tool to use to find open access articles relevant to your subject. It has over 1.8 million peer-reviewed articles from more than 10,000 journals.

E-newspapers

For a single access point for all of the UK's national and regional newspapers you can go to *British Newspapers Online* at www.britishpapers.co.uk. As well as providing a directory of the newspapers (and links to them), this website includes a page giving information about each of the papers included. However, not all of the newspapers included have their own archive searching facility.

NewsUK has been updated and has become *ProQuest UK Newsstand*. It is an online database providing a search facility for more than 300 national and regional newspapers and magazines. Some of the newspapers contain archive material for around 25 years, but for many the coverage is more recent. Your library needs to subscribe to this service.

The *British Newspaper Archive* at www.britishnewspaperarchive.co.uk is a new digitization partnership project between the *British Library* and *'findmypast'* (DC Thomson Family History) to digitize over the next ten years up to 40 million newspaper pages from the *British Library*'s vast collection. It covers nearly 200 years, but predominantly the nineteenth century to the mid-twentieth century. In May 2015 nearly nine million pages had been made available from more than 400 titles. Individuals can access the archive by subscription (the first three pages are free), and there are plans to introduce a subscription service to libraries and schools 'in the near future'. In the meantime, whilst you can also see what is available in the *British Library* itself via its catalogue, you can only access the newspapers for free in the *British Library*'s Reading Rooms or online through *British Newspapers 1600–1950* and other packages, available for subscribing institutions. See more at: www.bl.uk/collection-guides/newspapers.

You will find a list of online newspapers around the world at www.newspapers-list.com/. From there you can link to the websites of the individual newspapers, where many of them can be accessed for free, but some must be paid for.

E-books

Many libraries now subscribe to some of the growing number of e-books available. Some will do this via various online collections, such as the *Oxford Reference* (covering 25 different subject areas), *EBSCO* eBooks and Audiobooks, or *netLibrary*, which is a collection of e-books covering a wide variety of subject areas, including business, management, economics, history and literature. Where there is an electronic version of a book available, the library catalogue will provide a web link and the book will then be displayed on your PC for you to browse through. (You will need a username and password to use e-books in subscription collections.) *Science Direct* (as well as providing access to articles from e-journals – see above) gives access to chapters from more than 17,000 e-books at www.elsevier.com/online-tools/sciencedirect/books#ebooks.

An increasing number of e-books and other texts, particularly classic works of history and literature, are now freely available on the web. For example, the *Online Library of Literature* at www.literature.org and the *University of Oxford Text Archive (OTA)*, which 'develops, collects, catalogues and preserves electronic literary and linguistic resources for use in Higher Education, in research, teaching and learning' (http://ota.ox.ac.uk).

Searchable lists of web resources

In addition to the library's own online literature resources, such as databases, e-journals and e-books, you may need to search for other websites that contain up-to-date information relevant to your course. You can find information on the web yourself using search engines (see below) but there are also other sources of details of websites available. Your library may well have compiled a list of quality free websites, selected by specialist subject librarians in consultation with academic staff. These may be called subject indexes or subject directories and provide lists of websites organized into subject categories. There are also tools through which you can search far more widely for information on the web. These tools are sometimes known as subject information gateways, subject portals or subject trees. They will provide descriptions of web resources in particular subject areas, such as *Biz-Ed* (www.bized.co.uk) for business education and *Chemdex* (http://chemdex.org/) for chemistry. If you discover one for your subject area, add it to your list of favourite websites and always try it first. You are likely to find much higher quality material for academic study (although less of it) using a subject portal than you will with a search engine, since portals have the advantage of having been reviewed by experts in the field. Search your library website for details of subject information gateways in your subject area.

The virtual training suite (www.vtstutorials.co.uk) provides tutorials to help you learn how to find information on the web for your field of study and research. These are interactive, teach-yourself tutorials that take around an hour to complete. You can simply work through the material in your own time at your own pace. As well as providing materials to help you to develop your Internet research skills, there is a tour of resources for each of the wide range of subject areas, from aeronautical engineering to women's studies.

Your course tutor or module tutor may also be able to recommend current sites in your particular field. For some of your assignments, though, and certainly for any research project, you will be expected to discover such information for yourself. Various resources are available to help you do this.

Activity Twenty-Two

Explore the list of subject portals that are available on your library website. Choose a service that is relevant to your subject area and explore the resources it contains by searching or browsing. Bookmark any resources that may be useful for future reference.

Search engines

If you do not manage to find all the information that you need through databases or subject information gateways, you may need to search more widely on the web, but care is needed when doing this as many websites contain information that is too generic for academic purposes. Although the web is full of useful information to help you when doing assignments or research projects, it also has, unfortunately, rather a lot of totally irrelevant information as well. It is very easy to fall into the trap of thinking that spending hours 'surfing the net' is the equivalent of doing real work for your assignments. It is probably advisable to set yourself limits on the amount of time you spend searching and *stick to them!* In order to spend your time most effectively you are best off avoiding searching the web at busy times of the day *and* you need to make use of the growing number of 'tools' which are now available to help you search for relevant material.

Search engines will search the web for web pages and documents (including pdfs) and for *PowerPoint* files (indicated by .ppt after the filename). They will generate a list of addresses of websites (URLs) where you will find information on a very specific subject. If you make your search terms too broad, a search could generate hundreds if not thousands of URLs. Some search engines are better than others for a particular subject area and there are those that are more appropriate to use for academic purposes, since they control the web pages that are included in their databases. There are also those that are easier to use than others because they have more flexible search query language and features such as phrase searching, Boolean searching and restricting the search by date. (Boolean searching is searching according to a set of rules about word order and use of symbols to aid the search.) *Bing, Google, Yahoo* and *Ask* are four examples of search engines that incorporate many such features.

Most search engines will only search a proportion of the total web, with different search engines searching different parts of it. However, some search engines are 'meta' search engines (for example *MetaCrawler, Ixquick* and *1-Page Multi*

Search) that search multiple engines simultaneously. While this may save time, you may lose some control over your search if you cannot be as specific in your search terms. To save time, if you are resident in the UK, consider using UK search engines as they will probably be less busy than the ones sited in the US and you will be searching in a smaller database. For instance you could try using *Yahoo UK and Ireland* rather than the full American equivalent.

You can restrict your search to academic or scholarly websites by using *Google Scholar*. This searches scholarly literature across many disciplines and sources, including theses, books, abstracts and articles. If you want to find images to include in your assignments you can use the main *Google or Bing* search engines, but restrict the results to images by clicking on the images tag at the top of the page. You could also use a search engine that only searches for images, such as *Picsearch*, which will find pictures, images and animations. Remember that if you reproduce these in your work you must acknowledge the source of the images, so as not to be accused of plagiarism (see Section 7.3), and there will be some images that you are not allowed to reproduce, because of copyright issues, without paying a fee to the artist. There are also issues of the quality of the image after reproducing it, so care is needed in this area.

Whichever search engine you are using, the following tips will prove useful:

- Plan your search beforehand
- Read the help pages of the search engine
- Use the advanced search option
- Use phrases
- Search in the titles of web pages
- Don't look beyond the first couple of pages of results
- If it looks useful – bookmark it (that is, add to your list of favourite sites)

Activity Twenty-Three

Access the *Yahoo* search engine, either via your library website or direct at www.yahoo.com or http://uk.yahoo.com (with the option of searching UK sites only or Ireland sites only, or of restricting the search by time period).

Click your mouse inside the search form and type some keywords that describe your topic of interest. Try to use several words and use uncommon words if possible. Then click on the find button to start your search. Bookmark (that is add to your list of favourites) any pages you come across which may be useful for future reference.

Search strategies

Whichever tools you are going to use to search the web, it is crucial that you first develop your search strategy – planning your search carefully will mean that you retrieve the material that suits your purpose more quickly. If you do not achieve the results you would like, you will need to look at your search results to see if they indicate how you can modify your initial search. Searching the web may yield full text documents, but often you will be retrieving references to other sources, sometimes in paper format, which you will then need to trace using your library catalogue.

In planning any search there are a number of steps to take:

1 Define your topic, that is, establish its scope and the keywords for searching
2 Structure your search
3 Choose appropriate information sources to search
4 Perform your search
5 View the results
6 Review your results and refine the search if necessary

If you don't find the information you need at first, you may need to go back and revisit some of the steps.

Define your topic: scope and keywords

Think carefully about the sorts of words you could use to describe your topic effectively. Thought-storm the topic, so that you write down as many keywords as you can think of that describe it. Use both broad terms and more specific ones, so that you can decide if you want to focus on a particular aspect of the topic. The narrower terms might also be useful if your first search finds too much information, or information that is too general for your needs.

Think also about the time period in which you are interested. Do you want current information or information that describes what has gone on in the past? Also relevant is the geographical context of your search. Are you interested in country-specific aspects of a particular topic, or are international perspectives of interest to you?

Structure your search

Once you have a set of keywords, you need to think about how you are going to use them to formulate a query in order to perform your search. Searches can be broadened or narrowed depending on how you combine your terms. The different tools you will use for searching databases on the web will each have a set way for you to combine your search terms.

Search terms can be combined using the operator AND, in order to narrow a search, or they can be combined using the operator OR, in order to broaden a search. However, different search tools will express the concepts AND and OR using different symbols. Some may use the words, others a comma for OR, or a plus sign for AND. On-screen help is always available for you to check how to express these operators.

The operator NOT is sometimes available to exclude terms. For example, if you found that you were retrieving a lot of material on science education by searching for *mathematics AND secondary*, you could rerun the search explicitly excluding science *(mathematics AND secondary) NOT science*. Brackets are used to make sure that the sense of the query is clear where more than one operator is used.

In some instances you may want to *truncate* your terms, to pick up singular and plural forms of a term, or you may want to allow for alternative spellings by inserting *wildcard characters*. Often truncation and wildcard characters are expressed using an asterisk, a question mark or a dollar symbol, depending on the search tool or database being used. For example, where an asterisk is used for truncation, *child** will pick up the terms *child, children* and *childhood* (as well as *childless*), and where a question mark is used as a wildcard, *organi?ation* will pick up *organisation* and *organization*.

Some search tools and databases allow you to *search for specific phrases*, often by enclosing the phrase in quotation marks, such as '*University of Leeds*'.

Field searching is a function which many search engines offer. Field searching enables you to search for a particular word or phrase in a specific field of a document (such as the title). It is likely that a document which has your chosen keyword in its title will be more relevant to your needs than one that simply mentions the word in passing somewhere in the body of the document. Most search engines use the title of a website or document when inputting to their system. Make sure only to follow the links in the search results to those items where your chosen term(s) are in the title.

Choose appropriate information sources to search

See 'Databases', 'Searchable lists of web resources' and 'Search engines' above.

Perform your search

Only once you are satisfied that you have a good structure for your search and have selected the appropriate sources should you actually perform the search. Searching can be time-consuming and it can also be very expensive if you are paying for an Internet connection by the minute or via a mobile device.

View the search results

Once you have performed your search, take a look at your search results displayed on screen. Most search engines use a facility known as 'relevancy ranking' in order to rank your search results in 'best match' order, so that the documents that are most relevant to your keywords appear near the top of the list of your results. This means that the first page of results is likely to be more relevant to your needs than subsequent pages.

Review and refine your search

Once you have looked at your results, any flaws in your search strategy should become apparent. If you have retrieved an unmanageably large number of results, think about repeating your search using more specific terms, or incorporating more terms using AND. If you are finding very few relevant items, are there other terms you could use? Are you making full use of the tools available to you? If you are still not retrieving items, think about other sources you could search.

There are various online resources available that will help you to improve your search techniques. Your own university library should provide some that are specific to your institution and are likely to be password-protected and available for their own staff and students. Some, such as the *ASK* materials (Assignment Survival Toolkit) developed at Staffordshire University Library, are on open access (www.staffs.ac.uk/ask/), although at times they link to their own further resources.

Record-keeping

You will probably find it useful to keep a record of the searches that you perform, so that you don't needlessly repeat work, and so that you can look back at the notes and be reminded of the more useful sources that you used. Start by writing down in your own words the information that you are seeking, including the subject for an essay, any particular authors you are looking for, and so on. Then keep a note of each date when you perform a search, which databases you searched, the terms (keywords and phrases and/or authors) that you used in the search, and any years by which you restricted the search, such as 2010–2015. It is useful to record how many results you retrieved for each search and note any comments about the results, such as whether or not a particular database produced far too many or too few results. This may seem quite a lot of work, but you will find it helpful to be this organized, especially if you are doing searches for a large assignment or research project.

Once you have generated lots of references, which lead you to resources, you will need to be just as careful in how you manage those references (see Section 6.8).

Current awareness services for resources

It is potentially very time-consuming to have to keep going back to the databases and running searches in order to keep up to date with new publications and developments in your field, although some databases (for example *MEDLINE*) allow you to store search strategies to rerun at a later date. Many multidisciplinary (for example, *Web of Science*) and some more subject-specific databases (for example, *Sociological Abstracts*) now offer alerting services.

Automated alerting services can also take away some of the effort of scanning and browsing journals, bulletins, newsletters and websites by doing this for you and sending you updates on new developments in your subject. There are a number of such services available, some of which are outlined below.

The *Zetoc Service* (http://zetoc.mimas.ac.uk) from the *British Library* is an automated alerting service that emails information about new publications direct to your mailbox. *Zetoc* is free to use for members of JISC-sponsored UK higher and further education institutions. *Zetoc* covers over 29,000 journals and more than 52 million article citations and conference papers through the *British Library's* electronic table of contents. The database covers 1993 to date, and is updated on a daily basis. You can receive:

- Electronic tables of contents from your favourite journals
- The results of regular searches on current journal and conference literature on any subject of your choice
- RSS feeds for journals in *Zetoc*

Copies of all of the articles and conference papers in the database are available *at a charge* from the *British Library*, and can be ordered direct or through the document supply service in your library (see Section 6.3).

Science Direct Personalization and Alerting Services (which grew out of *Elsevier Contents Direct*) are available at www.sciencedirect.com. After registering for free with the service, you can save a list of journal titles in the fields of science, technology and medicine for which you would like 'alerts' or automatic notification of the latest tables of contents. You can also ask to be notified when new books in your subject area are published. The notification is sent to you by email whenever the database is updated and new books or journal issues are added. You can link from the email to the full-text version of the article. This will be free to you if your library has a subscription to the journal and you have the relevant username and password or access via *Athens*.

The Taylor & Francis publishing group provides a service whereby you can register to regularly receive, by email or an RSS feed, the contents pages of individual journals or clusters of journals which they publish in your subject field. This service is part of their complete 'Alert' service, which includes:

- New Content Alert: when new issues are added to a particular journal
- Latest Article Alert: when new articles are available
- Citation Alert: when a new article on Taylor & Francis Online cites a particular article
- Saved Search Alert: when a new article on Taylor & Francis Online matches a particular search query

They have a wide range of titles in the following subject areas: education, gender, healthcare and biomedicine, law, management, science and technology, social sciences and humanities. You will find their website at www.tandf.co.uk/journals/alerting.asp.

In addition to sending contents pages updates, Taylor & Francis also offer 'eUpdates', which provide information on journals, books, conferences and other news within your areas of interest. For more information, go to www.tandf.co.uk/journals/eupdates.asp.

The Scout Report is a guide to new web resources in the fields of the sciences, social sciences and humanities, and is published weekly on the web or by email by the Internet Scout Research Group. Their team of professional librarians and subject matter experts select, research and annotate each resource. You can use it to keep up to date with new web resources in your subject area. The home page of the *Scout Report* website is https://scout.wisc.edu/report.

To find out when your favourite websites have been updated you can register with *ChangeDetection.com* or *Google Alerts* who will monitor websites for you for free on a daily basis and notify you by email of any changes. Alternatively, you can set up your own alerts to be notified when specific websites are updated by using RSS feeds/news feeds (see Section 5.14).

You can also receive alerts from booksellers when new books in your field are published (see Section 6.4).

Electronic networking

You can keep in touch with other people in your subject area via newsgroups and mailing lists on the Internet but, be warned, you can waste a lot of time reading messages posted to such groups and lists when the information is very peripheral to your research. You would be advised to be very selective in the groups and lists that you join. For more details about mailing lists, see Section 5.5.

Newsgroups

A newsgroup is a discussion area on the Internet. Newsgroups are a public area (a bit like a notice board) where people can post information on a variety of topics and discuss their interests with other people. Newsgroups are organized into subjects. They are also organized by type, for example News, Recreation, Society, Science and Technology, Computers, and so on (there are many more), as well as geographically. Users can post to existing newsgroups, respond to previous posts and create new newsgroups. You can use a service called *Google groups* to search the recent archives of newsgroups or to post your own mes-sages to newsgroups (see: http://groups.google.com).

Social Networking services

As the name suggests these services (such as *Facebook* and *Twitter*) are pro-vided for keeping in touch socially, but can just as easily be used for members with common subject interests to exchange news, views and resources on a less formal basis than in a newsgroup. If you cannot find a space relevant to your spe-cific subject area, you could always take the initiative and set one up yourself. However, you need to beware of how you use the information that you find in such a source – it is much less likely to have the authority of, say, a posting to a peer-reviewed wiki. (See 'Evaluating websites for quality' below.)

Professional communities

A growing number of professional groups maintain their own websites and data-bases of researchers and academics in their field. For example, the *Community of Science (COS)* lists experts and funding opportunities across all fields. You can search *Community of Science* to find a researcher doing work in a particular field. *COS* is now accessed via *Pivot* (http://pivot.cos.com/).

ChemWeb.com is the website of the World Wide Club for the Chemical Commu-nity. The site includes: databases containing abstracts, selected full text articles, chemical structures, patents, other websites, and so on; *The Alchemist* – ChemWeb's own magazine; and a conference diary for the latest events and conferences.

The Feminist and Women's Studies Association (FWSA) UK and Ireland 'is dedicated to the advancement of research into feminism and women's studies. The organization promotes both students and established academics in their research by organizing conferences and events, writing competitions, and maintaining networks with other related research communities' (www.fwsa.org.uk).

The International Union of Architects (UIA) 'is a non-governmental organisation, a global federation of national associations of architects, that are its members' (www.uia.archi/en). 'The UIA's goal is to unite the architects of the world without any form of discrimination. [It] has grown to encompass the key professional organisations of architects in 124 countries and territories.' It publishes an 'Accord on Recommended International Standards of Professionalism in Architectural Practice and Recommended Guidelines' and an 'International Code of Ethics on consulting Services', and the 'UNESCO-UIA Charter on architectural education', which lays out a series of guidelines aimed at ensuring that young architects are capable of meeting the professional, social and cultural challenges of the modern world. The UIA global network for young architects and students of architecture has recently been set up to stimulate and enrich exchange among its members.

Evaluating websites for quality

Anyone with access to an Internet server can set up their own web pages. This means that there is little control over the quality of material that appears. If the information you find on a website is going to have any legitimacy/authority/ validity, you need to ask, and be able to glean satisfactory answers to, the following questions:

1 *Can you find out who is the author of this website?* This could be an individual or a corporate author. Is this information clearly available? Is there an email address available at which you could contact the author?

2 *Is there any indication of the designation or authority of the author?* Can you establish their credentials – for example, are they a member of staff in a university department? Is there evidence that their organization supports the information on the web page? Is there a copyright statement or is a disclaimer visible on the page?

3 *Can you establish the corporate owner of the information?* This could be, for example, a university or a commercial company. Can you establish this from the URL if it isn't immediately obvious on the page? For example: does the URL end with '.ac.uk' (a UK university), '.edu' (a university in the US), '.edu.au' (an Australian university) or '.gov' (a governmental organization)?

4 *What is your impression of the reliability of the information?* On what basis can you form this impression (for example, from prior knowledge of the subject area, from looking at the bibliography or linked information and so on)?

5 *How up to date is the information?* Is there a date when the document was last modified or updated?

6 *What do you think about the way in which the information is structured?* Is it easy to find your way around the website? How have graphics been used? Does the text follow basic rules of grammar, spelling, and so on?

From the answers to the above questions you will be able to form an overall opinion about the quality of any site you visit.

> **Activity Twenty-Five**
>
> Revisit a couple of the sites you bookmarked in Activity Twenty-Three and ask the above questions of each one.

For a free online tutorial offering more practical advice on evaluating the quality of websites go to the '*Internet Detective*' at www.vtstutorials.ac.uk/detective/. This 'critical' approach to websites is required for all of your reading, whatever the source of the information. You will look in detail at reading and writing 'critically and analytically' in Chapters 7 and 8 respectively.

6.8 Managing references

Keep a record

Once you begin to locate useful information for one or more of your assignments using the above methods, it is important that you keep accurate records of all that you find and to organize those records appropriately. This is particularly important for a larger assignment, and especially so if you embark upon a substantial research project. This is for two reasons. First, when you re-read your notes at a later date you may need to return to one of your documents or web pages to recheck something. It can take a very long time or even be impossible to rediscover where you read something several weeks or even only days or hours earlier. Second, you will need to include information on all of the resources you have used in your assignments – and especially those you have quoted from directly – at the end of each of your assignments in a bibliography. Not only does this avoid plagiarism on your part, but it also provides you with the opportunity to demonstrate how extensively you have read about the subject and clearly show the authorities on which you have based your arguments and your conclusions.

Since keeping records of your references can be an onerous task, it might be advisable to learn how to use one of the personal bibliographic software packages now available for helping students and researchers keep track of their references. These allow you to create and organize a database of references imported from a library catalogue or bibliographic databases (*Web of Science*, and so on), or those entered by hand. They automatically create in-text citations and bibliographies in your word processor on your PC or laptop in your chosen style. Examples of such packages are *Endnote* and *Reference Manager*, both available from *Adept Scientific* (www.adeptscience.co.uk). You may find that one or the other is available on the PCs in the computer clusters of some universities or colleges, and that there will be online training materials to learn how to use them, and face-to-face sessions if you attend the university from time to time. (There are also guides to using *Endnote* available at http://library.leeds.ac.uk/skills-endnote.) You can also purchase your own student copy of the software at a discount, although some universities and colleges do now make *Endnote* (and a lot of other software) available for off-campus use by staff and students as well, using technology such as *Desktop Anywhere* or *Application Jukebox*. For those of you using the *Firefox* web browser, there is a free downloadable extension called *Zotero* to help you collect, manage and cite your sources (see www.zotero. org). If your library uses a single-search tool such as *Discovery* or *NORA* for finding books and journals in its subscribed resources, you can also use this software to save the results of your searches to your computer. Some universities provide automatic access to *RefWorks* – the online Bibliographic Management Tool.

'I wish I'd got to grips with bibliographical management systems such as *Zotero* or *Endnote* earlier on in my course. So much more efficient than my reams of paper and card system!'

'Spending time gaining an understanding of bibliographical style at the outset is highly recommended. The devil is in the detail, and consistency is key. So getting to grips with this at the very beginning will save hours of time trying to correct errors later on.'

Styles of references

There are many different styles that can be used for citing (mentioning or quoting in the text) and listing references. Individual academic institutions and even different departments within those institutions may prefer you to use different styles. It is important that you know before your first assignment which style is required for your particular module, otherwise you may lose marks. The Harvard system is very popular and it is a particularly helpful one to use, since you can gradually build up your list of references in alphabetical order as you find and use them in your assignment. This list then becomes your bibliography, which should be included at the end of your assignment. The author references cited throughout the main text and listed at the end of the book you are currently reading use the Harvard system, and so provide an example of that system.

To cite references using the Harvard system, you provide the author and date of publication (plus the exact page numbers when you are directly quoting from the publication) in the main text, then include the details of each publication in the bibliography at the end of the assignment. For the numeric system (another popular choice), you use consecutive numbering of your references in your citations in the text, using (brackets) or superscript, and a numeric list in the same order at the end of the assignment (or sometimes at the bottom of each page as footnotes). Where the same reference is cited on several occasions in the text, the number used the first time in the text for that reference may be repeated throughout the text, or you may use a separate number each time it is cited (check which method is preferred by your tutor/institution).

Various guides (online and hard copy) to citations and to the Harvard and other systems of referencing are available. Some of these may be available via your college or university library's website, but the following are two examples.

At www.staffs.ac.uk/support_depts/infoservices/learning_support/refzone/ you will find useful pages about referencing and plagiarism, and links to different citation systems including Harvard, APA (American Psychological Association) and OSCOLA (Oxford Standard Citation of Legal Authorities). There are also links to two referencing quizzes.

There are also examples on open access of how to reference virtually any format of resource in the Harvard, Numeric, MHRA and many other styles at the following Leeds University Library web page: http://library.leeds.ac.uk/ skills-referencing. These materials are especially useful in showing how to cite and reference what are termed 'irregular' sources, such as an e-book via an e-book reader, a poem, an image or a law report.

Other useful guides on how to write citations and references are the Modern Humanities Research Association (2013) *Style Guide, Chapter 11* and Pears and Shields (2013) *Cite Them Right: The Essential Referencing Guide.* The latter includes examples of referencing sources using the Harvard and other styles including e-books, personal and virtual learning environments (e.g. *Blackboard*), web pages, blogs, wikis and social networking websites such as *Facebook*, as well as print books and journal articles. (*Cite Them Right* is also available online at www.citethemrightonline.com/.) See also Neville (2010) *The Complete Guide to Referencing and Avoiding Plagiarism* and the referencing section of the online *LearnHigher* resources at www.learnhigher.ac.uk/writing-for-univer sity/referencing/advanced-referencing-exercises/. (For more on recording and using sources, and on when to reference and so avoid accusations of plagiarism, see Section 7.3.)

6.9 IT support

It may well be the case that access to a PC with an Internet connection was stated as a prerequisite for your course, in which case you will have had ample time to either purchase your own equipment or arrange access to the necessary equipment at work or elsewhere. Even if it is not stated as a prerequisite, the advantages of having access to such equipment must be clear by now, especially for accessing information, for writing your assignments, and for reducing isolation by being able to communicate electronically with tutors, students and the course administrator.

Computer viruses can be spread very easily through distance learning contacts. Once again let me emphasize the wisdom of installing a proprietary brand virus checker, such as McAfee *VirusScan*, and checking all files sent to you before opening them.

Computer services helpdesk

Any help in dealing with problems with your hardware must come from the supplier of that hardware, but you will usually be entitled to support from the helpdesk at your university or college with any aspect of their networked computer services, including passwords. Whether you are using a PC in a computer cluster on campus or using a PC, laptop, tablet or other mobile device at home or work, you should be able to ask for help with accessing electronic sources, provided you are using them via the institution's network. Helpdesks have a duty to support all students in accessing and using digital services on a personal device, wherever you are studying. You should therefore be entitled to help with and advice on all of the services that your computer services department supports, as specified in their service level agreement.

Activity Twenty-Six

It would be useful to discover at an early stage what 'helpdesk' support is available to you. It could take quite a while to find out the specific telephone number you need to ring or email address you need to use for help with a computer network problem. It is much better to have this information already to hand at the time of any mini-crisis in that area.

Many helpdesks will publish frequently asked questions (FAQs) and longer guides on using IT. Try searching your study institution's website using the terms 'computer services' or 'information systems services' for links to the support available.

Chapter summary

In this chapter you have:

- Investigated what sources of resources are available to you
- Explored some of the recommended resources
- Made arrangements (if necessary) to access other resources
- Learned how to evaluate web resources
- Given some thought to how you are going to manage references
- Been encouraged to discover what IT support is available from the institution where you are registered

7 Reading and note-making

Introduction to Chapters 7–10 • Reading • Note-making from reading
• Recording and using sources • Chapter summary

Introduction to Chapters 7–10

With limited time and restricted access to resources the distance learner in particular needs to make the most of their learning experience. While it is widely acknowledged that the overall experience of the full-time 18-year-old entering higher education encompasses much more than their learning, the distance learner is often far more focused on the specific task of studying, successfully fulfilling the assessment requirements of the course of study, and obtaining some form of accreditation. That said, most distance learning courses include some element of human contact and it is to be hoped that there is an opportunity for enjoyment and stimulating company (if only in a virtual way) for all of you studying by this mode of delivery.

In the following four chapters we focus on the detail of the reality of studying, namely:

- Reading and note-making (Chapter 7)
- Writing essays (and other prose assignments), revision and exams (Chapter 8)
- Other forms of learning and assessment, including working with others (Chapter 9)
- Doing a research project (Chapter 10)

What follows is a relatively brief guide to those aspects of studying for which you may feel in need of a bit of a refresher. However, there may be some sections that you don't need to work through in detail, especially if you have recently been a student. Conversely, if you feel after reading these chapters that you need more help with these study skills, you will find links within the text to other resources, and details of more paper and electronic resources in the Further Resources section at the end of the book. In particular I would recommend the online resources to support you in your studies that are made available by *LearnHigher*.

7.1 Reading

Since so much time on a course of study is spent reading, it is crucial that none of that time is wasted. It is essential that you:

- Read with a purpose
- Read selectively
- Read critically and analytically

Doing background reading before the start of a course or by way of preparation for an essay or other assignment can sometimes be seen as an overwhelming experience, largely due to the enormous amount of information that is available. The task can be made more manageable if you start with introductory texts on a subject, or use secondary sources such as a review article where the literature of a subject is discussed. Some students are fortunate enough to be given an annotated bibliography or reading list at the start of their course, which instantly provides more information about each item on the list. The purpose here is to help you to familiarize yourself in general terms with the subject and to learn some new vocabulary. Not everyone is this lucky though and you need to develop your own strategies for deciding what you want (or need) to read. No one will be this 'spoon-fed' throughout their course in any case, and certainly when it comes to researching for an assignment, some of the marks are likely to be awarded for evidence of your ability to select relevant literature and other sources yourself. (The information provided in Chapter 6 will help you do this.)

Relevance

With the help of catalogues, indexes, abstracts, databases and the development of good searching strategies, you will eventually find what you hope are relevant items of literature and electronic sources to read. However, once you finally have the item on the desk, PC, laptop or tablet in front of you, it is worth spending a few minutes employing the following strategies to confirm that it is going to be worth spending many more minutes, or even hours, reading a particular book or article which could turn out to be unsuitable after all. Try to put yourself into a questioning frame of mind by asking questions such as: Why am I interested in this item? How will it contribute to my essay/assignment/group work preparation?

It is not recommended that you set out to read an academic book from cover to cover. Even if it turns out that the book is very relevant to your studies, you will get far more out of it if you find out a bit more about it first.

Cover

Read the dust jacket or back cover of a book. Although this is provided by the publisher primarily to encourage sales, it can also provide a useful indication of its overall relevance to your needs. It tells you about the author – their standing in the academic community, their qualifications for writing the book and their contribution to a particular field.

Abstract

An abstract at the start of a journal article or of an item on a website is likely to be more informative than a book cover. In the case of academic journals the abstract should conform to the protocol of academic writing and provide an accurate, brief account of what is in the article. Indeed you may have obtained the article only after reading an abstract in a database, but if you have come across it via an index or search engine or by browsing through a journal, it is well worth reading the abstract first. An abstract will provide information such as how the item adds to the body of knowledge, what methodology was used in any research, and the main conclusions.

Contents

Read the contents page of a book or website so that you can select only the relevant chapters/sections or even a few pages, using the chapter/section subheadings to guide you.

Index

Scan the index of a book for appropriate or relevant vocabulary. If none of the terms used there are familiar to you (for example, the words that are used in an essay title), it may be that the book isn't worth reading after all. An index can also provide an overview of the key concepts covered in a book and help you build up an idea of the structure of a subject.

Bibliography

Scan the bibliography to see if you recognize some of the references. Once you become familiar with your subject area you will come to know at least a handful of authors that you would expect to see there.

Introduction

Read the introduction to a book. This can sometimes be the author's preface or it may be the first chapter. In the case of a collection of essays or papers that have been put together by an academic editor, the introduction will be especially useful, since the key points of each chapter usually will have been picked out by the editor. The introduction may also give you an idea of the author's point of view or perspective on the subject of the book, which will help you to read critically and analytically.

Conclusion

Read the final chapter of the book. It's not like reading the end of a novel when you don't want to know what happens. In fact the opposite is true: you want to read a summary by the author of what has gone before or read the overall conclusions that they have reached by the end of the book, to know if you want to read the detail. As with the introduction, the conclusion will provide a rich source of information to enable critical and analytical reading.

Chapters

Use scanning and skimming to delve into chapters to assess how much of each chapter to read. Read the first and last paragraphs of a chapter and read the first and last sentences of a few other paragraphs. Scanning is used when you look quickly down a page or website for specific words or phrases with which you are familiar, and which you want to find. Skimming is used when you are not looking for anything in particular, but want to get a general impression of the writing, and to discover what keywords, phrases or arguments have been used by the writer.

Double check

Don't just rely on one of the above strategies in isolation. You will need to employ two or three to ensure that you don't reject something potentially useful.

Take stock

Some people find it helpful to start a mind map or spider diagram at this point, before progressing to the more in-depth stages of reading. (See the section on the design of notes later in this chapter for more on mind maps.) This involves noting down the keywords for the knowledge you have gained from your reading up to this point. This can make your reading from now on faster and more effective.

An example of what the core part of a mind map might look like is given in Figure 7.1 for the essay title shown there. You will see that this first version of the mind map covers only the key concepts from the first part of the question. These have been arrived at after some preliminary reading around the subject. Figure 7.2 in Section 7.2 shows the more developed version of the mind map in response to the second part of the essay title, after more detailed reading has taken place.

Order of reading

If, after employing the previous strategies, you decide that you will read some or all of the book or article, don't assume that you need to read the chapters or sections in the order that they are provided. This is especially true of edited collections of different papers. Where the book is by a single author, however, it may be possible that they develop a theme or argument as the book progresses (rather like a good essay – see Section 8.1), in which case you will only get confused if you don't read in a logical order. You should have been able to find out whether or not this is likely to be the case by following the suggested earlier strategies. A lot of information on websites is not intended to be read in a linear way (indeed the flexibility of access to information via the web is one of its assets), but beware of getting lost by going off to other, less relevant, sites. A good website will help you keep track of where you are by providing helpful navigation tools or 'breadcrumbs', usually across the top of the page.

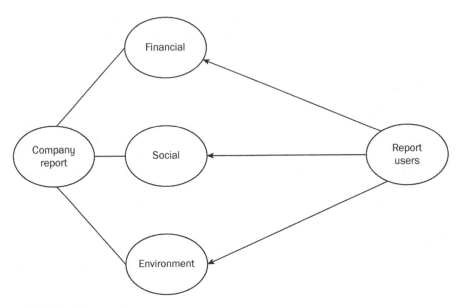

FIGURE 7.1 Mind map 1

Note: Essay title: 'Identify and explain the major classifications of company information required by users. Outline the reports typically required by various types of user, justifying your linkages.'

Speed reading

Once you have identified that a chapter is relevant, one strategy you could employ rather than reading each section thoroughly (as below) to begin with, is first to skim read the chapter rapidly several times, looking for clues, and building up a picture of what each section is about. You will not be able to fully comprehend the meaning of the chapter, but you will be able to decide if it is worth reading it more carefully in order to do so. If you are unfamiliar with this technique, you might want to consult one of the books available on the subject, such as the study skills books by Tony Buzan.

Critical and analytical reading

Whatever order you eventually decide to read a book in, try not to be tempted to simply read what's written, passively accepting everything that's there. To do so is a bit like watching a television programme without listening to the sound. When we read we need to really engage with the writer and 'hear' what the author is saying. To do this we need to stop and think from time to time about what we have just read and consider whether or not, and in what respects, we agree with it or believe it to be based on sound evidence. In other words we need to make a considered response to what we've read. It is a good idea to employ the tactic of *double reading*: first doing a quick skim of the page, or several pages, to get the gist of what is being said, and then returning for a second reading, going over the content much more carefully and making notes on the key points as you go. It is also useful to note your response to what you have read at these key places.

If you are to read critically and analytically you need to compare different points of view that are presented in different books and articles and to be able to make judgements about what is being said. You can start to make judgements by asking the following questions about something that you are reading:

- How much of what is written is fact and how much is opinion?
- Where the author expresses an opinion, is it backed up with evidence or is it simply their latest idea?
- Where evidence is cited, is it recent evidence?
- Does the author have a lot of experience in this particular field?
- Are the author's conclusions based on what is written earlier?
- What are the logical outcomes of following that person's point of view or belief? Are they reasonable and desirable?
- Can you identify the 'school of thought' of the author? (Academics tend to be divided up into groups or 'schools' of people who have the same way of thinking about a subject. For example, psychologists might be 'Freudian' or 'Jungian', depending upon whose opinions they share.)
- Does anyone else in the field oppose the author's view?

Activity Twenty-Seven

You may be able, at this point, to add to the above list, giving some of your own examples of how to read critically and analytically in your particular subject area.

Just because an author has been published does not mean that everything written in a book or journal is academically sound or conforms to current thinking on a subject. This is especially relevant now that there has been a dramatic increase in self-publishing on the web, where material is rarely reviewed. It is therefore important to make judgements about what you read on web pages, since there is often no academic publisher involved to give credence to what is published on the web. (See towards the end of Section 6.7 for a checklist of how to critically evaluate websites.) In particular check out the academic credentials of the author of the materials. The material written by most academics and found on the web will be on sites produced by their academic institution or by the organizers of conferences where papers have been presented. The clue is often very simply in the URL of the website.

Even though academic publishers will always have commissioned peer reviews of the content before publishing a book or journal article, it is nevertheless possible to question what is written, especially if it is not supported by evidence. However, it is important not to be a lone voice disagreeing with several academically renowned authors who agree with one another. Challenging the accepted wisdom of a specific subject is generally reserved for doctoral or post-doctoral study!

More help

The following materials available online will help those of you who need more information on academic reading:

- *LearnHigher* materials at www.learnhigher.ac.uk/research-skills/reading/
- *Skills Plus* materials from Northumbria University at www.northumbria.ac. uk/static/5007/llspdf/skills/academicreading.pdf
- *Skills@Library* materials at the University of Leeds on critical thinking, reading and writing available at http://library.leeds.ac.uk/tutorials/skills-for-suc cess/. These include video clips of academic staff talking about what critical thinking is
- The University of Toronto at www.writing.utoronto.ca/advice/reading-and-researching/critical-reading has some very useful materials entitled 'Critical Reading Towards Critical Writing' as part of their 'Writing at the University of Toronto' website

You may want to read in greater depth about critical thinking, especially if you are a postgraduate student, since a significant part of your work will need to reflect this approach. See the relevant section of 'Further Resources' at the end of this book. You will find Cottrell (2011) a particularly useful book, with chapters on critical thinking, critical reading and critical writing, plus Chapter 8 of Davies (2011) is very thorough on this subject, as are the Open University 'Skills for OU study' materials at www2.open.ac.uk/students/skillsforstudy/reading-skills-for-postgraduate-study.php. If you decide to move on after a taught master's degree to a research degree, you will find the in-depth analysis of critical reading and writing provided in Wallace and Wray (2011) very helpful, especially if you also use the supplementary online self-study materials provided at www. sagepub.co.uk/wallaceandwray.

A note on academic criticism

Criticism in general terms is regarded as something negative, but in an academic context it has a rather different meaning. Criticism does not have to imply negativity; rather it is an opportunity to state what is good about something too. Where something isn't good, it is constructive if you can point out precisely what is wrong and in what ways it could be improved. As you will read in the next chapter, constructive criticism of your essays by your tutors is to be welcomed (even though it might not initially feel like it!). If you are able to develop a critical and analytical approach to listening, thinking and reading, you will be better equipped to write critically and analytically.

Academic criticism is fully accepted as a crucial component of study in higher education at institutions in most parts of the world. In particular, if you are registered for a course with an institution in the UK or other European country, in the US, Canada or Australia, you will be expected to adopt this approach. This may be difficult for you to do at first if you have a different cultural background, but be assured that it will not be interpreted as a rude, personal insult to the author when you include academic criticism in your essays or your contributions to online or face-to-face discussions.

Stopping reading

It is important to recognize when to stop reading. This will be when the items you are reading are not providing you with any new material and/or your research questions have been answered.

Key points to remember when reading

- Ensure that the item is relevant
- Do not read an academic textbook from cover to cover
- Read the 'blurb' or description on the back cover of a book first
- Read the abstract of a journal article or item on a website
- Read the contents page of a book or website
- Scan the index and the bibliography of a book
- Read the introduction and the final chapter of the book
- Use scanning and skimming to assess the relevance of each section
- Decide on your order of reading
- Speed read each section
- Read each relevant section critically and analytically and make notes
- Stop reading when you are not discovering any new material

7.2 Note-making from reading

It is crucial to make notes from your reading as it assists the mind to engage with the material and to process what you have read. People's choice of how they make notes varies considerably. However, although it is quite a personal activity, the following strategies have worked for many.

Highlighting

If you are the sort of person who likes to mark key passages of what you are reading by using a highlighter pen, by writing in the margins or underlining, you will need to make photocopies of the relevant pages of books and journals or make printouts from electronic sources. Never make notes on a library copy of a book or journal.

Copyright

Of course, you need to ensure that the material you are photocopying falls within the limits of what you are allowed to copy for personal use under the terms of the current law on copyright. The licence agreement of the institution where you are doing the copying will usually be displayed near the photocopier.

Additional notes

If you need to write more notes than will fit into the margins of the photocopies, it is a good idea to use a card or a piece of paper and to staple this to the photo-copied article. In this way you ensure that you keep all the notes together.

Physical means

You may choose to record your notes on cards or sheets of paper or you may want to input them directly onto a PC, laptop or tablet. The latter, though time-consuming, means that you may later be able to use some of your notes in the body of your essay without repeating the writing activity, but there is a danger then of including everything you have collected, just because it's there.

Summarize your thoughts

In making the initial notes, don't be tempted to write down everything you have read. Rather, read through a section at a time, think about it, then write a brief summary of what you have read in your own words, only looking at the origi-nal text to check for accurate spelling of new words and to record the names of people and so on. State the main idea at the start of the summary, citing the source of the information, then re-state the other important points. Include only the key points from the reading, checking that you have listed these points in the most logical order. After this, re-read the original work to check that you have not missed out anything important. You may want to think about creating your summary using a mind map rather than by writing a paragraph of text (see next section on design).

Design

You may choose to make notes in a linear fashion or using some kind of pictorial representation of your ideas. Those who are more visual according to the VARK categories of learning preferences (Fleming and Bonwell 2006) will probably find the latter more appealing (see Section 2.10 for details). Some people make linear notes initially as they read through source materials, then they read their notes and produce some form of mind map or spider diagram from them, pick-ing out the key points/themes and highlighting them. This involves writing down the main theme drawn from your reading in the centre of the page and drawing connecting lines from there to other relevant ideas, as well as lines to show the connections between the various ideas. This has the added advantage of helping you to absorb or digest what you have been reading and to start to think about your response to it.

An example of what a mind map might look like is given in Figure 7.2. It is a more detailed version of the one given in Figure 7.1 in Section 7.1. It is based

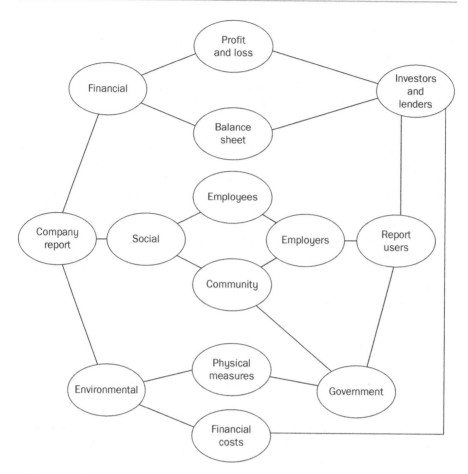

FIGURE 7.2 Mind map 2

Note: Essay title: 'Identify and explain the major classifications of company information required by users. Outline the reports typically required by various types of user, justifying your linkages.'

on the essay title shown. You will see that in Figure 7.2 the more extensive mind map indicates the development of the concepts in response to the second part of the essay title, after further reading has taken place. This is just one example of how to link up your ideas. With practice, you will develop the sort of design that best suits you. Only you will see your design, so don't worry if it is not the neatest piece of work you have ever produced. Some people like to use colour to emphasize the most important points, or to draw the lines that link ideas together.

The mind mapping resource from James Cooke University provides an excellent introduction to how to create a mind map and gives very clear examples of mind maps produced from reading, for writing an essay, and in a lecture.

See www-public.jcu.edu.au/learningskills/resources/lsonline/mindmapping/index. htm. There are also hundreds of examples of colourful and entertaining mind maps to give you inspiration in the *Mappio* mind map library, which you can access at http://mappio.com/.

There are a growing number of electronic mind mapping software programs available. Many of them are available as free downloads (some only as free trials of proprietary brands prior to purchase). Open University (UK) students can download the software *Compendium* via *Moodle* (the VLE). Students who log in (for free) to the Open University's OpenLearn Learning Space are also allowed to download the software (see http://openlearn.open.ac.uk/). Non-OU students should be able to access the *Compendium* tool via the *Compendium* website at http://compendiumld.open.ac.uk/. A tutorial is available to help you learn how to use *Compendium*. You will also find details of software, such as *FreeMind*, *Inspiration* or *MindMeister* via a *Google* search.

The *NoteMaker* tool, which is available from the Research Skills: Note-making section of the *LearnHigher* materials, gives the opportunity to create notes in 'linear', 'pattern' or 'Cornell' formats. The 'pattern' format is very similar to that used in Figure 7.2. In addition, there are now numerous apps for creating mind maps on your mobile device.

To use or not to use

After reading and note-making you should consider splitting the copies of any articles/chapters and sets of notes into different categories: those that you definitely want to use; those that you might possibly use; and those that you reject. It is better to discard irrelevant material at this stage than be tempted to include everything in your essay just because you have it. If you've made notes directly onto your computer, you may have some deleting to do at this stage. If you're not quite sure, create another version of your data file with a new file name, so that if you change your mind, you can retrieve your work.

7.3 Recording and using sources

Bibliographical details

At the start of any reading and note-making session, record the full bibliographical details of the item you are about to read, if you don't already have them from the literature searching stage, and the source of the item (library, website and so on). You could do this on index cards but if you have the opportunity it is much better to use some form of software to record the details on a PC or laptop. This could simply be done in *Word* or some other word processing program, but specialist software is available specifically to record bibliographical details, and this is a much faster and more accurate way to do it. You may decide to export the results of your searches using software such as *Cite Them Right Online*, *End-Note*, *Reference Manager* or *RefWorks*. You will need to find out which software your particular college or university subscribes to, but there will usually be a link to it from your library's website. (For more information on managing references see Section 6.8.)

Whichever means you use to record the details, it is advisable to use the Harvard system of referencing so that you gradually build up your bibliography in the course of researching and reading for your essay (again see Section 6.8 for details of referencing). However, the choice of referencing system will be determined by your institution and may even vary from one department to another within the same institution. Check their guidelines at an early stage.

At the top of each page of notes write the author, date and title of the item, so that you have a clear record of the source of your notes.

Cite your sources/plagiarism

Be meticulous about citing and referencing your sources and quotes so that you avoid being found guilty of plagiarism. In some countries and cultures, copying word for word the work of others who are revered in academia, without acknowledging the source, is perfectly acceptable and is even considered flattering (Introna et al. 2003). In other cultures (predominantly western), however, plagiarism (that is taking and using another person's published thoughts or writings as your own) is not allowed. You may have a whole assignment or examination disallowed if you do plagiarize another person's work. You may even be dismissed from your whole programme of study. The penalties for plagiarism at your institution are likely to be laid out in the college or university student handbook. Copying is not allowed from paper or web or other electronic sources. Sometimes plagiarism can be unintentional, in the sense that you forget to cite the source. However, in many institutions this excuse does not constitute an acceptable defence and you would still suffer the consequences. The sophisticated plagiarism prevention software *Turnitin* is used by institutions to check whether your work contains material from websites. Increasingly they insist that students check their own assignments with the software before submitting them to their tutors, so you have no grounds on which to base mitigating circumstances that you used unattributed materials accidentally. Whatever your personal views are on the rights and wrongs of plagiarism, you need to ensure that you abide by the rules of the particular institution where you are registered.

Some people may be unclear as to when it is necessary to cite a reference. An excellent guide covering why, what, when and how to reference is available: Neville (2010) *The Complete Guide to Referencing and Avoiding Plagiarism.* The author has kindly given permission to reproduce here a quiz from that publication (see Figure 7.3). (Only fill in the boxes if this is your own copy of the book. If you have borrowed the book, you may want to photocopy the quiz, and then complete it before checking your answers against those in Appendix One.) If you score poorly in the quiz, you need to seek further help with the subject. Either refer to the Neville (2010) book or go to one of the many online learning resources on referencing and avoiding plagiarism linked from the *LearnHigher* website at www.learnhigher.ac.uk/. (Go back to Section 6.8 for guidance on different styles of references.)

To test your understanding of when to reference, try answering the questions in the quiz in Figure 7.3. Look at the following situations that can occur when writing assignments and decide if a citation is needed.

	Yes	No
1. When you include tables, photos, statistics and diagrams in your assignment. These may be items directly copied or a source of data collation which you have used.	☐	☐
2. When describing or discussing a theory, model or practice associated with a particular writer.	☐	☐
3. When you summarise information drawn from a variety of sources about what has happened over a period and the summary is unlikely to be a cause of dispute or controversy.	☐	☐
4. To give weight or credibility to an argument that you believe is important.	☐	☐
5. When giving emphasis to a particular idea that has found a measure of agreement and support amongst commentators.	☐	☐
6. When pulling together a range of key ideas that you introduced and referenced earlier in the assignment.	☐	☐
7. When stating or summarising obvious facts, and when there is unlikely to be any significant disagreement with your statements or summaries.	☐	☐
8. When including quotations.	☐	☐
9. When you copy and paste items from the Internet and where no author's name is shown.	☐	☐
10. When paraphrasing or summarising (in your own words) another person's work that you feel is particularly significant, or likely to be a subject of debate.	☐	☐

FIGURE 7.3 Quiz on understanding when to reference
Source: Reproduced, with permission, from Neville (2010) *The Complete Guide to Referencing and Avoiding Plagiarism*, p. 15, figure 3.1.

Quotations

If you decide that a short section of the original text of a book or article is going to provide a really useful quote in your essay, be especially meticulous about recording your sources. You can spend hours returning to the library to rediscover the exact page number of a quote. Don't, however, let your essay or other written work become just a series of quotes. If an author expresses something very clearly it is reasonable to quote them, but you have to explain in your own words why the quote is relevant to the essay and how it supports your own reasoning. Even when you are not quoting an author verbatim you should acknowledge the source of ideas/evidence/theories to which you refer in the text of your essays.

There are various ways of laying out long and short passages of text. Again guidance may well be provided by your department, and there are also guides such as those referred to in Section 10.7 that help you do this, and those linked from the *LearnHigher* website.

Chapter summary

In this chapter you have:

- Had the opportunity to revisit two of the most important study skills that you will need to successfully complete your distance learning course: reading and note-making
- Given particular thought to how to read critically and analytically in your subject area
- Learned more about how to make notes from reading using a mind map
- Assessed your own knowledge about when to cite references and, by doing so, avoid plagiarism

8 Essays and written examinations

Introduction • Essay writing • Revising for examinations • Sitting
examinations • Chapter summary

Introduction

Although the style of writing required to complete all of your assignments is likely
to vary during the course and may include reports, observations, numerical or
scientific exercises, case studies and essays, it is often the writing of traditional
essays that creates most anxiety among students. This is especially true of those
who are returning to study after a gap of some years. I am, therefore, going to concentrate on essays here. Most of you reading this book have probably done some
sort of study in further or higher education in the past and have therefore written
essays before. What follows is a reminder list of strategies to help you plan and
write successful essays. Some of the more general strategies suggested are applicable to all assignments, irrespective of the form of writing needed. Some strategies will apply to writing essays for unseen written examinations as well as to
writing essays submitted throughout the course. Clearly, however, some aspects,
such as asking someone else to read a draft to check that you have made yourself
understood, are luxuries not afforded in the examination environment!

8.1 Essay writing

Created not born

Remember that you are not born a good essay writer. Rather you develop into
one – but only through:

- Reflecting on your strengths and weaknesses
- Gaining feedback to use in that reflection
- Using resources such as this book, people and computers to tackle your weak-
  nesses
- Using checklists
- Giving your reading and writing plenty of time
- Reflecting often on what you have written

Start early

Allow plenty of time to research and write each essay – a good essay will take many hours of reading, note-making and writing. If you leave it too close to the deadline you will be too pressured to do a good job and you are likely to find that the key books that you need to read will already have been requested by others from the university or college library. As with other aspects of your studies, you need to plan backwards from the deadline for each assignment and add to your chart when you need to start your literature searching for each one. (See the *Gantt* chart, Figure 3.1 in Section 3.6.)

Assessment criteria

Find out what the assessment criteria are for your assignment/essay/report and how many or what percentage of marks are allocated to each criterion. Depending on the subject, some tutors award marks for good spelling/punctuation/grammar or conversely subtract marks if these aspects of an essay are poor. Most (or all) marks are likely to be awarded for your ability to:

- Express your ideas clearly
- Provide evidence that you have conducted sufficient research, that is, read widely and deeply about the subject
- Show that you can analyse and critically appraise what you have read, moving away from being purely descriptive
- Present and justify your own argument and conclusions

> 'Having spent much of my working life producing management type reports, I had to learn a new written style for my academic work. The fact that bullet points were frowned upon in my area of study, was something of a shock!'

How many words?

Take note of the minimum and maximum word allowance for each piece of work. If you do not meet these requirements, you may be penalized and marks might be deducted. Such word limits are imposed to provide you with an indication of the level of detail required in your answer. It is also a test of your ability to structure a balanced and concise argument.

Read the question

Some tutors (examiners) are more helpful than others in the way they formulate essay/assignment questions. However it is worded, read and re-read the question and break it down into its various component parts if it is complicated. Pick out the keywords from the title. Add your own words and phrases as you think through exactly what is being asked in the question. These words and phrases will help you in your literature search. Include the full range of concepts you will need to cover. With the increasing emphasis on learner-centred learning, it will sometimes be possible to negotiate an essay title, making it more relevant to your work context, country or culture, whilst still meeting the required learning outcomes. This should increase your motivation for the task in hand and ensure that you have at least a basic knowledge of the subject right from the start.

Read the literature

Perform your literature search for the assignment and obtain useful books and articles. (Chapter 6 will help you do this.) Don't forget to check reading lists from your tutor where such lists have been provided. The length of the assignment and the marks allocated to it will largely determine the time you spend on your literature search and the number of items it is necessary to obtain and read to meet the assessment criteria. Don't be tempted to try to read everything there is on a subject – each assignment is not a research project. Although you will probably have some materials provided by your tutor(s) that are relevant to the title of the essay, tutors don't want simply to receive back a reordered version of these materials. They want to see that you have been thinking about the information they have given you and are developing your ideas. It is also important that you show you have read more widely than the notes they have given you.

Make notes

It is important that you make notes from the literature as you read it. How you might do this was explored in Section 7.2. Ensure that you record all of the bibliographical details of everything you read, especially the page numbers of any phrases or short passages you may want to quote verbatim.

Make a plan

Plan your essay before you start to write the substance. Note down keywords or features/ideas/arguments you want to make, and the reference(s) you want to use to support those ideas. This has sometimes been known as 'brainstorming' or, more recently, 'thought-storming' your ideas. Don't worry about the order of these individual points initially. Again people vary in the way they find it helpful to note down their essay ideas, just as they do in making notes on their reading. Some will write in a linear way, while others will use mind maps or spider diagrams. The latter has the advantage of showing the relationship between the main points, and may ultimately help you decide on the order in which you will write about these points in your essay. In practice your mind map will be developed during the combined tasks of planning your essay and doing the background reading for it (see Figure 7.2 in Section 7.2 for an example). Re-read the essay question and ensure that you have ideas that address each part of it.

Make your points

Expand each of the keywords or features into one or two paragraphs, commenting critically and analytically (that is, questioning and justifying) on what you have read, and citing the sources. (See Section 6.8 for guidance on *how* to reference and Section 7.3 for help on *when* to reference.) Keep reminding yourself of the question/essay title and check that what you are writing is relevant. Write concisely and succinctly, yet using enough words to be able to summarize unambiguously the theories and/or the arguments in what you have read, and to express your own opinions and ideas.

Link it all together

Put the various paragraphs into a logical order and write the linking text. This is the point at which the disjointed parts come together to form a coherent whole. It is also where you gradually develop your line of reasoned argument throughout the essay. It is in writing the linking text that you may well decide to change the order of the different parts of the essay or to rewrite some of the paragraphs to make more sense in view of the developing argument. Writing down everything you have learned about a subject does not constitute a good essay – you *must* answer the question. Sometimes what you leave out is as important as what you leave in.

Conclusion

Draw your conclusions based on the points you have made earlier, combining sound evidence from your reading with some original thoughts of your own.

Introduction

The introduction is very often the last thing to be written, providing as it does an outline of what is to follow and a hint of what your conclusions are.

Critical and analytical writing

There is a very useful resource entitled 'What's the difference between description and critical analysis?' on the *LearnHigher* website at www.learnhigher.ac.uk/learning-at-university/critical-thinking-and-reflection/. If you look at these materials, you will notice that the key words in the list for 'Descriptive writing' are: 'explains', 'notes', 'lists', and 'states'. Whilst these are valid characteristics to be found in the introductory section of an essay, it is crucial for a higher level piece of work that you build on these. This means implementing the suggestions given in the 'Critical/analytical writing' list in the resource: such as 'argues according to evidence', 'evaluates', 'identifies the significance', 'shows the relevance' and 'draws conclusions'. This vocabulary will hopefully be familiar to you, since it takes us right back to the descriptions used in Bloom's higher levels of 'Analysis', 'Synthesis' and 'Evaluation' in his cognitive domain of learning outcomes, which we looked at in Chapter 2. If you skipped this more theoretical part (Section 2.5), now might be an appropriate time to consider it, since it will undoubtedly have a beneficial effect on your essay writing skills if you are clear about the meaning of the learning outcomes for your assignments.

For example, if your assignment asks you to 'evaluate the main causes of the First World War', it will gain you little credit if all you do is provide a list of the causes. It will be essential that you also analyse each cause in terms of its relative influence, bringing in evidence to support your analysis, and then synthesize your analysis, that is, bring together the points you have made to provide an overall evaluation.

Use of first person

It has traditionally been accepted in most academic subjects that we avoid using the word 'I' in academic writing when expressing our views. This has been seen as a way of encouraging you to focus on the argument and the evidence. However, the rules seem to be changing and now vary from one academic discipline to another. Reflective writing in particular requires that you personalize it, so the rules will change depending upon the nature of the assignment. It is worth checking out at the start of your course what the accepted practice is for your subject and for different types of work.

Use plain language

Don't be tempted to use long words or complicated sentences in the essay: they do not equate with intellectual ability – often the opposite is true. The ability to write clearly and understandably is far more impressive!

Understand what you write

Don't use words that you don't understand. If you come across a word or phrase in a reading that you want to quote, ensure that you understand its meaning before using it. Your tutor or other students may ask you about it in a discussion of your essay.

Use drafts

You will need to write more than one draft. Once again, the number of marks allocated to a particular assignment will help determine just how much time you spend on this task and therefore how many versions you will produce, but there comes a point when you have to stop and be prepared to submit it. (Often the deadline will impose this discipline in any case.) Word-processing packages on PCs and laptops are wonderful (especially the spellchecker!) and it may be possible that you are constantly amending your copy as you work through your document. However, it is a good idea to stop at some point and print off a full draft. Leave it for a while (preferably until the next day) and return to it with a more detached and self-critical approach to what you have written. Make final amendments.

Reviewers

If possible, ask someone who is not on your course to read and review a fairly advanced draft of your work to ensure that they can understand what you have written. Clearly with higher-level courses a non-specialist will not be able to understand all of the meaning, but they may be able to point out, for example, where your argument has not been presented in a clear and logical way. While it would be wrong for someone else to actually contribute to your work, it is generally accepted practice that others are allowed to view your drafts and to point out where more evidence is required or when some references are not provided. For some assignments the tutors themselves may be prepared to read your draft and give advice before you submit the final version. Write down the feedback and use it as a reminder for other essays.

Read the feedback

For some programmes of study you will be writing essays at various points throughout your course and before a final examination or assignment. This is sometimes called formative assessment and may or may not count towards the final mark for your course. In such cases the feedback you receive from the tutor who reads your essay is almost as important as the mark itself. Good feedback will be supportive, giving constructive criticism of your essay and providing advice on how to improve your performance in your next essay (and for this reason is also sometimes called 'feedforward'). If you don't understand any of the feedback provided by your tutor, don't be afraid to ask for clarification, or even to question or challenge it. Discussion of your work is good – it will help you see how to improve it and it will help you to recognize where and how to make your argument more clearly. Feedback is also important because it is one of the key opportunities for contact with your tutor, which should help you to feel motivated and give you a sense of belonging.

Your tutor may also suggest key readings that you have not discovered for yourself. Don't be tempted just to look at the mark and be relieved that you have passed – read the feedback. The process of writing an essay and reading the feedback is as much a part of learning as reading study materials or attending lectures. As was stated in Section 2.6, the principal purpose of formative assessment is development rather than judgement.

When writing your next essay get out the feedback on previous essays and use it as a checklist – especially to spot your spelling and grammar mistakes.

Practice for exams

Every time you prepare for and write an essay, it is good practice for writing examination answers. The key points of reading the question, doing a plan and linking your points together to develop your argument are all crucial elements of writing good examination answers. These combined with taking heed of the feedback received are all essential preparation for final exams. Effort put into writing essays will be rewarded twofold – in the marks received for the essay itself and in the marks received in an exam.

Key points to remember when writing an essay

- Start early
- Read the assessment criteria
- Check the minimum and maximum word allowance
- Read the question (repeatedly!)
- Read the relevant literature carefully
- Make notes from your reading
- Make a plan for your essay
- Make individual points
- Link it all together
- Cite your sources
- Write a conclusion
- Write an introduction
- Use plain language
- Write what you understand
- Write drafts
- Ask someone to review your draft
- Read feedback from your tutors

More help

For further advice on other forms of writing, see Section 9.2 on report writing and Section 10.7 specifically on writing a research report. For citations and referencing, see Section 6.8. Your department or university/college may also issue its own guidelines. See also the details of other resources at the end of this book. If you require more than a reminder about writing essays and need more in-depth advice about the process, an excellent book is Creme and Lea (2008). Another is Rose (2012). For guidance for international postgraduates on writing, see Part VI of Davies (2011). You will find Chapters 10 and 14 especially useful for writing critical reviews, and Chapter 9 on writing style and language very practical. Section 5 of Chapter 8 (on Critical Thinking) of Davies (2011) provides a useful example of how to apply critical thinking when writing an assignment by using a real postgraduate essay topic from a class in International Business. For more help with writing analytically and critically see Chapter 10 in Cottrell (2011). (See 'Guides to reading, writing and referencing' in Further Resources for details of these and other resources on writing, as well as checking out the *LearnHigher* materials on academic writing at www.learnhigher.ac.uk/writing-for-university/.)

8.2 Revising for examinations

Although many tutors are now choosing to use more innovative forms of assessment (including electronic means) and are providing continuous assessment throughout the course, a lot of importance is still attached by many to the final written examination at the end of a module.

Even where assignments have been submitted by post or email at regular intervals through your course, many distance learners are expected to attend a final examination in person, not least to satisfy your study institution's requirements regarding authentication/identity of the registered students. Even if you don't have to attend your host institution, you are likely to be asked to sit an unseen written examination paper at a local study centre. With advances in technology, some students are now able to sit examinations of various kinds (online assessments) using their own PC or laptop, and so do not need to attend in person. Some systems are able to verify the identity of the student using retina and iris identification, although it is likely to be some time before the use of such a system is widespread.

While some people thrive in an examination situation and welcome the opportunity to demonstrate all that they have learned, the vast majority of us do not readily embrace the prospect of final exams, and the pressure and concentrated period of effort associated with them. Nevertheless, with a little forethought and a calm approach, the experience does not have to be quite as traumatic as many would have us believe. The key to being successful in exams is good preparation for them, namely – revision.

The skills required for the combined process of revision and sitting exams are essentially those that have already been addressed in this and the previous chapter – reading, making notes and writing. In addition, while it is not something everyone (especially distance learners) has the chance or desire to do, some people also use their skills of working with others to help them to prepare for exams. Some people find it helpful to revise with one or more other person and/or to have someone test them before their exams by asking them questions.

Planning

While serious planning for revision and exams is naturally going to begin towards the end of your module, there is a sense in which planning needs to begin right at the start of it. If you are organized in the way you make and store notes from your reading and from any lectures you might attend, this will make your task of revising a little easier. Filing together all material related to each topic being covered on your course means that you know where to find it all when you come to revise.

When to revise

Well before the actual period of revision needs to begin, you need to make a revision diary or chart. You need to note on this a timetable or a schedule of the weeks over which you will revise and what topics you will revise in which weeks or days. Similarly, just as you have to decide as a distance learner at what time of day or night you are going to do your studying and complete your assignments, you need to consider realistically when you are going to find time in your week to revise.

Activity Twenty-Eight

Although you may already have done a study schedule and a weekly planner for your whole programme of study, it is probably a good idea to do separate and more detailed versions of these for the period of revision. Clearly this will be an activity to which you will return once you know more about the exact nature of your course, and if and when any exams of this sort are scheduled. Remember though that the key to time management is knowing when to amend your schedule.

The overall period of time that you devote to revision and how many weeks ahead of the exams you begin to revise is going to be something for you to work out for yourself. Some people are very systematic and start some revision many weeks before the exams; others find that if they start too early, they can't remember everything on the day. However, I would advise that you don't leave it too late to begin: most people find they don't leave enough time. If you follow the strategy for revision suggested later in this section, you will hopefully find that you can do the different stages of revision over an extended period of time and ultimately discover that you can recall it all.

What to revise

The best advice to give is that you should revise everything included in each module on your programme. However, as a part-time student you may need to be strategic in your choice of revision topics, especially if you know that it is unrealistic to revise every element of your course. Be aware, though, that deciding which topics to revise and which ones to set aside is a very risky business. Another approach used by some students is to revise most but not all topics in greater depth, and to revise the remaining topics to a lesser extent. This at least means that if you really do have to answer a question on a topic that you hadn't really anticipated you will not be completely devoid of ideas. Your own interests, and your strengths and weaknesses, will also help you to decide which topics need most work, which ones you should tackle and which ones to avoid if possible. You may even get some hints from lecturers, so don't miss out on any online discussions, tweets or face-to-face elements of the course as examinations draw closer. (See the information on cue consciousness in Section 2.9.)

While not foolproof, you can often see from past exam papers which topics always or nearly always come up for a particular module. Looking at past papers also helps you to become familiar with the structure of the paper: how many questions have to be answered; which ones are compulsory; and so on. (Of course this can change from year to year, so always read the instructions on the top of your paper when the time comes.)

Reading

Revision essentially consists of doing a lot of reading and trying to absorb what you read in order to be able to reproduce the ideas, points of view, theories and so on in a written examination. It doesn't often mean committing to memory in a rote-learning sense, but in the case of mathematical or scientific formulae or passages of literature, for example, you may have no choice but to do so. How each individual does this varies a great deal, but for most of us repetition is a major element of the process.

What you should read will vary according to your particular course. For some courses the tutor will make it clear that if you thoroughly know all that is in a detailed study manual or included in online learning materials you will be well prepared. For most courses, though, you will also need to re-read your own essays or other assignments and even some of the articles or extracts from books that you used to prepare to write those assignments. If you have made and kept good summary notes of your topics as you worked through the module or as you prepared an assignment, use these as a starting point for your revision.

Making notes

Most people find that it helps to make notes when they are revising. This can ensure that revision reading becomes a more active rather than simply a passive activity. As with note-making when reading as you prepare to write an essay, it is better to read a section at a time, think about what you have read, and only then make notes that summarize what you have read, using whatever style of writing that best suits you and your subject. Again, as when preparing for essay writing, try as a second stage to reduce the longer version of your notes to some diagrammatic form (a diagram is easier for showing the relationship between elements), or simply a list of related topics (you might want to do this using whatever form of technology you are most comfortable with). Finally, extract a few keywords or phrases from each list or diagram and commit these to memory – by rote, if necessary. Hopefully (if you have done the revision thoroughly in the earlier stages), by recalling these keywords in the examination room, you will remember the diagram in your head, which in turn will lead to a whole chain reaction of thought, and you will find that all the knowledge that you need will be 'unlocked'.

It is probably better to go through each of the three stages of note-making in different weeks if possible, and certainly on different days within your revision schedule. This way you are revisiting the subject at regular intervals and 'topping up' the store of knowledge in your head. Some people, however, prefer to go through all three stages in one sitting for each topic, returning to the keywords a day or two before the exam, just to refresh their memory.

Key points to remember when revising

- Make plans for revision right at the start of your module by organizing your notes carefully
- Create a revision timetable
- Decide what topics to revise
- Read your notes, assignments and other materials
- Make notes on your reading
- Summarize your notes
- Pick out key words from your summary

8.3 Sitting examinations

I have already suggested towards the end of Section 8.1 that each essay or other form of assignment you write during your course is practice for your exams. Although the timing is of course far more restricted in the exam situation, which puts you under more pressure, the process of writing the answers is essentially the same as when writing for assignments. Some exams are even open book exams, where you don't have to rely completely on your memory to recall crucial information, and the examiner is looking for your appropriate interpretation of the data rather than your recall of them. It needs to be said, however, that this type of exam is still relatively rare. Whatever form your exam is going to take, there are some steps you can take beforehand to ensure that you are able to do your best.

Assessment criteria

Although you are unlikely to receive a list of assessment criteria for each exam question, it is not unreasonable to ask your tutor well ahead of the exam for a list of criteria that they will, in general terms, be applying when marking the exam answers. These are likely to be similar to those provided for each of your assignments, but there could be some differences so it's worth checking this out.

Handwriting/spelling/grammar

Exam markers are likely to be a bit more lenient about these than they would be in marking an assignment prepared in more time and with the use of a word processor. However, while you are not going to get extra marks added for neatness, you may lose marks if the examiner cannot understand your answer because of these factors. No examiner is going to spend very long struggling to try and work out what you mean by something you have written in an exam answer, if it is not immediately clear.

Planning for the exam

Well before an exam you should be aware of how much time you will be allowed in total and how many questions you will have to answer in that time. It is therefore possible to have decided beforehand how much time you can devote to answering each question. Don't be tempted to simply divide the total time by the number of questions, say three hours by four questions, which makes 45 minutes per question. It is advisable to allow, say, 10 minutes at the start of the exam to read through the whole paper and decide which questions you are going to answer (where there is a choice) and the order that you might prefer to answer them in. You should also try to allow another 10 minutes before the end of the exam to read through your answers, and check for and correct any errors that it is easy to make when you are writing at speed in exam conditions. So, subtracting 20 minutes from the total leaves you in fact with 160 minutes or only 40 minutes per question.

Beforehand

Some people can stay calmer than others at the time of exams. Although you will need to check your keywords the day or night before, it is best not to be revising for too many hours immediately before an exam. Instead, try to relax, perhaps by doing some form of physical exercise, followed by a soak in the bath, and try to get an early night.

On the day of the exam, allow plenty of time to travel to the exam centre. You don't want to arrive hot and flustered after rushing there, and you certainly don't want to be late – you may not be allowed to sit the exam at all, which would be a great waste of all that effort. If you have never been to the exam centre before and you are not sure where it is, it is probably a good idea to travel there on a previous occasion, if it is not too expensive or time-consuming to do so. Once you know exactly where it is, it is one less thing to worry about as the day of your exam approaches.

Remember to take with you whatever writing, mathematical or scientific instruments you are going to need, as well as your college or university identification card and/or exam entrance number, which may be needed to gain access to the exam centre. You may also need the details of the exact room number where your exam is taking place.

Don't allow others to make you nervous before the exam – if necessary wait away from the crowd. Similarly, don't analyse the paper at length afterwards.

Write your name or number

Most exams are now taken anonymously, so you will need to take with you your examination entry number or code and write this in the appropriate place on the exam script or cover sheet, whichever system is used by your institution. It would be a nightmare if, after doing so much work before and during an exam, you were not given credit for your answers.

Read the whole paper

Even if you think you know how long the paper is due to last and how many questions you have to answer, always read the instructions at the top of each exam paper before you start. It's very easy in a stressful situation to misremember the more straightforward things. Check too if there is any choice on the paper – you don't always have to answer all of the questions. Take care here as sometimes you have to answer a set number of questions from each section of the paper or all questions from section one and three more from the rest of the paper. Take your time and recalculate, if necessary, how many minutes you definitely have for each question, allowing yourself time at the beginning and at the end of the whole paper, as suggested above.

Take note too of any instructions about using the answer sheets. In most exams you are expected to start your answer to each question on a new sheet of paper. This is usually so that different people can mark individual questions at the same time.

Read through all of the questions and make a mental or preferably a written note as you read through the paper about which ones you think you could answer most successfully. Note too if you think you could answer two or three better than the others and decide the order in which you are going to do them. Beware: if you don't write your answers in the same order in which the questions are set, it is possible to forget to return to an earlier one and realize with horror after the exam that you didn't answer the required number of questions. Write at the top of the paper which ones you decide to tackle. Put the numbers clearly on your first sheet.

Read each question

Having decided upon the questions you are going to answer and the order in which you are going to do them, read through each question twice before starting to plan your answer, and again from time to time *as* you write your answer. As you read through the question the second time, pick out the component parts and note them down separately or divide up the question with oblique strokes on the question paper.

Planning each answer

Keep in mind how much time you have per answer, but allow the first five minutes or so to plan each answer. This will be time well spent.

As when planning an essay, note down the key elements that need to be included in your answer, thinking about the relationship between the elements and the order in which you want to include them in your answer. If it is an essay-type answer, jot down the keywords that you need to include in your conclusion. Even where it is not an essay answer, still note down the key parts that you need to include in your answer so that you don't forget to complete all parts of it.

Writing your answer

Unlike when writing an essay in a non-exam situation, you are going to have to write your introduction right at the start of your answer for an exam. But unlike when you are writing an essay, you already know the subject matter, you have noted down what to include and how to conclude the answer. Once you have these, you are ready to write the introduction and thereafter to continue into the body of your answer.

When writing an essay-type answer in an exam you don't have time to have the luxury of writing the component parts and then rearranging them. That's why your plan is so important. Hopefully you will have collected your thoughts together at that stage and you can be confident of writing your answer in the time available, in a logical and well-argued way. You will be able to show, not just what you know, but that you are capable of using that knowledge in an appropriate and well-structured way.

Tick off each part of your notes when you have written about a particular topic and at the end of writing your answer put a line through the whole of your notes for that question. Rules will vary according to who has set the exam, but generally you are expected to hand in everything you have written in the course of the exam, even if you don't want it to be seen as part of your final answer. You need to ensure that it is very clear which part of the script contains your notes and which is your final answer.

As well as planning the content of your answer, you need to think about how much time you will spend writing about each aspect of the answer. Although you don't want to spend too many valuable minutes on the planning stage, it is probably wise to jot down very quickly on your plan before you start writing how many minutes you intend to use for writing each part, so that the sum of the parts is not greater than the time available for answering that one question. You need to be constantly aware of the time as you are writing. Even if you don't have time to include all aspects that you had intended, it is better to ensure that you have written your concluding argument at the end of an essay, or come up with a solution at the end of an answer that involves calculations or theories.

That said, marks are often awarded for the processes involved in completing calculations, even if the final solution is not accurate in every respect, so don't be tempted to cross out your workings if you feel that the solution is not correct. Again, any rough workings or notes that ultimately you don't want to be considered should be clearly crossed out.

If it looks like you are going to run out of time, ensure that you have made an attempt at as many of the required number of questions as you can. Remember it is always harder to get the last 30 per cent of the marks for a question than it is to get the first 30 per cent. Avoid perfecting your answers and not leaving yourself enough time to attempt all the questions that you need to.

At the end of the exam

Ideally there should be ten minutes left after you have finished answering your last question to skim read all of your answers. Although this isn't enough time to amend anything you discover that is seriously wrong, it does give you time to spot minor errors in spelling or use of words or phrases or calculations and to put them right. You could pick up a few extra marks this way – marks that could make the difference between passing the exam and not doing so.

Key points to remember when sitting an exam

- Find out beforehand what, in general terms, the examiner will be looking for in your answers
- Take care with handwriting, spelling and grammar
- Plan well in advance of the exam, and check again on the day of the exam, how many minutes are available for each answer. (This is after allowing ten minutes at the beginning and another ten minutes at the end of the total time allowed for the exam.)
- Find out beforehand exactly where the examination will be held and take with you your identification card and/or exam entrance number
- Remember to write your number or code on the exam script
- Before you start to write your answers, take ten minutes to read the whole paper, including the instructions at the top of the paper, and decide which questions you are going to attempt

- Read each chosen question very carefully, when you get to each one, and divide up the question into its component parts
- Use the first five minutes for answering each question to plan the answer, noting down the key parts that you need to include and the keywords that should be in your conclusion
- Write your answer, starting with the introduction, and checking back frequently to the question and to your notes to ensure that you include everything that is relevant
- Cross out each part of your notes after you have used them as the basis of your answer, finally writing your conclusion
- Use the last ten minutes of the exam to quickly read through your answers and make any necessary amendments

Chapter summary

In this chapter you have:

- Had the opportunity to revisit two more of the most important study skills you will probably need to successfully complete your distance learning course: writing essays and revising for and writing examination answers
- Begun to think ahead about the time that will be needed for revision

9 Other forms of learning and assessment

Introduction • Working with others • Report writing • Maths and data collection and analysis • Labs, workshops and field work • Posters, presentations and literature reviews • Chapter summary

Introduction

Although their use is widespread, essays and written examinations are far more prevalent as forms of assessment in the humanities and social science subjects than they are in what might be called the more 'applied' subjects, such as science and engineering. In these subjects other forms of learning and assessment are growing in popularity, particularly now that developments in technology mean that the choice of methods available has expanded. For some of your assessments you may be expected to write a more factual report (see Section 9.2), perhaps less analytical than an essay; make a presentation to your peers and tutor (including in mathematical or diagrammatical formats – see Sections 9.3 and 9.5); or conduct practical work of some form in a laboratory, a workshop or on a field trip (see Section 9.4). Producing a poster or giving a presentation is becoming a popular form of assessment in many subjects, as is writing a literature review (see Section 9.5). While some of these forms of assessment are less prevalent in distance learning situations, you are increasingly likely to come across them in some form or another even when attendance at your study institution is fairly limited (or non-existent). In particular, working with others in groups is an increasingly popular form of learning and assessment with distance learning tutors in all subjects.

9.1 Working with others

The role of the tutor in higher and further (tertiary) education has changed significantly in recent years. In many instances there has been a shift towards the tutor as a facilitator of learning rather than, or in addition to, a teacher. Although much of your learning as a distance learner will be done by you as an individual, facilitated or helped by materials provided (and probably written) by your tutors and other experts, it is now widely acknowledged that we also have much to learn from our fellow students or peers. The tutor (increasingly referred to as an 'electronic moderator' or 'e-moderator'; Salmon 2011: 3) will adopt the role of facilitating that learning between students, but may not necessarily directly involve themselves in the process. In a few instances whole courses are delivered in this manner, but most courses are likely to include some element of group work at some point. In many cases the group work will be assessed.

Student handbook

'Participants work together in small groups on an agreed topic. They generally use a private bulletin board forum for discussions and a separate area within the course for uploading files and making presentations as web pages.'

Although working with others on some aspect of your coursework is perhaps more difficult, and certainly different, when studying at a distance, for some courses you may nevertheless need to demonstrate that you possess an appropriate set of skills to do so. Learning to work co-operatively and collaboratively with others in a 'community of practice' (Clarke 2008: 9) to complete a project not only benefits you during your time of study but also develops much needed skills for the workplace. When collaborative work is successful, it brings benefits to all group participants, since it can reduce the workload of individuals and bring fresh ideas and perspectives to group members. Group working can help you learn more effectively because you will be challenged about your own ideas – thus improving the learning outcomes in Bloom et al.'s (1956) 'affective' domain (see Section 2.5).

What skills do you need?

While the categories of broad skills needed are essentially the same whether working face-to-face on campus or at a distance, the methods used to work together will obviously vary and the specific skills required will differ. In general more effort is required in group work at a distance and it can be slower and more complicated than working alone. Most significantly, the majority of your communication with others may be by technological means, including the use of emails, synchronous and asynchronous electronic discussion groups (some of which may be accessed via a VLE), and increasingly by contributing to blogs and wikis (see Chapter 5 for more details of these methods). You may also be able/expected to use telephone, text messaging, *Facebook* or *Twitter*. In addition, Asynchronous Voice Boards might be used to facilitate group work (Salmon 2011: 87). (See the Glossary in Section 5.3 for a definition.)

The list of skills that you will need to possess to benefit from working with others includes:

- Good communication and interpersonal skills
- Good computer and information technology skills
- Ability to work with others to produce and develop good ideas
- Ability to work with others to achieve outcomes
- Willingness to offer and receive constructive criticism
- Ability to reflect upon your own behaviour in group situations and to be prepared to take steps to change inappropriate or ineffective behavior

The principles of good listening and speech skills that are essential for telephone communication can be transferred to the electronic environment. They equate in some respects with good message writing and message reading. However, there are specific skills required to communicate effectively electronically and guidelines that need to be followed.

Emailing

The more practical 'dos and don'ts' of emailing were included in Section 5.5. However, you also need to consider some of the more 'ethical' issues of using email: what Salmon 2011: 252–3 calls 'netiquette'. The following guidelines are loosely based on some of Salmon's suggestions.

- Only address email messages to people who really need to know something and/or need to take action or reply to you. You might want to use the 'copy' facility for others who might be interested in the information, but who don't need to respond to the message.
- An email will be more appropriate than a message posted to a discussion room when the information is directly relevant only to one person (or a small number of people) in the group. Use their individual email addresses instead.
- If you know that your message might be upsetting to the recipient, first of all consider if it is really necessary to communicate it at all, and, if you decide that it is, try to communicate with that person face-to-face, or by 'real time', synchronous technology such as *FaceTime*, or by telephone, if neither of those is possible.
- When replying to a message that has been sent to a number of people but your response is only relevant to the original sender, ensure that you reply only to that one person.
- It is frustrating to receive irrelevant messages that have been inappropriately sent using the 'reply all' function, but avoid the temptation to vent that frustration by doing another 'reply all' message and making the problem worse.
- Strictly speaking, the sender of an email message holds the copyright on that message and, as such, you do not have the right to forward it to other people, especially if it contains personal or sensitive information. If in any doubt, it is polite to get the original person's permission before doing so.

Group discussions

Tutor comment
'Students are urged to visit the forums regularly and to post their results and observations for discussion.'

- Some of your contributions will be your responses to tasks set by your tutor, others will be reflective responses to what other people have posted.
- Generally your contributions will need to be short and to the point.

- You may want to take some time to think about your contribution and write it out in draft before posting it. It also takes less time to paste in a message previously written in, say, *Word*, than to type it out there and then on the message board. This ensures that you are able to post your contribution before the discussion moves on.
- Whilst making it clear to which message you are responding, don't repeat the whole of the previous message in your response.
- When wanting to respond to two different aspects of the same discussion, it is better to post two separate messages.
- Be constructive. Giving critical feedback to other group members is fine if it is accompanied by suggestions of ways to improve their work.
- Sometimes it is more appropriate to email an individual directly to their private email address about something they have posted, rather than to the public discussion forum.
- Beware of hiding behind the anonymity of an electronic discussion group and perhaps including something in a message that you wouldn't say face-to-face. This is just common courtesy, plus in many courses there will be opportunities for face-to-face sessions where you will meet up with other group members and therefore have to face those to whom you have mailed messages.
- Everyone needs to take their share of responsibility for making a group discussion work. Try to resist the temptation to only browse or 'lurk' – that is to only read the messages and not participate by making contributions.

Tutor comment

'The cut-and-paste brigade must be identified as soon as possible and set on the correct path. The cut-and-paster's typical contribution to the discussion forums is to paste something from the Internet, possibly prefaced with something like, "Here's something I found on the Internet. Cheers." I expect comment and analysis as much as possible.'

Causes of concern, anxiety and frustration

Most of us have concerns or experience some anxiety and frustration when asked to work co-operatively with others.

'Online discussion boards are a very mixed blessing. It seems very easy to misunderstand or misinterpret meanings of posts and get bogged down in quite aggressive and competitive disputes. As tone and nuance are missing online and people tend to be on the defensive and anxious, this seems to happen frequently. For example, irony and subtle humour are easily mistaken for outright hostility – especially where multicultural groups are involved. My experience is that it's best to avoid any kind of nuance in online language and save it for private posts that might develop. The use of "smileys" and those silly punctuation icons like :-) and such like just seem to make the situation worse!'

Activity Twenty-Nine

Make a list of any concerns, anxieties or frustrations you have experienced in the past or currently have about group work.

Commentary

Among others, you may have included some of the following:
- You felt that you didn't have much to offer.
- You felt that you could have done the task better on your own.
- Other group members have had too little to offer.
- No one in the group really took the lead or chaired the group and no real progress was made.
- One or two group members dominated the group and didn't listen to the views of others.
- One or two group members did very little work but were awarded equal marks to those who had worked hard.

Group working strategies

How you deal with your anxieties and frustrations will vary enormously from person to person and for the same individual in different situations, but the following might prove helpful:

1 Ask the group tutor to provide guidelines on group work to all participants. They might include things such as a minimum and maximum percentage of contributions to discussions that each individual must make, or guidelines regarding (in)appropriate language in electronic discussion rooms.
2 Find out what the assessment criteria are, what marks will be awarded for meeting each of the criteria and if there are any penalties for lack of participation, or for deliberately jeopardizing the success of a project.
3 Ensure that the group sets out a clear list of tasks, with the name(s) of those responsible for completing the tasks and the time schedule for doing so.
4 Suggest (if it hasn't been done by your tutor) that for different group projects different people assume different roles and that these roles are recorded at the start of each project. For example: the chairperson takes responsibility for encouraging other members and ensuring that every member makes their contribution; the project manager records the schedule for the project and checks that all tasks are completed on time; the purchase or resources manager ensures that all resources are available for the appropriate stage of the project; and so on.
5 Share any anxieties about group working or about a specific project with the group, but beware of turning a discussion into a moaning session rather than focusing on the work itself.
6 Don't get too upset if people disagree with you: it is very stimulating, if you can avoid being too defensive, to have your own views challenged by others. It is best seen as an opportunity to learn of other people's perspectives on a subject. At times you will have the thrill that comes from letting go and taking

on new views and beliefs. At other times it can ultimately be reassuring, having listened with an open mind to others' perspectives, to conclude that you still hold the same view and to feel that you have satisfactorily 'defended' it.

Group members working effectively together form a valuable resource that can be tapped by each individual member. While you may not feel that you have a great deal to offer for every activity, there will be times when your contribution might be one of the most significant. Remember that working with others is all about 'give and take' and mutual support. Some frustration is probably inevitable from time to time, but hopefully the overall experience will be very positive. As Clarke (2008: 9) states,

A community of practice is more than a simple group of individuals. The members share common interests, experiences, aims and objectives. Participants in a community of practice will support each other to achieve the common goals. Communities of practice do not simply come into existence when people meet online; people need opportunities to work and collaborate together so that structures, methods, communication channels and commitment evolve.

Tutor comment

'The tutor's role is to facilitate discussion, answer queries when they arise and generally help the students integrate with each other.'

Online group work has been used very effectively in many different learning situations. Below is a case study of online group work used for four consecutive years with undergraduate mechanical engineering students at the University of Leeds. It was used for an assignment which was part of a 'Computer Aided Engineering' (CAE) module, with very positive results. It is included here with the permission of the module tutors. Although this particular case study is of a campus-based module, you may well be asked to participate in something similar in a totally online context.

Case study

The assignment was introduced in a face-to-face setting but executed online with the aid of discussion rooms in the VLE. The details of the assignment were also posted on the departmental website. The VLE was also used to obtain feedback about the module from the students. The discussion rooms used to support the assignment were private to students and tutors on that module only. The assignment involved the students working in groups to define a process by which to produce a specific product: a plastic fishing game. One of the discussion rooms contained multiple-choice tests, which were designed to help students learn the material associated with workbooks provided for the whole of this module. There was no limit to the number of times students were allowed to attempt the tests.

This assignment was intended to provide students with concrete examples and experience of a real process and supply chain, and a realistic product and organizational environment. It was also intended to provide students with opportunities to use at least one CAE system, to experiment with the functionality that is available and experience some of the limitations of shape-based CAE systems.

The students were divided up into two teams, with each team further subdivided into smaller groups, each of which had responsibility for a particular aspect of the project. The subgroups communicated with each other via the VLE discussion rooms. Twenty-five per cent of the module mark was based on the usage of the team's discussion room. Teams were encouraged to raise and resolve issues and queries with their customers and suppliers in this room. Twenty-five per cent of the mark was awarded for presentations at scheduled design reviews and 50 per cent for the final report. It was estimated that the assignment should take each student round 25 hours of private study time. Face-to-face tutorials on the assignment were offered throughout the module.

Each team had to select and/or define its own process, using the product requirements (as provided by the tutor) and produce an electronic product definition, including information that a design team would pass to a manufacturing planning department. The process had to create the outputs in a timescale that fitted in with the specified timescales of the entire supply chain process.

Multicultural group work

A great deal has been written about the cultural differences of students working together on projects (see, for example, Carroll and Ryan 2005). Although some multicultural group work situations can become problematic, the problems are minimized when all members of the group appreciate, value, respect and even celebrate the cultural differences of group members. There are some specific issues relating to online group work that it may be appropriate to address here. Many of you, after finishing your current studies, could find yourself working in multicultural groups in your chosen profession, and similar issues to those outlined here will need to be addressed.

Group membership

You will probably be allocated learning groups by your tutors. Don't be tempted to try and arrange to move into a group where all of the students are from the same cultural background as you – we all have much to learn from those from cultural backgrounds different from our own, especially about the social, political and economic situation of other countries (Ladd and Ruby 1999). All students need to make a big effort not to cause offence to students from different cultural or religious backgrounds. Mutual sensitivity is needed to customs/beliefs/practices of others and to what are (un)acceptable language phrases to use. Institutions have their own rules about the content of emails and contributions to discussion rooms, and there could be serious consequences for any student using inappropriate or inflammatory language. Take care too with using humour – what might be hilarious to you may appear extremely rude to other members of the group.

Students from some cultural backgrounds may be unfamiliar or uncomfortable with any form of group work and will need encouragement from those of you who are. It is important that all students feel that their contributions are valued.

> 'I was concerned about whether the teaching style would be different enough that I [would] have problems adapting. While [it] is certainly different, I actually found I preferred it to what I had become used to in [this country].'

Socialization

Introductions in any group work are important, but they are especially significant in online communication. Many tutors in facilitating online group work will begin by suggesting that each group member posts a few introductory sentences about themselves as a way for students to get to know one another. Salmon (2013: 16) refers to this as 'Online Socialization', being Stage 2 of her five-stage model of online communication: 'Stage 2 involves individual participants establishing their identities and then finding others with whom to interact. They start to understand the benefits and requirements of working with others in their online environments.' In some ways online learning is advantageous in this respect, because participants do not make instant value judgements about group members based on appearance or accent, which could lead to stereotyping and negative expectations. It is important that you reveal as little or as much about yourself as you feel comfortable with in this context. Show respect for one another's contributions at this (and each subsequent) stage and take care not to ask inappropriate personal questions. Try to help each student feel validated by your responses and try to ensure that one or two students do not dominate the discussion.

Language

Some of you may struggle with the English language where it is not your first (or even second) language. Many may find that you have more of a problem with listening and speaking than you do with reading and writing. This makes face-to-face group work difficult, as you need longer to digest what has been said and to formulate your response. Online group work may therefore suit you better. When posting messages asynchronously (not at the same time as others) to a discussion room you have the opportunity to think about what you want to say and the time to check through spelling and grammar before posting. It may be wise to read the contributions of two or three other people before submitting yours. It would give you the opportunity to become more familiar with the language so that you can use the most appropriate English words and expressions for a particular context.

   Contributing to synchronous discussions is rather more challenging if you are not working in your native language (and hard enough even when you are!). It is, however, possible to do some preparation beforehand. Try to familiarize yourself with the appropriate terminology for a particular task and have some words, phrases or even sentences and paragraphs typed into your word processor, ready to cut and paste into the discussion at the appropriate time. It is easy to lose the thread of a synchronous discussion when more than two people are participating, especially if you have a fairly slow Internet connection, and this is exacerbated if you are scrabbling to find the correct spellings of words in a hurry. Remember, too, that when working with students from a number of different countries there is the issue of different time zones to address. Some tutors run each synchronous session twice to accommodate students from across the world.

For those of you whose first language is English, you need to be patient and encouraging to those who may be struggling a bit to make a contribution to group work in whatever form. Don't be tempted to pick up on language mistakes in contributions for the sake of it. If you genuinely need to ask one of your fellow students to restate something in order to clarify the meaning of their contribution, try to do it in a constructive and not sarcastic way (see note on tone of voice, and so on, above). Try not to use colloquialisms, which students from a different country or cultural background may not understand.

'I did not realize that there would be British terms that people take for granted that left me totally unknowing what they were saying. Most of the time I could look the phrases up on the Internet and get a good feel about the meaning. But a couple of times I had to ask the professor and it was cleared up. Especially for the subject matter lingo, the Internet searches became a useful learning tool since I could not only define the terms but also learn a little context that turned out to be useful.'

Critical thinking and academic criticism

As was discussed in Section 7.1, there is often more than one perspective on a subject, especially when you are studying at postgraduate level. Academic criticism (a critical and analytical approach to listening, thinking, reading and writing) is a crucial component of study in all levels of higher education. This applies equally to group work. When holding 'discussions' either face-to-face or online, the aim is rarely to arrive at a consensus of opinion on a topic. Rather it is to be able to express and support with evidence your own point of view, based on yours and others' knowledge and experience. To this end, try to use your own cultural background in your course and your assessments where possible. You could influence what you learn and on what you are assessed by suggesting things important to you (and your country or culture) that are relevant to your course. At the same time, you must be ready to accept that there are different perspectives to most subjects, and to respect those who hold a perspective different from your own. Increasingly, online group work is being seen as a forum for constructing new knowledge, as well as for discussing existing perspectives on a subject.

For further ideas about group work, see the document 'Group Work Tip Sheet' available on the *Skills Plus* website of Northumbria University at www.north umbria.ac.uk/static/5007/llspdf/skills/Groupwork.pdf. More materials are also available on the *LearnHigher* website at www.learnhigher.ac.uk/working-with-others/group-work-working-with-others/.

9.2 Report writing

As mentioned in the introduction to Chapter 8, some of the more general strategies suggested there for essay writing are applicable to all written assignments, irrespective of the form of writing needed. These include things such as allowing plenty of time to write your assignment, finding out what the assessment criteria are, carefully planning your work, and citing your sources. However, there are times when your assignment will need to be very different from the traditional academic essay. This will include the need to write a project report after working on a small-scale project, either on your own, or in a group situation. Such reports will essentially be giving details of what you did in your project and what are the outcomes of the project.

One of the main differences between an essay and a report will be the style of writing used. There will need to be a move away from writing in one continuous prose style and a move toward presenting information in various styles, including diagrammatic, graphical or tabular forms, in different sections of the report. Another key feature of a report is that it needs to be written for a very specific purpose and with a particular reader or readers in mind.

There are some excellent interactive online materials on report writing written originally by Judy Turner and her colleagues at the University of Reading. They can be found on the *LearnHigher* website at www.learnhigher.ac.uk/writing-for-university/report-writing/. As suggested by the website authors: 'A good way to understand the key features of reports is to see how they differ from essays as a type of academic writing' (see Table 9.1).

Table 9.1   Differences between reports and essays

Reports...	Essays...
Are formally structured	Are semi-structured
Are informative and fact-based	Are argumentative and idea-based
Are written with a specific purpose and reader in mind	Are not written with a specific reader in mind
Are written in style appropriate to each section	Are written in single narrative style throughout
Always include section headings	Usually do not include sub-headings
Sometimes use bullet points	Usually do not include bullet points
Often include tables or graphs	Rarely include tables or graphs
Offer recommendations for action	Offer conclusions about question

Source: Reproduced, with permission, from the *LearnHigher* Report Writing online materials

Of course, there is a lot more to writing a good report than knowing the differences between a report and an essay. For more on report writing see Section 10.7, which is particularly relevant if you will have to write a research report or dissertation. There are also many other resources on the subject of report writing and some of these are listed in the Further Resources section at the end of this book. However, the following activity is highly recommended.

Activity Thirty

Either now, or later in your course when you know you will have to write one or more reports, go to the *LearnHigher* Report Writing materials. As well as reading through the online materials, try out the Report Writing exercises that are provided on the website. This is the best way to develop your report writing skills. This activity will also be relevant to those of you who have to do a larger research project. (See also Section 10.7.)

There are also some excellent *Skills Plus* materials on report writing available via the Northumbria University Library website at nuweb2.northumbria.ac.uk/library/skillsplus/categories.html?12-1, including a web guide and an interactive tutorial as well as the document 'Effective Reports' at www.northumbria.ac.uk/static/5007/llspdf/skills/reportwriting.pdf. This guide includes a really useful 'report checklist'. See also Davies (2011), Chapter 11.

9.3 Maths and data collection and analysis

Many students, in the course of their studies, find that they need to use skills in mathematics, especially numeracy, and in data analysis for some of their assessments. These could be skills that you may never have possessed, or skills that you have not used for a long time. If you are studying in the area of engineering, for example, you will expect to have to use such skills, but so will social science students studying subjects such as business studies or psychology. Even if you are studying a course in the field of the arts or the humanities you may need at some time to work on some mathematical calculations or to read and interpret data. A student in any subject area may also be expected to present, in a written or verbal report, information that you have collected, perhaps as part of a small research project.

The best way to acquire or to refresh such skills is by having the processes demonstrated to you. For the distance learner, studying away from your educational institution, this is more problematic. However, remote demonstrations of mathematical calculations, and so on, can now be made using technology such as pencasts, which are broadcasts using a digital 'pen' on a whiteboard, using software such as *Livescribe*. There are also a growing number of excellent resources available online, and some of these are detailed below. Your own education provider may also have produced some online materials – check out the study skills website of your institution.

Mathematics

Improve your maths

These are materials created for students by the 'Skills@Library' team at the University of Leeds. They consist firstly of *Maths Solutions*, which feature 'experienced teachers demonstrating solutions to a series of maths problems that are known to challenge students. The solutions are presented as a series of short video clips displayed on the screen in a step-by-step format; in the same way as a teacher writing on a page or whiteboard' (from the Introduction). These can be found at: http://library.leeds.ac.uk/tutorials/maths-solutions/. Secondly, there are *Maths Quizzes* which feature 'a collection of diagnostic tests in a range of maths areas. The quizzes are for your own benefit – no scores will be recorded and you can try them as many times as you like. If there is an area which you are struggling with, you may wish to also visit the corresponding section of the *Maths Solutions* site, a link to which can be found on each page' (from the Introduction). Both solutions and quizzes cover the areas of: numeracy; algebra; vectors; trigonometry and geometry; calculus; complex numbers; and maths for nurses. In addition there are *Maths Solutions* materials on: sets; mechanics; and statistics and probability. *Maths Quizzes* can be found at: http://library.leeds.ac.uk/tutorials/maths-quizzes/.

MathTutor

These materials, which are available on the *MathTutor* website at www.mathtutor.ac.uk, are intended 'To bridge the gap from school to university study, to revise or find the maths topic you missed, you will want to meet *mathtutor*. Video tutorials, with diagnostics, summary text and exercises, take you through more than eighty topics in the way you choose' (from introduction on website). The makers are 'a group of teachers, mathematicians and new media producers from the Universities of Leeds, Loughborough and Coventry and the former EBS [Educational Broadcasting Services] Trust'. The contents include seven areas: arithmetic; algebra; trigonometry; functions and graphs, sequences and series; differentiation; integration; geometry, vectors. You can work with the materials online or purchase a set of DVD-Rom disks. For a list of printed text and electronic resources including 3GP mobile phone downloads, which are useful short clips from the *MathTutor* video tutorials, visit the *Math Centre* at www.mathcentre.ac.uk/.

The Open University UK's 'OpenLearn' website

OpenLearn at www.open.edu/openlearn/ is 'the home of free learning from the Open University'. It 'aims to break the barriers to education by reaching millions of learners around the world, providing free educational resources and inviting all to sample courses that our registered students take – for free!' (from introduction on the website). *OpenLearn* offers more than 800 free courses, including some in 'Science, Maths and Technology' at www.open.edu/openlearn/science-maths-technology, ranging from 'Introductory' to 'Advanced'. See especially, 'Numbers, Units and Arithmetic' and 'Succeed with Maths', Parts 1 and 2. For an alphabetical list of all the free 'Science, Maths and Technology' courses see: www.open.edu/openlearn/free-courses/full-catalogue?source=freecoursespage.

BBC Study Guides materials

The BBC *Bitesize* materials website at www.bbc.co.uk/education/subjects/ has materials on many subjects including maths (see: www.bbc.co.uk/education/subjects/z6vg9j6). Don't be put off by the fact that these materials appear to be aimed at school students, as there are some really useful introductory materials if you are new to a particular subject field. There are also some excellent revision materials at www.bbc.co.uk/education/subjects/z6pfb9q aimed at GCSE students that will prove useful as a quick refresher for those who have studied a subject before. BBC *Bitesize* is also available for your tablet or mobile phone. There is also a 'Skillswise – Numbers' site at www.bbc.co.uk/skillswise/topic-group/numbers/ for adults who want to improve their basic maths skills.

LearnHigher

'Numeracy, Maths and Statistics' Student Resources are available at www.learn higher.ac.uk/learning-at-university/numeracy-maths-and-statistics/. There you will find a glossary of 'Maths instruction words', including words such as 'differentiate', 'integrate' and 'verify', materials on 'Revising for maths assessments' and 'Using graphical data', plus links to several external online resources in the fields of mathematics, numeracy and statistics.

Data collection and analysis

LearnHigher

For online materials on data analysis, see the interactive tutorial at www.learn higher.ac.uk/analysethis/. The tutorial is divided into the following sections:

- Introduction to data analysis: the story, the scenario, what comes before
- Introduction to Qualitative and Quantitative data
- Qualitative data analysis
- Quantitative data analysis

The Open University UK's 'OpenLearn' website

As well as the OU maths materials mentioned above, you will also find on this website units relating to representing data in 'Diagrams, charts and graphs', and to ways of summarizing data numerically in 'Exploring data: graphs and numerical summaries'. Go to the alphabetical list mentioned above to locate these resources.

You will find a lot more about data collection and analysis in Chapter 10.

9.4 Labs, workshops and field work

In many subjects (especially in the fields of science and engineering) it is far more appropriate to use labs, workshops and field work as part of the learning and assessment process than it is to use essays or exam papers. Clearly these present some challenges for distance learning students and their tutors. In some cases you will be expected to attend either your study institution itself, or a local agency study centre, to participate in practical learning and teaching sessions and examinations (see Section 2.6). It is also likely that, where field work is an integral part of a course, distance learners will be expected to make arrangements to attend. Such face-to-face requirements will have been included in the course information you received prior to registration. More details (including dates) should be included in the student/course handbook issued at the time of registration (see Section 3.8).

Labs and workshops

Many successful attempts have been made to replicate the 'real thing' for those students at a distance from their institutions when it comes to practical work and assessment. For years the Open University has provided or recommended home experiment kits so that students can gain practical 'laboratory' experience at home, and record the outcomes of their work as part of their assignments. Kits are used for subjects such as general science, environmental subjects, geology and robotics.

More recently, more sophisticated learning technology has meant that tutors in many universities can create labs and workshops online. In many cases this is done with the use of simulations, where the student can use their PC, laptop or tablet (online via their web browser) to manipulate data that affects the outcome of a process, such as selecting the most appropriate drugs to prescribe for a patient with particular symptoms. (It is much safer for the patients of new medical students to practise in this way!)

It is also now possible to set up a system that allows remote access to real experimental equipment via a web interface. Students can remotely select appropriate actions that affect physical components set up in a real laboratory. One example of this, developed by staff in the School of Mechanical Engineering at the University of Leeds, is a system called *ReLOAD* (Real Labs Operated at a Distance). Both student and system evaluations have been very encouraging and a growing number of experiments are being developed within the university and in partnership with academics in other institutions, both in the UK and abroad. The following case study provides a summary of the system, including the background to its development.

Case study

Engineering is by its nature a very practical subject and extensive use is made of laboratory-based teaching sessions, particularly in the first few years of a typical undergraduate degree programme. These sessions are ideally suited to develop both cognitive skills (knowledge, information analysis and so on) and psychomotor skills (physical skills, such as the use of tools and equipment). In addition, well-designed laboratory sessions can enthuse, motivate and inspire students, as well as having the potential to allow them to work at their own pace and take ownership of their learning material. However, multiple sets of the required equipment (needed for large groups of face-to-face students) are expensive, and the difficulties of distance learners accessing the equipment are clear, so the *ReLOAD* system was developed to overcome the limitations on access.

The *ReLOAD* system was initially used by Level 2 undergraduates studying vibration and control, using the School's intranet, but was soon adapted for more widespread access via the Internet. Although the system cannot be used to develop psychomotor skills, it does allow students to develop higher cognitive skills such as planning experiments, collecting and analysing data and conducting further experiments if required. It offers greater accessibility, can be run 24 hours a day, 365 days a year, and allows many students to access a single piece of high quality equipment. Subsequently the *ReLOAD* system was used successfully as a key part of a distance-delivered master's module, allowing experimental validation where none would otherwise have been possible.

Briefly, the system works as follows. A client (student) computer sends a request to a central web server (the *ReLOAD* web server) for experimental data across the Internet from any location with an Internet connection. Depending on the type of experiment requested, the *ReLOAD* web server redirects this request via a local area network (LAN) to one of several experiment server computers physically connected to either a single or multiple pieces of experimental equipment. The experiment server converts the request into a series of commands appropriate for the specific equipment being run. Upon completion of the experiment, the experiment server computer sends results in the form of data images and video clips back to the user on the client computer via the *ReLOAD* web server, providing virtually the same level of information as would be obtained by performing the experiment locally.

Student feedback has been very positive, with students particularly appreciating the virtually unlimited access and the ability to easily visualize the output via the use of video clips simultaneously with near real-time analogue data and the reinforcement that they are accessing real experimental data these clips provide.

Some people have developed 'virtual laboratories' using 3D MUVE technologies. (See Glossary in Section 5.3 for a definition of these.) See, for example, the description of the work of the University of Leicester in Salmon (2011: 82–6).

Virtual field work

Field work is an integral and important part of learning and assessment in many subjects, perhaps most obviously geography, geology and archaeology, but in others as well, such as architecture and botany. The experience of field work, most often conducted in the context of residentials, brings social as well as intellectual benefits and is not to be missed if it is at all possible to participate. However, the realities of the distance learning student are often such that spending several days (and nights) away from home and/or work is simply not possible.

Over the years there have been developments in the whole area of virtual or simulated field work, using computers to 'explore virtual physical and social environments' (Jenkins 2004). This has been prompted in part because of economic considerations but also because of the need to provide the opportunity for disabled students to meet the requirements of their coursework in a number of subject areas, when they cannot physically participate in the field. They can also be used in preparatory work by those who do later go to the locations in person. Known as virtual field courses (VFCs), programs range from a set of web resources (including video) to sophisticated 'software that enables simulated movement through and analysis of a landscape, such as flying through or over a landscape in two or three dimensional space' (Jenkins 2004). Following extensive research, the developers of such VFCs can now claim that there are strong educational grounds for their development.

Case study

The Ecology of the Maltese Islands Field-Sim package is a web-based interactive learning package to assist in the development of field work skills and the acquisition of specific knowledge sets relevant to the chosen field work location. It was developed by John Stainfield, in the School of Geographical Sciences at the University of Plymouth (now retired).

The link http://78.158.56.101/archive/gees/projects/outputs/fieldsim/index.html takes you to the 'Malta Virtual Field Sites' page. The package provided on this web page is an extension of materials developed at the University of Plymouth to support field work in the Mediterranean. The aims of this package are: to introduce the student to the ecology of the Maltese Islands and permit the student to carry out simulated or virtual field work; to simulate data collection and species identification in the field; to give students the opportunity to acquire field work, identification, data analysis and interpretative skills before going into the field. It includes concepts and methodology of Maltese field work trips, a quadrat tool and information on field sites and ecosystems.

(Details of the above case study were originally taken from the resource database on the website of the Higher Education Academy's Subject Centre for Geography, Earth and Environmental Sciences, accessed 28 October 2009. However, that website is no longer in use, and the Malta Virtual Field Site is no longer being maintained and is now a little dated. Nevertheless the materials are archived and can be seen at the above address (as of March 2015) and are still an interesting example of such materials.)

In some cases VFCs can be used by way of preparation for the real thing (as above), but in other cases what can be presented via computer surpasses what can be achieved in reality. This is especially significant given the restriction in time and money available for field trips, and in some instances the sheer practicalities (or danger) of accessing various environments, such as 'Antarctica or Mars' (Jenkins 2004). This is now provided by the Lunar and Planetary Institute (see www.lpi.usra.edu/education/explore/LifeOnMars/).

Such developments are significant for the distance learner – those of you studying in a variety of subjects may find yourselves visiting places as part of field work that you thought would be impossible. It seems highly likely that ever more sophisticated virtual reality technology will enhance the experience of virtual field trips and perhaps students will prefer the virtual experience conducted in the warmth of their own homes to the cold and wet of the real thing.

9.5 Posters, presentations and literature reviews

Posters and presentations

Whilst your own institution should have a 'study skills' section on its website (which may or may not be password-protected), several universities have materials that are on open access. '*Skills Plus*' is Northumbria University's program of interactive online materials and guides for developing study skills, IT skills and information literacy training to help each student 'to become a more effective learner'. In addition to those materials already cited earlier in this chapter, there are some interactive online materials and a study guide on giving presentations, and a guide on producing a poster. See http://nuweb2.northumbria.ac.uk/library/skillsplus/azlist.html for details. Whilst these last two methods of assessment may not be as prevalent in distance learning courses as those on campus, the technology (such as *Skype*) exists to make presentations at a distance perfectly feasible, and posters can be created and saved in digital format for submission online.

The University of Leeds also has some excellent online tutorial materials on presentations in its '*Skills at Library*' program at http://library.leeds.ac.uk/skills-online-tutorials. It is interesting to note that there are three sections – 'Planning to present', 'Preparing to present' and 'Practising your presentation' before the fourth and final section on 'Delivering presentations'. This demonstrates the importance of good preparation for presentations and how necessary it is to spend time on this to ensure that your presentation is a success. Within 'Practising your presentation' there is a very useful ten-minute video showing a voice training session. There are also links to materials on poster presentations at http://library.leeds.ac.uk/skills-presentation#activate-creating_poster_presentations.

Literature reviews

A review of literature in a specific subject of study is a popular means of assessment, especially in conjunction with the preparation for conducting and writing up a research project. Where it is an integral part of your research project it is likely to be awarded at least 10 per cent (and possibly as much as 30 per cent) of the total marks awarded for your project – it being regarded as such an important element of your work. In some degree programmes, however, coursework assessment of a module may also include writing a literature review. Once again, you are likely to find resources on the skills website of your own institution, or you will be given guidance on the requirements for a specific assessment by your tutor. Newcastle University, for example, has materials available at www.ncl.ac.uk/students/wdc/learning/essays/literaturereview.htm where it states that: 'A literature review is a comprehensive survey of published research on a particular topic. It summarises, synthesises and critically evaluates relevant research. It reveals trends and controversies, and identifies areas where further research is needed.'

The key to a good literature review is critical analysis rather than description (so requiring good critical thinking, reading and writing skills: see Sections 7.1 and 8.1), but it also involves being able to summarize and evaluate the information retrieved. It is a prime example of demonstrating Bloom's levels of learning 4, 5 and 6 (see Section 2.5). It is important to be able to generalize from your conclusions, identifying key concepts in the subject field, including the direction in which current thinking is going.

Northumbria University has produced a quick guide on literature reviews (found at: http://nuweb2.northumbria.ac.uk/library/skillsplus/loader.html?55388245). This will help you plan the stages involved in conducting your literature review, including how you will structure the review after planning and conducting your literature search, and reading, making notes, evaluating and summarizing the information you find. Davies (2011) provides a very useful chapter (14) on 'Writing a literature review', including examples, see Further Resources. This builds on Chapter 10, 'Writing critical reviews', which provides a detailed, step-by-step guide to this form of assessment, including numerous examples of the sort of language structure and vocabulary that you need to use. This will prove to be especially useful to those of you who are studying in English, when it is not your first language.

Since a literature review will be needed for any research project with which you are involved, this form of assessment in one of your earlier modules will be good preparation for when you begin the 'real thing' (see Section 10.4). The next chapter takes you in detail through the things that you need to consider in preparing to conduct and report on your research project.

Chapter summary

In this chapter you have:

- Considered how to make the most of any group working experience you may have
- Had the opportunity to learn more about forms of learning and assessments that you may encounter on your distance learning course
- Received guidance on where to find online materials that will help you improve your skills in report writing and for completing assessments that include mathematics and data collection and analysis
- Received reassurance that, whatever subject you may want to study, there is a way of doing just that by distance learning, even where it includes labs, workshops and field work
- Learned about how to conduct a literature review

10 Doing a research project

Introduction • Preparing to do research • Ethical issues • Feasibility • Literature searching and reviewing • Evaluating other people's research projects • Managing your research project • Reporting your findings • Chapter summary

Introduction

There is no set pattern for every programme of study, but most (whether you are studying full- or part-time) will include at some stage a major assignment, or a large or small research project. This chapter (together with Chapter 6 and Section 9.2) should help you to prepare for the experience. Conducting a research project and writing the research report or dissertation are likely to be the largest single piece of academic work that you do, especially if you are studying at postgraduate level. It will dominate your course (and most aspects of your life) for at least the second half of your period of study. As with all other aspects of your studies, planning ahead for your research project will reap major benefits. Time spent beforehand exploring your ideas for research and the feasibility and practicalities of putting your ideas into practice will be time well spent.

This chapter cannot hope to provide everything you need to know about doing a full-scale research project (indeed in some respects it will barely scratch the surface). However, there are many excellent and comprehensive books available to help you explore all of the issues raised here in much more detail. Some of these are included in the Further Resources and References and Author Index sections at the end of this book, and many are referred to within the main text. In particular this chapter does not look at specific methodologies or techniques for actually doing the research. Rather it is an attempt to provide the practical framework within which you will need to work to conduct and report on your research successfully. I do hope that by working through the chapter at an early stage in your studies and considering some of the issues raised, you will be better prepared for the task ahead and will be able to avoid some of the pitfalls in doing research that can be both painful and very time-consuming to tumble into. You may well wish to return to some parts of it at a later stage in your programme of study when you have had time to get to know your subject better and have received some initial guidance from your course leader.

While there are obviously some added difficulties in conducting research when you are at a distance from your study institution, the continual development of electronic resources means that you are less disadvantaged than distance learners used to be in this task. Access to the web and the use of email and other forms of electronic communication mean that, in many cases, data collection is considerably easier than it used to be. Access to bibliographical resources on the web will to some extent depend upon the subscriptions paid by your institution for off-campus access, for example to electronic journals, databases, and so on. However, as already indicated in Section 6.7, there is a lot available electronically to assist you in your studies.

All of us feel somewhat daunted at the prospect of embarking upon a research project, especially when approaching the task for the first time. There is nothing for it but to breathe deeply, relax, keep a clear head, listen to advice from others and *begin*.

10.1 Preparing to do research

What is research?

Phillips and Pugh (2010) distinguish research from what they call 'intelligence gathering' (p. 54). They emphasize that research is concerned with more than answering the 'what' questions: 'Research goes beyond description and requires analysis. It looks for explanations, relationships, comparisons, predictions, generalizations and theories. These are the "why" questions' (p. 55). For a more detailed commentary on the nature of research see Blaxter et al. (2010: Ch. 1).

The research process will vary considerably from one subject discipline to another, and from person to person within the same discipline. What all research has traditionally had in common is the following process:

1 Definition of the research question or hypothesis
2 Data collection
3 Data analysis
4 Interpretation of findings
5 Presentation and dissemination of the results

This is still the standard approach for a lot of research. However, as Blaxter et al. (2010: 7–10) point out, there are other far less 'linear' views of the research process, which can be represented by a circle or as a spiral.

What is 'good' research?

A debate exists about what constitutes 'good' research. Opinion is roughly divided along pure science versus social science lines, or pure versus applied research. Whatever type of research you ultimately choose to do, that research must be academically rigorous. Exactly what constitutes academic rigour in your subject discipline will become apparent as you progress with your programme of study, but essentially it involves substantiating your arguments with evidence.

Approaches to research

Much is written about research methodology. 'Methodology' literally means the study or science of method. Within the context of conducting research it means rather more than this. It refers, not simply to a list of different research methods that you employ to collect and analyse data, but rather to the overall approach that you take to conducting research. It is really a combination of the principles or perspectives behind the research, and the appropriate practical skills or tools required to conduct the research. For many researchers their approach to research is very much influenced by their ideology, which in turn both influences and is influenced by their views on *epistemology* (the study or theory of knowledge) and on *ontology* (theories about what exists or the study of being).

There is no one straightforward way of categorizing research, and it is beyond the scope of this chapter to try and do so. But, crudely put, natural scientists traditionally have been seen as doing *pure* research, which is concerned with the creation of theories and the testing of those theories in laboratories, and social scientists have been the ones who have done *applied* research, testing theories in the real world. These approaches have also been known as 'positivist' and 'interpretive' and are largely concerned with the collection and analysis of quantitative and qualitative data respectively. Many researchers today find that a combination of the two broad approaches is more appropriate. Robson (2011) refers to these approaches as needing 'fixed' or 'flexible' research designs or a combination of the two.

Within social science the debate still rages about whether, when essentially *people* are the subjects of the research, such research can be totally objective, therefore requiring a positivist approach, or whether subjectivity inevitably creeps in. There are also those that believe that no research, however 'scientific', can be totally objective. Some people would argue that it is possible to arrive at objective 'truth' and that research helps to establish and reinforce that truth. Such people may feel threatened by the idea that there can be several different perspectives to 'truth'.

May (2011: 7–25) and Robson (2011: 13–41) both provide an introduction to the major perspectives in social research. May explores the view that the methods and theories employed in the natural sciences are inapplicable to the social sciences 'because there are important political and value considerations that relate to how we live' that will affect our practice' (May 2011: 8).

Robson explores what it means to be scientific and argues for its advantages, but goes on to consider the standard positivist view of science and rejects it as a basis for real world research. He also discusses relativist views and similarly rejects them. He goes on to review two main current approaches to social research: post-positivism and constructivism; considers a realist approach; and concludes that 'critical realism' or 'scientific realism' is an acceptable approach for real world research.

There is also a keen interest within the social sciences in the approach known as 'grounded theory' where explanation and theory are fashioned directly from the analysis of data, rather than the research starting out with a theory or hypothesis. This is based on the qualitative research of Glaser and Strauss (1967).

You may consider that such theoretical considerations are secondary to the actual doing of research. If you are studying and researching in a scientific discipline, then you will probably find less discussion of these issues. However, such principles form the foundation of any social research and must be understood before moving on to other considerations, such as choice of methods. When doing further reading about approaches to research, try to relate the ideas to your own research ideas, as well as to your own inclinations, and try to decide which perspective or combination of perspectives best suits you and your research.

Methodological approaches

You will at some stage need to look at the specific types of methodology which are available for you to choose from. Some approaches or strategies are those described as:

- Experimental research
- Survey research
- Qualitative research
- Quantitative research
- Comparative research
- Longitudinal research
- Documentary research
- Secondary data analysis
- Action research
- Evaluation research
- Case study research
- Ethnography (study of groups or communities)
- Feminist methodology
- Grounded theory research

These categories are not mutually exclusive, indeed some involve the use of others. For instance: ethnography is regarded by some (but not all) as a type of qualitative research and may use a case study approach; comparative research may use survey research; and action research may be quantitative.

Several items listed in the Further Resources section provide a detailed description of different methodologies. For example, Robson (2011: Ch. 4) explores the question of research design by developing a framework for design that links purpose, conceptual framework, research questions, methods and sampling strategy. He considers fixed (experimental and non-experimental), flexible and multiple research strategies. In particular he looks at the three flexible strategies of case studies, ethnographic studies and grounded theory studies. He provides a clear and useful guide to selecting the most appropriate strategy for your project, and illustrates the section with several examples. Having looked at the question of research strategy using this broad approach, Robson then devotes the following four chapters to looking in detail at design: in Chapters 5, 6 and 7 there is a more detailed discussion of fixed and flexible designs, concentrating on design issues specific to each strategy; and in Chapter 8 evaluation research and action research are discussed.

In addition to Robson, you will find relevant chapters in May (2011). For instance: Chapter 7 on participant observation (an alternative term for ethnography); Chapter 8 on documentary research in social research; Chapter 9 on Case Study research; and Chapter 10 on comparative research. Documentary research is covered in more detail in Sapsford and Jupp (2006: Ch. 6). The above books are taking you into a great deal of detail about strategies for conducting research and go on to provide very helpful detailed advice on the choice of actual methods to use to collect data, for example: surveys and questionnaires; interviews; observational methods; and analysis of documents (including secondary data analysis in Robson 2011: 358–61) .

If you want to cover similar ground but in considerably less detail, a book such as Robson (2014) *How to Do a Research Project: A Guide for Undergraduate Students* or Denscombe (2014) *The Good Research Guide for Small-Scale Social Research Projects* would probably be more appropriate. You will also find various online guides to research useful, for example those on the *LearnHigher* website, such as those on data collection at www.learnhigher.ac.uk/research-skills/doing-research/collect-this/and those on data analysis at www.learnhigher. ac.uk/research-skills/doing-research/analyse-this/.

Your project proposal

At some stage, you will need to write a project proposal. Essentially this will state not only *what* it is you are going to research, but also *why* you have chosen this particular topic, *how* you are going to go about conducting the research, within what *timescale* and with what *resources*, and how you are going to *analyse the findings*.

Choosing the topic

Some of you reading this book may already have quite definite ideas about what the subject of your research project will be. Others (probably the majority) will not. Some of you in the latter category will, however, know the broad subject area in which you want to work. The task before you is to narrow down that broad area to a fairly narrow topic for consideration. If you are reading this book at the beginning of a two- or three-year course you may feel that you have plenty of time to consider this – after all the dissertation is the final piece of coursework to be submitted. In fact it is important to try and decide on your topic at quite an early stage. The practicalities of obtaining resources or collecting data can sometimes take months, so the sooner you begin to plan the project the better. That doesn't mean to say that you will know what the title of your dissertation is going to be. For most people the final version of the title is decided upon at the last minute, having been through many variations along the way. Most people arrive at their exact choice of topic after a considerable amount of reading and discussion with other students/colleagues at work/their supervisors.

> **Activity Thirty-One**
>
> For now make a note of the topic you have in mind at the moment. Don't worry too much if it is still a fairly broad topic, there will be plenty of opportunity to narrow it down later, especially as you conduct your literature search.

10.2 Ethical issues

As Robson (2011: 197) points out: 'It is vital that, at a very early stage of your preparations to carry out a research project, you give serious thought to the ethical aspects of what you are proposing.' Broadly speaking, ethics refer to a set of principles or rules that affect or control our behaviour. We each tend to develop our own code of conduct by which we live our lives (usually within the context of a set of laws of the land in which we are resident), but in research, as in various other areas of our lives, that code of conduct will often be imposed on us. Often the ethical issues with which you must be concerned are imposed on you by a professional body, by your employer (if your research is to be done within your place of work), by your sponsor (often a government agency) or other funding body (for example, the Economic and Social Research Council, ESRC, which publishes its own *Framework for Research Ethics* – latest version 2015 – see www.esrc.ac.uk/about-esrc/information/framework-for-research-ethics/index. aspx – which includes a useful example initial checklist in Appendix A), or by your research institution (such as the university where you are registered). There are no easy answers to the ethical questions that are raised in research.

> **Activity Thirty-Two**
>
> Skim read the *Code of Ethics and Conduct* (2009) published by the British Psychological Society (BPS). This is available to read online or in a file to download from the BPS website (www.bps.org.uk). It raises major issues that are applicable to many fields of investigation: respect, competence, responsibility and integrity.
>
> There is also a useful chapter in Cryer (2006: Ch. 9) on 'Handling ethical issues', and a more detailed exploration of ethical issues as they relate to student researchers can be found in *The Student's Guide to Research Ethics* by Paul Oliver (2010).
>
> What ethical issues do you need to consider for your own project? Obtain your own copy of the ethical guidelines likely to be most relevant to your area of research. Your tutor or workplace mentor should be able to provide you with other examples appropriate to your subject area from the British Sociological Association (BSA) (www.britsoc.co.uk), the Socio-Legal Studies Association (www.slsa.ac.uk), the Medical Research Council (www.mrc.ac.uk) and so on. Failing that, your academic department is likely to issue its own guide for students conducting research. Although the issues identified in the guidelines may not be identical to the ones that you may raise, you may find that the guidelines prompt you to think of similar issues that need to be considered.

> **Activity Thirty-Three**
>
> What steps do you need to take to resolve each of the ethical dilemmas that have been raised by reading the guidelines?

10.3 Feasibility

It is crucial that you are realistic about what can be achieved in the timescale available for your project. Before committing yourself to your project and completing and submitting your research proposal, you should ask yourself the following questions about the feasibility of the research:

1 *Do I have the time?* What is the timescale for the research? Is it possible to complete all the negotiation of access/data collection/data analysis/report writing that the project would involve? Be realistic.
2 *Do I have the money?* Do you have the money for travel and accommodation, during data collection away from your usual residence; preparation of questionnaires; cost of phone calls; analysis of data by external agents; stationery/equipment?
3 *Do I have access?* Do you have access to buildings/institutions/individuals/documents, within the timescale available, to be able to collect the data you require? Blaxter et al. (2010: 156–60) looks in some detail at how to gain access to data and offers some strategies to consider if access is refused.
4 *Do I have the skills?* Do you have the keyboard skills, analytical skills? Do you have the required skills to do the research or the time to acquire them?
5 *Do I have the knowledge about the subject?* Do you have the required knowledge to do the research or the time to acquire it?

In all cases you need to identify in advance any potential problems and consider finding solutions or alternatives.

Robson (2011: 399–406) provides further advice on issues of feasibility, especially on negotiating access.

10.4 Literature searching and reviewing

Anyone beginning research for a module assignment or for a much larger research project needs to carry out comprehensive literature searching and reviewing for the following reasons:

* To discover what research already exists in the broad subject field
* To rule out the possibility of someone having already done the same research
* To help you decide upon the exact nature of your research
* To increase your knowledge and understanding in the subject field

This book cannot possibly give a detailed guide to literature searching in every field. What it can do, however, is to indicate in general terms the sort of searching tools that are available in most libraries, especially in academic libraries. What you *must* do is go to the library that will be your main resource centre (either in person or visit the website) and collect from there the various guides on literature searching that the library produces. If these do not appear to be available ask to speak to or email the librarian in your subject area. They will be able to give you more specific help. Also, your fellow students/colleagues/supervisor should be able to guide you.

You were introduced in Chapter 6 to ways of finding relevant resources for your assignments and in Section 9.5 to how to write a literature review. While you may need to go into greater depth of searching for resources and reviewing them for a research project, the basic tools for doing so are essentially the same. You should be able to find details of books, journal articles, conference proceedings and dissertations using the various tools that are available, and to review them using the critical analysis skills that you will develop in the course of your studies.

However, before embarking upon a very detailed and time-consuming literature search, it would be as well to discover if anyone else has done or is currently doing research in your chosen area. It is unlikely that someone will have done exactly what you plan to do in exactly the same context and geographical location, but it is best to check. In any case, as you explore other people's current research, it will give you ideas for your own topic.

Current research

It is important to try to establish what research is currently being conducted in the same general subject field as your own. This is actually very difficult to do. One way is to try and attend relevant conferences and talk to people making presentations who will know what is happening in the field. Ask your research supervisor for advice on the best conferences to attend in your subject field. You may also need to enquire about possible grants for conference fees. You can also receive free email updates of conferences matching your interests, available dates and preferred destinations by registering with *Academic Conferences Worldwide* at www.conferencealerts.com. If you cannot meet people in person at conferences, it is possible to keep in touch with others working in your subject area via electronic networking (see Section 6.7).

Another way of keeping up to date is to consult various indexes of current research. There are indexes for particular subject areas, such as *Current Education and Children's Services Research in the UK* (CERUKplus) maintained by the National Foundation of Educational Research (NFER). (Unfortunately, at the time of writing (January 2015) this database is not being updated. However, it is still a useful resource of research in this area in the recent past.)

CERUK*plus* is a free, online database of...education and children's services research in the UK. It covers individual PhD studies, as well as long term, large-scale research such as national surveys. CERUK*plus* is a resource for commissioners and users of research, and researchers...conducting studies.

(www.ceruk.ac.uk)

For details of ESRC funding opportunities and the publications and research activities that are the product of these awards, you can use *ESRC Society Today* at www.esrcsocietytoday.ac.uk.

You could also look at the websites of other big funding bodies and research centres in your subject area, for example, the Centre for Research and Action in Public Health at the University of Canberra (www.canberra.edu.au/centres/ceraph/research) and the Joseph Rowntree Foundation (www.jrf.org.uk), where you can also subscribe to receive emails of a weekly round-up of new research and blogs.

Most libraries will have a number of other compilations of research published in various subject fields by different bodies/publishing houses. Unfortunately, by the time they are published they are already out of date, but if you want to see what has been researched in the recent past they are a useful source. Search your library's catalogue for details (see also information on databases in Section 6.7).

Those working in the scientific and technological fields can use patents information to help avoid duplicating existing research and development work. A huge amount of patents information is now available for free on the web. For example, you can receive regular free email notification about inventions recently patented in the US by subscribing to Patent Alert at www.patentalert.com. For older patents material and a more thorough search of worldwide patents literature you can visit one of the Patent Information Centres across Europe. Known as *PATLIB* (PATentLIBrary), the Europe-wide network of patent libraries comprises the national patent offices of each of the 38 member states and all regional Patent Information Centres. In total, over 323 such centres in Europe can help you with free information and competent advice (www.epo.org/searching/patlib.html). In addition, the free European patent applications and specifications (EPAB) online search tool is designed for people who need to monitor European patent applications and granted patents. The tool offers advanced search capabilities, including full-text searching.

In the UK alone there are 14 *PATLIB* centres around the country. You can see the list at www.epo.org/searching/patlib/directory/bycountry-item_2.html. They are based mainly in the public libraries of large cities and towns around the UK from Aberdeen to Plymouth. On the web page of the Business and IP Centre of the *British Library* at www.bl.uk/bipc/ there is a list of databases for international collections of patents, though unfortunately (due to licence restrictions) many of these databases can now only be accessed from within the *British Library*'s London Reading Rooms, where some of the content of some of the databases can be downloaded. However, there are links from the BL BIPC website to some databases that are freely available online, including the *US Patent and Trademark Office* (patft.uspto.gov) for searching US national utility patents and design patents and *Patentscope* (patentscope.wipo.int/search/en/search.jsf) where you can search 43 million patent documents including 2.5 million published international patent applications (PCT) with the option of searching in nine different languages.

Grey literature

Unpublished papers about current research are one form of so-called 'grey literature' which is very hard to trace. An initiative developed at the British Education

Index (BEI) Office, University of Leeds, is the Education-*line* Project (www.leeds. ac.uk/bei). The primary purpose of Education-*line* is to maintain a freely accessible database of pre-print and grey literature in education and training, providing a forum for discussion and facilitating early access to over 6000 significant unpublished and pre-published research texts. The database contains full-text reports, conference papers, working papers and electronic literature that supports educational research, policy and practice. Some records previously available in the free collections that were accessible from here are now only included in the main BEI database delivered by *Proquest Dialog* since BEI was sold by the University of Leeds in 2013 to *EBSCO* Information Services.

The *arXiv e-print archive* (arxiv.org) operated by Cornell University provides open access to over a million e-prints in the fields of physics, mathematics, computer science, quantitative biology, quantitative finance and statistics.

The US Department of Energy (DoE) and the Office of Scientific & Technical Information (OSTI) in the US have developed the *E-print Network* which is:

> ...a vast, integrated network of electronic scientific and technical information created by scientists and research engineers active in their respective fields, all full-text searchable. E-print Network is intended for use by other scientists, engineers, and students at advanced levels.

> ...a gateway to over 35,300 websites and databases worldwide, containing over 5.5 million e-prints in basic and applied sciences, primarily in physics but also including subject areas such as chemistry, biology and life sciences, materials science, nuclear sciences and engineering, energy research, computer and information technologies, and other disciplines of interest to DOE.
>
> (www.osti.gov/eprints)

The *E-print Network ALERTS feature* will provide automated emails to you with updates in your specified subject area. (OSTI also hosts a blog at www.osti. gov/home/ostiblog to accelerate science discovery.)

Science.gov 'searches over 60 databases and over 2200 selected websites from 15 federal agencies, offering 200 million pages of authoritative US government science information including research and development results' (www.science. gov).

Theses and dissertations

To discover what research has recently been completed you will need to consult an index to theses/dissertations. You may be able to search for theses produced by former students at your own institution using the library catalogue and restricting your search to 'thesis'. Or your library may hold a separate index to the theses/dissertations that it has in its own stock, as at SOAS, University of London (www.soas.ac.uk/library/using/finding/theses/).

There are also various published indexes to theses/dissertations. Details of these will be available in your library or via its website. For example: the electronic version of what used to be called *Index to Theses* and now called *ProQuest Dissertations and Theses – UK and Ireland* provides:

the entire bibliographic record of dissertations written in the United Kingdom and Ireland from as far back as 1716, with full abstracts for titles available from 1986. This product currently comprises over half a million records, with some additional 15,000 citations added annually.

(www.proquest.com/products-services/pqdt_uk_ireland.html)

The electronic resource *ProQuest Dissertations and Theses—Global* (PQDT Global) (formerly *Digital Dissertations*) lists doctoral (PhD) and some master's dissertations (theses) in all subject disciplines and covers the US, Canada and some European countries (some British universities are not covered). It:

simplifies searching for dissertations and theses via a single access point to explore an extensive, trusted collection of 3.8 million graduate works, with 1.7 million in full text. Designated as an official offsite repository for the U.S. Library of Congress, PQDT Global offers comprehensive historic and ongoing coverage for North American works and significant and growing international coverage from a multiyear program of expanding partnerships with international universities and national associations.

(www.proquest.com/products-services/pqdtglobal.html)

Once a free service, the *ProQuest* database can now only be accessed via subscription, so you will need to obtain a username and password from your own educational provider to be able to access it.

The National Library of Australia's *Trove* (trove.nla.gov.au/) is a free repository of Australian material, including almost a million Australian theses produced by postgraduate research students at Australian universities. This incorporates the *Australasian Digital Theses* database which ceased operation on 28 March 2011.

Theses Canada, launched in 1965 at the request of the deans of Canadian graduate schools, is a voluntary programme between Library and Archives Canada (LAC) and nearly 70 universities accredited by the Association of Universities and Colleges of Canada. It strives to:

- acquire and preserve theses and dissertations from participating universities
- provide free access to Canadian electronic theses and dissertations in the collection
- facilitate access to non-digital theses and dissertations in the collection.

(www.bac-lac.gc.ca/eng/services/theses/Pages/theses-canada.aspx)

In 2008 there were approximately 300,000 theses and dissertations on microform in LAC's collection. Of these approximately 50,000 were also available electronically.

DART Europe is 'a partnership of research libraries and library consortia who are working together to improve global access to European research theses. [It] provides access to 585357 open access research theses from 575 Universities in 28 European countries' (as of 28 April 2015) (www.dart-europe.eu/basic-search. php).

Activity Thirty-Four

The literature search and review. This task once begun will be ongoing and it would be unwise to concentrate solely on this and neglect your other studies. However, it is crucial that you make a start on this process at an early stage in your studies. For an introduction to conducting a literature review, see Section 9.5.

You may already have made an initial visit to the library that will be your main or sole resource centre to discover what information sources are available (see Activity Twenty). If you haven't you would be well advised to do so sooner rather than later. When you make that visit (in person or via its website) you need to make a note of those sources of information likely to be most relevant to your field of study.

Once you have some ideas for your research topic, and indeed for other assignments in your programme of study, and you have identified the sources, you need to begin to carry out searches systematically in order to discover what is available in your field. Make sure that you keep careful notes of the search strategy, the sources searched and of those items that the searches produce. You may want to input notes directly into your computer, thus beginning what eventually will become your bibliography. There is now software available to help you do this (see Section 6.8). Even without such software, it is recommended that you download the results of any electronic searches to your PC (or data pen, mobile phone or tablet if working away from home). You will then have an accurate record of the search together with the search terms used.

Using index cards, while still an excellent low-tech (and extremely portable) way of storing bibliographical information, does carry with it the potential for error. Great care needs to be taken in noting down accurately the bibliographical information. Don't forget to note the source of information for each item. It could save you hours trying to track down this information at some future date when you discover, for instance, that you don't have the volume number for a journal article.

Once you have located the items identified as potentially relevant and begin to read them, make notes about them, their usefulness, point of view, conclusions and so on. This will form the basis of your literature review when you write up your dissertation/research report and in the intervening time act as a very useful annotated bibliography.

A specific time cannot be set for this task – it will take you several hours, days – even weeks. Even after you have started to conduct your own research you need to continue to keep up with what else is happening in the field.

10.5 Evaluating other people's research projects

You can discover a lot about how to do research (and how *not* to do it) by looking at other people's research reports/dissertations. It will help you to further formulate your ideas about your own research. Whenever you read a report (and indeed plan your own research and report), the following questions need to be considered:

1 Has the study been done before? (You will know the answer to this from your literature search and search of current/recent research.)
2 Does the study end up answering the question set at the beginning?
3 Are the conclusions justified by the results?
4 How do the results relate to the findings of others?
5 Do the findings fit to an existing or proposed model?
6 Could you repeat the study from the information given?
7 Do the authors set out the implications of their work for your subject area and for further research?

In addition, consider the following questions about the data collection and analysis:

1 Were the data collection methods suited to the subjects being researched and the question being addressed?
2 Are the results reliable?
3 Are the results valid?
4 Are the results generalizable?
5 Is there any bias?
6 Are the findings clearly presented?

Activity Thirty-Five

Critically evaluate two or three project reports/dissertations written about research carried out in your subject area. You should be able to obtain access to these in your local university library or via its website, or (for reports of smaller research projects) in the department of the institution where you are registered as a student. Ask the above questions as you read the report and make a note of the answers.

In the light of your findings, make a note of issues that you need to consider more carefully about your own research before you begin it.

10.6 Managing your research project

You need to think carefully about managing the project – planning ahead, managing your time and keeping accurate records of any number of things. Don't always be in a hurry to do things. Time spent in reflection or contemplation is time well spent – provided, of course, the ideas that are generated are eventually translated into action!

Plan/do/review

Making plans is all very well but they are only of value if you have some way of reviewing where you have got to in your plan. It is a good idea, therefore, to make arrangements with your tutor(s) about who is going to monitor your progress and how this is to be done. Ideally it should be a joint effort, though the primary responsibility is yours. If you are the sort of person who values some external pressure to help you meet deadlines, you could perhaps ask your tutor(s) to build in regular monitoring sessions when they ask to discuss a piece of written work with you or a report you have written on your own review of your progress. If you do not have easy physical access to your tutor(s), it may be possible to *Skype* or *FaceTime* them, if they have the same video chat application on their PC or mobile device.

You will need to be realistic about the workload here – yours and theirs – and be clear about the purpose of each meeting. Don't be tempted to review too often: you need the time in between to get some real work done.

'The time given for the dissertation is in proportion to the length of the work but be aware it is a much more intense and complex experience.'

'Assignments/dissertations *always* take longer than anticipated.'

Managing your time

We looked in some detail in Section 3.6 at the question of time management for the duration of your whole period of study. At this point you need to pay particular attention to the time management issues of conducting your research project.

Research schedule

Bearing in mind the issues raised in Section 3.6 and your responses to the activities there, draw up a *realistic* and more detailed schedule for the whole of the research project. Remember that you need to allow plenty of time for data analysis and presentation (especially if you are transcribing and editing from tape recordings of meetings or interviews) and for the writing of the dissertation or research report. The preparation of tables and graphs (even using computer software) and the final editing of your report can be very time-consuming. The deadline for finishing all of this is usually imposed by external factors, such as the submission date of your research report for your course of study or the date stated by your employer if you are planning work-related research. For some part-time programmes of study, course leaders may be happy for the dissertation or report to be submitted some time later than the official end of the period of study, well after other assignments and any formal written examinations have been completed. Be sure to check what the regulations are for your particular course (and institution) and also to enquire whether or not any additional fees will have to be paid if you extend the course in this way.

Using the submission date as your end date you can calculate how many months you have between now and then and design a work schedule. This might simply be a list of tasks with proposed completion dates against them, but in order to see the relationship between different tasks, including the rest of your studies, it is better to draw up some form of table or chart that is divided up into monthly, weekly or even daily sections on one axis and by a series of tasks on the other.

Month	1	2	3	4	5	6	7	8	9	10	11	12
Literature search and review	➡	➡	➡									
Finish this book	➡											
Plan own research	➡	➡										
Observe research of A. N. Other	➡	➡	➡									
Conduct pilot tests				➡								
Analyse and reflect on pilot tests					➡							
Collect main data						➡	➡	➡				
Analyse data								➡	➡			
Write dissertation										➡	➡	➡

FIGURE 10.1 Research schedule

Although you may have included your research project and/or the writing of the dissertation in the earlier *Gantt* chart for your whole course, it is important to look in more detail at the research project and the tasks associated with it. One example of what a research schedule might look like is given in Figure 10.1.

'I was awarded a scholarship and a research grant in my second year, which I used to...cover my work one day a week for three months while I did my research.'

Activity Thirty-Six

Although you will not be able to fill in the 'tasks' in detail until you have decided upon the exact methods you are going to use, make a start on drafting your schedule. You could even include the reading of this book as one of the tasks. You could also make an entry for assisting on someone else's research or reading about other research and you could certainly include the literature search and review, which you may already have begun and which will be ongoing for a few more weeks yet. Clearly this and many other tasks will overlap and will therefore appear in the same week or month of the schedule. Other tasks will have to be completed consecutively rather than concurrently, since the commencement of one is dependent upon the completion of the other. The data collection needs to include time for the execution and analysis of the pilot and for reflection on these before scheduling the main data collection time. You also need to build in some allowance for a degree of slippage. For instance, you may have to modify your strategy in the light of the results of the pilot work. The new strategy will need to be piloted if there are more than just minor changes.

Commentary

Other suggestions for charting your time schedule, together with ideas for making the most of your time, are included in Orna (with Stevens 2009: Ch. 5). As Orna points out (pp. 112 and 116) you are often dependent on other people to be able to meet your deadlines so you need to plan well ahead and make your arrangements in good time. There are also two useful chapters in Cryer (2006: Chs 13 and 14) on (respectively) planning your work and managing yourself and your time.

Record-keeping

Every step along the way you need to keep good records. They might take the form of notes on sources of information – be they people, addresses, references to literature or whatever – or a detailed report on progress (or lack of it!). The largest amount of data will be that which is generated in the process of actually doing the research. In every respect it is crucial to organize your data. Your means of doing this may take various forms, for example:

- Diary of research
- Card indexes
- Loose-leaf files
- Electronic files on PC or mobile device
- Audio and/or video tapes
- Notebook

We looked in Section 6.7 at the importance of record-keeping about your search strategy for bibliographic references for assignments. This is especially important when conducting a larger-scale research project.

Diary of research

A research diary can take different forms. For some people it can become a reflective journal, which serves a therapeutic purpose for the researcher as well as being a source of information/inspiration to return to at a later date. For others, although it may be reflective in some senses, it is kept very precisely for the purpose of building a record of the research process and forms the basis of various elements of the research report.

While a research diary can clearly be beneficial for a number of different reasons it is probably more relevant for a research student or where the research project is large-scale. For a smaller project the amount of time actually needed to write the diary may be better spent doing other things. Alternatively the diary might be a very brief record of progress of the project, perhaps written on a weekly basis. This can help the researcher to appreciate where more headway is needed.

Other records

You may want to create your *bibliographical database* directly onto your computer or mobile device. This is no bad thing, since you will gradually build up an essential element of your research report. (See Section 6.8 for details of personal bibliographic software.) However, a flexible, low-tech alternative – especially when out and about – are the index cards that you can buy from the stationers. They can also be used for a *database of people* you contact, possibly cross-referenced to another database containing *details of organizations, companies*, and so on. Obviously if you use the latter, they will then have to be transcribed onto a computer eventually.

Once you start actually collecting the *substantive data*, which is the subject of your research, you will need to be particularly organized. How you write up the results of, for instance, meetings or interviews is a question of personal choice. Eventually you will want to include at least a summary, if not a verbatim record, of interviews in your report so they will end up on computer, but in the short term (especially if you are out 'in the field' for several days) you will want to ensure you have an accurate record of what was said. If the interviews are recorded (audio or video) there is less urgency to write them up, but if you are making handwritten notes initially these should be done as soon as possible after the interview.

Don't be tempted to think that the very clear memory you have of what was said by a particular interviewee will stay with you. Even after two or three interviews the details all get a bit hazy and who said what becomes a bit confused. Since you might want to be able to rearrange the order of the information collected in this way you might be better writing on cards (for relatively brief interviews) or using a loose-leaf folder or typing them up on your PC or mobile device, rather than in a notebook.

Although you might not want to embark upon writing the research report until well into the project, you might consider keeping a file (either paper or electronic) containing headings and subheadings for the various sections of what will ultimately be your report and add notes to this from time to time. Again the low-tech version is more mobile (unless you're using a tablet or laptop computer) and you can use coloured dividers to mark the different sections, and new sheets can easily be inserted.

At the very least, always have a notebook handy. You never know when those brilliant ideas are going to come to you. What seems glaringly obvious and abundantly clear at 3:00 a.m. becomes a blur after a few more hours sleep.

Filing system

Whatever form your record-keeping takes, make sure that you have an efficient and effective filing system. In this way you will be able to locate the information you need when you need it. Classify the files you create in some way. On a computer you can do this by creating different subdirectories for documents covering the various components of your project. (Don't forget to keep backup copies.) If you are creating paper files you could use different coloured folders for separate topics as well as labelling the folders clearly. Keep a record of the classifications you have used so that you don't create a new folder when one already exists. Make sure that you label the documents in some way so that you know which folder they belong in, maybe by simply marking the top of each with a coloured pen. Since each folder will contain several documents, you might consider (especially for larger projects) using a simple card index system so that you know where each document is.

10.7 Reporting your findings

Writing your research report (or dissertation) is an integral and crucial part of the process of conducting research. The research has no real value unless what you find out is communicated to others. There are two stages to be considered here:

1 Writing up the results and the conclusions you have drawn from those results
2 Disseminating those findings to others

Both of these stages will be affected by your knowledge of who you want to read the findings and who needs/has a right to read them. It may be that different types of report will be needed to fulfil the different requirements. While it may seem a long way off before you need to have your report(s) ready, it is never too soon to start thinking about what is going to go in it (them). (You are likely to find much of what is included in this section on writing research reports also relevant to writing shorter reports and to your other assignments.)

Your audience

Most of you reading this book will be registered for an accredited academic course and one of the requirements of that course will be to conduct research and produce a dissertation. Clearly your primary aim will be to meet the expectations of your tutor(s) and of the external examiners. Different departments within universities issue their own guides to writing a research report. The rules and regulations regarding length of report, whether or not and how it is bound, how many copies are needed, and so on, will vary.

In addition, you may obtain some funding/sponsorship from an external body to help with the expenses incurred in conducting the research, or your employer may give you some form of grant. It is likely that someone somewhere will expect to be informed about the findings and that they will have their own expectations about how those findings will be presented.

Activity Thirty-Seven

Before going any further, discover (or recover) information about who will require a report on your research and in what format that report is needed. Read this information and make brief notes. Collect together into one folder any guidelines, documents and so on that you come across that include such information. If details about the format of the report are included in a larger document, photocopy (or copy and paste if available electronically) the relevant pages and keep them with other guidelines.

Commentary

You need to have such guidelines constantly in mind when writing your report(s). It may be that if you have to write more than one report you can use some sections in both/all of them.

The content of the report

While the exact format and final length of the report will vary according to the above factors, the basic outline will not. All that will change is the depth to which each aspect is analysed and the detail that is included. Essentially any research report will include the following:

- *What* the research was
- *Why* the research was done
- *How* the research was conducted
- *What* the results of the research are
- *How* you have interpreted those results
- *Where* you are going to go from here

You can start to gather together notes for the first three sections from a very early stage, indeed the content of these sections will be needed for your research proposal. The most significant change for the final report will be that you will change to using the past tense! If you are restricted in the number of words you may use, make sure that each one counts. Don't go into detail about peripheral matters and don't try to cram everything in just because you've got it.

Writing the report

Just because *you* know your subject inside out by the time you have finished your research, doesn't mean to say that everyone else does. Even when it is going to be read by others in the same field, it is important to keep the style of your writing simple and clear. It doesn't make your work more worthy or intellectual because you use long, complicated sentences. The opposite is quite often the case. Where you do use jargon, be sure to include a definition of the term in a glossary at the front or back of your report so that the uninitiated can check on meaning. It is especially important to remember this advice when writing a version of your report that will be read by a wider audience, say, by first-year undergraduates reading your article in a journal.

While there are conventions about most things to do with spelling, grammar, punctuation and abbreviations, there are many times when decisions are down to personal choice. (For instance, are you going to use full stops for 'e.g.', 'Dr', 'Mr' or 'USA'? Are you going to spell out 'seven' and 'nine' in full but use '11' and '46' in numbers?) In such instances make your mind up, note down your decision and stick to it. It is very irritating for all readers, but for examiners in particular, to see two or three different versions within the same document.

The ultimate aim of any writing is to enable the reader to grasp the meaning of what you are saying. This may be enhanced by the use of analogy and metaphor but don't set out to use them just for the sake of it. You may find that your reader won't be able to see the wood for the trees! Try to make your material straightforward and readable but interesting, so add a bit of variety. Gradually you will develop your own style that you will feel comfortable with. You might find it useful to ask a friend or helpful colleague to read some of your writing at a very early stage and to give constructive criticism of it. You will be less likely to be upset at this stage than asking someone to read your final draft when the deadline for submission is just two days away.

Robson (2011: Ch. 18) includes a section on reporting on case studies, writing a technical report, and one on how to present recommendations in evaluation reports. There are also useful guidelines for revising the first draft of your report, and some suggestions for further reading about reporting on the results of your enquiry can be found on the associated website at www.wiley.com/college/robson. On p. 498 of Robson there are some samples of anti-sexist language from the British Sociological Association's (BSA's) *Language and the BSA: Sex and Gender* (2004).You can download this document from the BSA's own website (www.britsoc.co.uk), as well as others in their Equality and Diversity series: *Ethnicity and Race* (2005) and *Non-Disablist* (2004).

The *LearnHigher* materials recommended in Section 9.2 on report writing are also highly relevant to anyone writing up the report on their research project. If you have not yet done Activity Thirty in that section, now would be a good time to do it.

Citations and references

For an excellent guide to the technical aspects of writing reports (including the presentation of bibliographic information) see Turabian (1982 and 2013). For a more up-to-date British guide, see *MHRA Style Guide: A Handbook for Authors, Editors, and Writers of Theses*, produced and published by the Modern Humanities Research Association (2013). The first chapter (on the preparation of copy) includes information on preparing copy for publication in any medium, on submission on disk, and on direct electronic submission. Other chapters provide the more traditional information on punctuation, references, footnotes, and so on. An electronic version of the guide is also available, downloadable in a pdf version for free for individual use, at www.mhra.org.uk/Publications/Books/Style Guide/download.shtml or by emailing mail@mhra.org.uk.

Various online (and paper) guides to citations and to the Harvard and other systems of referencing are available. Details of these are provided in 'Styles of references' in Section 6.8.

Disseminating the findings

In addition to distributing copies of the report(s) to various people already on your list, you need to consider using other ways of disseminating the findings to a wider audience. One way is to go to conferences in your field and present papers. This has the added advantage that, if the papers are published in conference proceedings, it also provides an opportunity for adding a publication to your CV. Another avenue (and one that you might consider before venturing out to the big conferences) is to hold a short seminar at which to deliver and discuss your findings. These are often held within various schools or departments of a university or at sessions organized by the various interdisciplinary research groups. The more you speak about your research in public, the more confident you will become (and the more familiar with the content!).

Getting published

It may be that in addition to submitting your dissertation for your diploma or degree your aim is to begin building up a list of publications. While you can make enquiries at the outset about getting a monograph published, the slightly easier and less onerous task is perhaps to aim at getting an article or two in relevant academic journals. You are not likely to be paid for such an article (indeed you may have to pay a fee to get the article published, especially if it is an 'Open Access' journal; see 'E-journals' in Section 6.7) but it will be a start. You have probably discovered (in the course of your own literature search) the sorts of journals that are likely to be interested in an article in your field. For ideas of other titles you can check the journals in your library and seek the advice of fellow students, colleagues and tutors. You will usually find guidelines within the current issue of a journal about how to submit your article for consideration. Take note of the suggestions on layout, length, referencing style and so on, or you may fall at the first hurdle. Your article is likely to be sent out to referees for scrutiny and may then come back to you with suggestions for improvement (which you may or may not be prepared to accept) so the whole process may take some time.

You may, of course, publish an article or research report on your own personal website or on your institution's website (if such a facility exists), although the former won't be refereed so will be unlikely to be cited by others, and the latter is less likely to be included in academic databases than if in a published journal, so won't reach a particularly large audience. However, some exposure of your work is better than none.

If you are already interested in finding out more about approaching a publisher about getting a book published, you might find it useful to read Ashcroft (1997: 121–7). If your work is within the broad field of educational research you will also find useful the annotated lists of education publishers and education journals provided in the same book, pp. 130–44. Sound advice is also provided in Luey (2010) and Thyer (1994).

Chapter summary

In this chapter you have:

- Begun your preparation for doing your research project by considering the nature of research and your approach to doing it
- Been alerted to the ethical and feasibility issues that need to be considered when conducting research
- Explored some of the numerous sources of bibliographical and other information that is available to assist you in that project, and begun to do your literature search
- Considered the practicalities of managing your research project and reporting your findings

Appendix one

Answers to the quiz on understanding when to reference. (See Figure 7.3 in Section 7.3.)

	Yes	No
1. When you include tables, photos, statistics and diagrams in your assignment. These may be items directly copied or a source of data collation which you have used.	☑	☐
2. When describing or discussing a theory, model or practice associated with a particular writer.	☑	☐
3. When you summarise information drawn from a variety of sources about what has happened over a period and the summary is unlikely to be a cause of dispute or controversy.	☐	☑
4. To give weight or credibility to an argument that you believe is important.	☑	☐
5. When giving emphasis to a particular idea that has found a measure of agreement and support amongst commentators.	☑	☐
6. When pulling together a range of key ideas that you introduced and referenced earlier in the assignment.	☐	☑
7. When stating or summarising obvious facts, and when there is unlikely to be any significant disagreement with your statements or summaries.	☐	☑
8. When including quotations.	☑	☐
9. When you copy and paste items from the Internet and where no author's name is shown.	☑	☐
10. When paraphrasing or summarising (in your own words) another person's work that you feel is particularly significant, or likely to be a subject of debate.	☑	☐

Reproduced, with permission, from Neville (2010) *The Complete Guide to Referencing and Avoiding Plagiarism*, Appendix 1, p. 194.

Appendix two: Example course study schedule

Year: Month	1:1	1:2	1:3	1:4	1:5	1:6	1:7	1:8	1:9	1:10	1:11	1:12	2:1	2:2	2:3	2:4	2:5	2:6	2:7	2:8	2:9	2:10	2:11	2:12
Introductory reading	↑	↑	↑																					
Residential			↑																					
Module 1				↑	↑	↑																		
Assignment 1						↑	↑																	
Module 2								↑	↑	↑														
Assignment 2										↑	↑													
Module 3												↑	↑	↑										
Assignment 3														↑	↑									
Module 4																↑	↑	↑						
Assignment 4																		↑	↑					
Dissertation																↑	↑	↑	↑	↑	↑			
Revision for finals																					↑	↑	↑	
Final written examinations																								↑

Appendix three: Template weekly planner

Hour of the day	Monday	Tuesday	Wednesday	Thursday	Friday	Saturday	Sunday

Note: Since people begin and end their days at different times no details have been included in the Hour boxes. A 16-hour day has been assumed, but if you sleep for considerably more or less than 8 hours you could always add or delete rows/hours accordingly in your own version of this planner. Half-hours could be created by dividing the boxes.

Further resources

Note

What follows is an indicative list of supplementary books and websites that will help you to further develop your study skills, should you need to do so. For convenience the materials are arranged in roughly the same order as the chapters of the book. Many more resources are already detailed within the main text of the book itself. In addition, an increasing number of book publishers now provide very useful websites to complement their published texts. The **titles** of online resources within these lists are given in ***bold***.

General study guides

Bourner, T. and Race, P. (1995) *How to Win as a Part-Time Student*, 2nd edn. London: Routledge Falmer.

Britton, A. and Cousins, A. (1998) *Study Skills: A Guide for Lifelong Learners*, 2nd rev. edn. London: Distance Learning Centre, South Bank University.

Buzan, T. (2010) *Use Your Head: How to Unleash the Power of Your Mind.* London: BBC Books.

Buzan, T. (2011) *Buzan's Study Skills: Mind Maps, Memory Techniques, Speed Reading and More!* London: BBC Active/ Pearson.

Cottrell, S. (2013) *The Study Skills Handbook*, 4th edn. Basingstoke: Palgrave Macmillan.

Drew, S. and Bingham, R. (2010) *The Guide to Learning and Study Skills*. Farnham: Gower.

Lashley, C. (1995) *Improving Study Skills: A Competence Approach*. New York: Cassell.

Lashley, C. and Best, W. (2003) *12 Steps to Study Success*. London: Thomson.

Lewis, R. (1997) *How to Manage Your Study Time*. Cambridge: National Extension College and Collins Educational.

Marshall, L. and Rowland, F. (1998) *A Guide to Learning Independently*, 3rd edn. Buckingham: Open University Press.

Moore, S. and Murphy, M. (2005) *How to Be a Student: 100 Great Ideas and Practical Habits for Students Everywhere*. Maidenhead: Open University Press.

Moore, S., Neville, C., Murphy, M. and Connolly, C. (2010) *The Ultimate Study Skills Handbook*. Maidenhead: Open University Press.

Northedge, A. (2005) *The Good Study Guide*, rev. edn. Milton Keynes: The Open University.

Open University Course Team (various years) ***Study Skills Books***. Milton Keynes: The Open University. Titles include: *Preparing Assignments*; *Revising for Examinations*; *Reading and Taking Notes*; *Develop Effective Study Strategies*; *Communicating and Presenting*; and *Thinking Critically*. 'These useful guides have been created by updating and revising the popular *Student Toolkits*, and offer practical advice and tips to help students improve their study skills. Each book is accompanied by A5 size cards that offer study advice and techniques in an easy to read bulleted format' (from the website). You can buy the full set of 16 cards on their own direct from the OU at www.ouw.co.uk/, from where you can also buy the guides in accessible PDF (Portable Document Format) files on CD-ROM. (See also *Studying with the OU: UK Learning Approach* in

'Guides for international students'; and various titles in 'Guides for Disabled Students' below.)

Powell, S. (1999) *Returning to Study: A Guide for Professionals.* Buckingham: Open University Press.

Pritchard, L. and Roberts, L. (2006) *The Mature Student's Guide to Higher Education.* Maidenhead: Open University Press.

Rowntree, D. (1993) *Teach Yourself with Open Learning*, new edn. London: Kogan Page.

Rowntree, D. (1998) *Learn How to Study: A Realistic Approach*, 4th edn. London: Warner.

Rowntree, D. (2015) **Learn How to Study: A Virtual Tutorial with Professor Derek Rowntree**, 5th edn. [Kindle edition]

Guides for disabled students
(see especially Section 4.7)

Hargreaves, S. (ed.) (2012) *Study Skills for Students with Dyslexia*, 2nd edn (with accompanying CD) (Sage Study Skills Series). London: Sage.

Jamieson, C. and Morgan, E. (2008) *Managing Dyslexia at University: A Resource for Students, Academic and Support Staff* (with accompanying CD) (David Fulton Books). Abingdon: Routledge.

Open University Course Team (Various years) **Study Skills Books.** Milton Keynes: The Open University. Titles include: **Studying when you are D/deaf**; **Studying and Staying Mentally Healthy**; **Studying with Little or No Sight**; and **Studying with Dyslexia.** 'This [last] booklet describes some of the challenges of studying with dyslexia and aims to help develop effective skills for studying. It has been printed on buff coloured paper, which many people who have dyslexia find much easier to read from as the glare that can be experienced when reading from white paper is reduced' (from the website). Hard copies of the booklets and pdf files are available at www.ouw.co.uk/. There is also an accompanying **Skills for OU Study** website www.open.ac.uk/skillsforstudy.

Guides for international students
(see especially Section 9.1)

Bailey, S. (2015) *Academic Writing: A Handbook for International Students*, 4th edn. (Routledge Study Guides). Abingdon: Routledge.

Davies, M. (2011) *Study Skills for International Postgraduates.* Basingstoke: Palgrave MacMillan.

Lowes, R., Peters, H. and Turner, M. (2004) *The International Student's Guide: Studying in English at University.* London: Sage.

Open University Course Team (2008) **Study Skills Books. Studying with the OU: UK Learning Approach.** Milton Keynes: The Open University. Although intended primarily for Open University students, this booklet is useful for all distance learning students. 'If you are a student who uses more than one language and your main language isn't English, this booklet is for you. Its aim is to give international students an understanding of how some cultural meanings go unstated in the English language and what is expected of students in a distance-learning UK university setting' (from the website). It is also available from www.ouw.co.uk as an accessible PDF file.

Subject-specific study guides

Chambers, E. and Northedge, A. (2008) *The Arts Good Study Guide*, 2nd edn. Milton Keynes: The Open University Worldwide.

The Language Learner's Good Study Guide (1998) Milton Keynes: The Open University. (This book is only available direct from the Open University, not from bookshops, except second-hand.)

Northedge, A., Thomas, J., Lane, A. and Peasgood, A. (1997) *The Sciences Good Study Guide*. Milton Keynes: The Open University.

Tyler, S. (ed.) (2007) *The Manager's Good Study Guide*, 3rd edn. Milton Keynes: The Open University.

Guides to learning technology
(see Chapter 5)

Clarke, A. (2005) *IT Skills for Successful Study*. Basingstoke: Palgrave Macmillan.

Clarke, A. (2008) *e-Learning Skills*, 2nd edn. Basingstoke: Palgrave Macmillan.

Cottrell, S. and Morris, N. (2012) *Study Skills Connected: Using Technology to Support Your Studies*. Basingstoke: Palgrave Macmillan.

Guides to reading, writing and referencing
(see Section 6.8, Chapters 7 and 8, and Report Writing in Section 9.2)

Bowden, J. (2011) *Writing a Report: How to Prepare, Write and Present Really Effective Reports*, 9th edn. Oxford: How To Books.

Buzan, T. (2009) *The Mind Map Book: Unlock Your Creativity, Boost Your Memory, Change Your Life*. London: BBC Active.

Buzan, T. (2009) *The Speed Reading Book: Read More, Learn More, Achieve More*. London: BBC Active.

Collinson, D., Kirkup, G., Kyd, R. and Slocombe, L. (2001) *Plain English*, 2nd edn. Buckingham: Open University Press.

Cottrell, S. (2011) *Critical Thinking Skills: Effective Analysis and Argument*, 2nd edn. Basingstoke: Palgrave MacMillan.

Creme, P. and Lea, M.R. (2008) *Writing at University: A Guide for Students*, 3rd edn. Maidenhead: Open University Press.

Davies, M. (2011) *Study Skills for International Postgraduates*. Basingstoke: Palgrave MacMillan.

Fairbairn, G.J. and Fairbairn, S. (2001) *Reading at University*. Maidenhead: Open University Press.

Fairbairn, G.J. and Winch, C. (2011) *Reading, Writing and Reasoning: A Guide for Students*, 3rd edn. Maidenhead: Open University Press.

Hennessy, B. (2000) *Writing Successful Essays*. Plymouth: How To Books.

Hilton, C. and Hyder, M. (1992) *Getting to Grips with: Writing*. London: Letts Educational. (Covers basic grammar, punctuation and spelling and writing for specific purposes, e.g. a letter. Slightly dated now, but still an excellent reference book.)

McMillan, K. and Weyers, J. (2011) *How to Write Essays and Assignments*, 2nd edn. Harlow, Essex: Pearson.

Neville, C. (2010) *The Complete Guide to Referencing and Avoiding Plagiarism*, 2nd edn. Maidenhead: Open University Press.

Pears, R. and Shields, G. (2013) *Cite Them Right: The Essential Referencing Guide*, 9th edn. Basingstoke: Palgrave Macmillan. (Details of both the printed book and the online version are available at: www.citethemrightonline.com)

Rose, J. (2012) *The Mature Student's Guide to Writing*, 3rd edn. Basingstoke: Palgrave Macmillan.

Seely, J. (2013) *Oxford A–Z of Grammar and Punctuation*, 2nd edn. Oxford: Oxford University Press.

Wallace, M. and Wray, A. (2011) *Critical Reading and Writing for Postgraduates*, 2nd edn. London: Sage.

Guides to sitting examinations (see Chapter 8)

Acres, D. (1998) *Passing Exams Without Anxiety: How to Get Organized, Prepare Yourself and Feel Confident of Success*, 5th edn. Oxford: How to Books.

McMillan, K. and Weyers, J. (2011) *How to Succeed in Exams and Assessments*, 2nd edn. Harlow, Essex: Pearson.

Orr, F. (2005) *How to Pass Exams: And How to Prepare for Them with Less Anxiety*, 2nd edn. Sydney, Australia: Allen & Unwin.

Tracy, E. (2006) *The Student's Guide to Exam Success*, 2nd edn. Maidenhead: Open University Press.

Guides to mathematics, statistics and science
(see Chapter 9)

See also the web resources cited within the main text.

Graham, A. (2013) *Mathematics: A Basic Introduction*, 6th edn. London: Hodder & Stoughton. (Teach Yourself Books)

Graham, L. and Sargent, D. (1981) *Countdown to Mathematics, Volumes 1 & 2*. Wokingham: Addison-Wesley and the Open University. (Still a classic basic introduction for non-maths students.)

Owen, F. and Jones, R. (1994) *Statistics*, 4th edn. Harlow, Essex: Pearson.

Rowntree, D. (1991, reprinted with corrections 2000) *Statistics Without Tears: An Introduction for Non-Mathematicians*, new edn. London: Penguin.

Rumsey, D.J. (2011) *Statistics for Dummies*, 2nd edn. Hoboken, NJ: Wiley.

Tennent, R.M. (ed.) (1971) *Science Data Book*. Edinburgh: Oliver and Boyd. (Basic scientific facts and figures.)

University of Edinburgh *The Really Easy Statistics Site* created by Jim Deacon is 'a user-friendly beginner's guide' to statistics. www.biology.ed.ac.uk/research/groups/jdeacon/statistics/tress1.html (accessed 15 May 2015; site archived and no longer maintained, but still useful).

Guides to doing research (see Chapter 10)

Ashcroft, K. (1997) Getting published, in M. Jones, J. Siraj-Blatchford and K. Ashcroft, *Researching into Student Learning and Support: In Colleges and Universities*. London: Routledge.

Bell, J. with Waters, S. (2014) *Doing Your Research Project: A Guide for First-Time Researchers*, 6th edn. Maidenhead: Open University Press.

Blaikie, N. (2007) *Approaches to Social Enquiry: Advancing Knowledge*, 2nd edn. Cambridge: Polity Press.

Blaxter, L., Hughes, C. and Tight, M. (2010) *How to Research*, 4th edn. Maidenhead: Open University Press.

Bryman, A. (2012) *Social Research Methods*, 4th edn. Oxford: Oxford University Press.

Bryman, A. and Cramer, D. (2011) *Quantitative Data Analysis with IBM SPSS 17, 18 and 19: A Guide for Social Scientists*. Hove: Routledge.

Cohen, L., Manion, L. and Morrison, K. (2011) *Research Methods in Education*, 7th edn. Abingdon: Routledge.

Cryer, P. (2006) *The Research Student's Guide to Success*, 3rd edn. Maidenhead: Open University Press.

Denscombe, M. (2010) *Ground Rules for Social Research*, 2nd edn. Maidenhead: Open University Press.

Denscombe, M. (2014) *The Good Research Guide for Small-Scale Social Research Projects*, 5th edn. Maidenhead: Open University Press.

Gray, D.E. (2014) *Doing Research in the Real World*, 3rd edn. London: Sage.

Luey, B. (2010) *Handbook for Academic Authors*, 5th edn. Cambridge: Cambridge University Press.

Mason, J. (2016) *Qualitative Researching*, 3rd edn. Thousand Oaks, CA: Sage.

May, T. (2011) *Social Research: Issues, Methods and Process*, 4th edn. Maidenhead: Open University Press.

McMillan, K. and Weyers, J. (2011) *How to Write Dissertations and Project Reports*, 2nd edn. Harlow: Pearson.

Modern Humanities Research Association (MHRA) (2013) *MHRA Style Guide: A Handbook for Authors, Editors, and Writers of Theses*, 3rd edn. London: MHRA.

Murray, R. (2011) *How to Write a Thesis*, 3rd edn. Maidenhead: Open University Press.

Murray, R. (2013) *Writing for Academic Journals*, 3rd edn. Maidenhead: Open University Press.

Oliver, P. (2010) *The Student's Guide to Research Ethics*, 2nd edn. Maidenhead: Open University Press.

Oliver, P. (2012) *Succeeding with Your Literature Review: A Handbook for Students*, 3rd edn. Maidenhead: Open University Press.

Oppenheim, A.N. (2000) *Questionnaire Design, Interviewing and Attitude Measurement*, 2nd edn. London: Continuum International Publishing Group.

Orna, E. with Stevens, G. (2009) *Managing Information for Research: Practical Help in Researching, Writing and Designing Dissertations*, 2nd edn. Maidenhead: Open University Press.

Petre, M. and Rugg, G. (2010) *The Unwritten Rules of PhD Research*, 2nd edn. Maidenhead: Open University Press.

Phillips, E.M. and Pugh, D.S. (2010) *How to Get a PhD: A Handbook for Students and their Supervisors*, 5th edn. Maidenhead: Open University Press.

Robson, C. (2011) *Real World Research: A Resource for Social Scientists and Practitioner-Researchers*, 3rd edn. Oxford: Blackwell.

Robson, C. (2014) *How to Do a Research Project: A Guide for Undergraduate Students*, 2nd edn. Oxford: Blackwell.

Rubin, H. and Rubin, I.S. (2012) *Qualitative Interviewing: The Art of Hearing Data*, 3rd edn. Thousand Oaks, CA: Sage.

Sapsford, R. and Jupp, V. (eds) (2006) *Data Collection and Analysis*, 2nd edn. London: Sage and The Open University.

Thyer, B.A. (1994) *Successful Publishing in Scholarly Journals* (Survival Skills for Scholars series). Thousand Oaks, CA: Sage.

Turabian, K.L. (1982) *A Manual for Writers of Research Papers, Theses and Dissertations.* Oxford: Heinemann. (Although there isn't a later edition of the British version, the American version published by the University of Chicago Press is now in its 8th edition, 2013.)

Study guides on the web

A number of universities in the UK and US have study skills and research skills guides on open access on the web; you could use a search engine such as Google to find these, or go via your library website. In particular, a growing number of university libraries provide a gateway to an ever-increasing number of good quality information skills materials on the web and other resources that support students. You may find that your university's website provides brief abstracts of and links to websites on:

- Citations and references
- Database searching skills
- Finding good quality information on the Internet
- Learning how to learn

A small selection of such resources are detailed below (and there are many more in Chapters 6 and 9, including some on citations and referencing in Section 6.8). Remember that the URLs to websites can change and you may need to find updated URLs by using a search engine.

Honey and Mumford Learning Styles Questionnaire (LSQ) Knowing about different learning styles and discovering what your preferred styles are can help you become a more effective learner. The Honey and Mumford LSQ can be accessed online for a 'Pay-As-You-Go' fee (c. £12 as of January 2015) at www.peterhoney.com. Your course leader, or even your whole institution, may have purchased a licence for all of their students to complete the questionnaire online. Each student will need to obtain the link to the test and an authorization entry code, and register their individual password in order to use the online tool. The LSQ Series and Peter Honey Publications are now owned by, and the tests administered by, Pearson.

LearnHigher originated in 2005 as one of 73 Centres for Excellence in Teaching and Learning (CETLs) in England and Wales, funded by HEFCE. With the end of CETL funding in 2010, LearnHigher activity is continuing under the auspices of ALDinHE, the Association for Learning Development in Higher Education. The materials are freely available to all on the LearnHigher website at www.learnhigher.ac.uk and include help and advice in more than twenty learning areas, including: academic writing; critical thinking and reflection; group work; information literacy; note-making; reading; referencing; report writing; numeracy, maths and statistics; assessment; and time management.

Ohio State University Libraries net.tutor 'offers interactive tutorials on basic tools and techniques for becoming an effective Internet researcher'. See: http://liblearn.osu.edu/tutor/.

Open University OpenLearn at www.open.edu/openlearn provides 'free educational resources' and invites 'all to sample courses that our registered students take – for free!'. The courses on offer include several under the 'Refresh your study skills' heading, including 'Reading and note taking – preparation for study' and 'Essay and report writing skills'.

Open University SAFARI (Skills in Accessing, Finding and Reviewing Information) at www.open.ac.uk/safari/ is 'an expedition through the information world'. You will need an *OU computer username and password* to access some of the materials.

Open University Skills for OU Study at www2.open.ac.uk/students/skillsforstudy/ provides an extremely useful set of materials in a variety of study areas. You will need an *OU computer username and password* to access some of the materials.

Study Guides and Strategies at www.studygs.net was created by Joe Landsberger of Academic Web Services at the University of St Thomas, in St Paul, Minnesota, USA. It is collaboratively maintained across institutional and national boundaries and regularly revised. The site covers guides to learning and studying in general (including a section on distance learning) as well as specific guides to learning with others, reading, writing and preparing for and taking tests. There are versions of the site available in many different languages.

Supporting Students at a Distance: Support for Tutors and Students Ormond Simpson's name is synonymous with providing advice on how to help students cope with distance education and so complete their courses. His recent book *Supporting Students for Success in Online and Distance Education* is complemented by his website at http://ormondsimpson.com/, which, as well as offering help to tutors on how to increase student retention, also includes resources for students themselves. The 'For Students' section of this web page – http://ormondsimpson.com/page4.htm – includes a number of downloadable files of helpful documents on a variety of study skills topics.

VARK: A Guide to Learning Styles The following website has been developed from where it is possible to take the VARK questionnaire interactively – www.vark-learn.com (accessed 12 August 2015). Copyright is held by Neil D. Fleming, New Zealand, and Charles C. Bonwell, USA. From the website you can also buy copies of Fleming, N.D. and Bonwell, C.C. (2006) *How Do I Learn Best? A Student's Guide to Improved Learning*, new edn. (published by the authors in New Zealand).

The **Virtual Training Suite** at www.vtstutorials.co.uk provides a set of online tutorials in various subjects to help students, lecturers and researchers improve their information skills for the Internet environment. You can work at your own pace – there is no one monitoring you! The tutorials take around an hour each to complete, and include quizzes and interactive exercises to lighten the learning experience. Learning how to use the Internet more effectively can help you with your coursework, literature searching and research.

References and author index

This is a list of items referred to in the text. The page numbers in **bold** indicate where reference to each item can be found within this book. The **titles** of online items are given in **_bold italic_**.

Ashcroft, K. (1997) Getting published, in M. Jones, J. Siraj-Blatchford and K. Ashcroft, _Researching into Student Learning and Support: In Colleges and Universities_. London: Routledge. **193**

Baroudi, G. and Marksbury, N. (2013) Becoming a mobile institution, in Z.L. Berge and L.Y. Muilenburg (eds) _Handbook of Mobile Learning_. New York: Routledge. **76 and 79**

Beetham, H. and Sharpe, R. (eds) (2013) _Rethinking Pedagogy for a Digital Age: Designing for 21st Century Learning_, 2nd edn. Abingdon: Taylor & Francis. **35**

Berge, Z.L. and Muilenburg, L.Y. (eds) (2013) _Handbook of Mobile Learning_. New York: Routledge. **34**

Blaxter, L., Hughes, C. and Tight, M. (2010) _How to Research_, 4th edn. Maidenhead: Open University Press. **174 and 179**

Bloom, B.S., Engelhart, M.D., Furst, E.J., Hill, W.H. and Krathwohl, D.R. (eds) (1956) _Taxonomy of Educational Objectives: Handbook 1 – The Cognitive Domain_. London: Longman. **20, 21, 23, 34, 143, 156 and 172**

Bonk, C.J. (2014) Foreword, in B. Sutton and A. Basiel (eds) _Teaching and Learning Online: New Models of Learning for a Connected World_, Volume 2. New York: Routledge. **33 and 35**

Cairns, L. and Alshahrani, K. (2014) Online learning: models and impact in the 21st Century, in B. Sutton and A. Basiel (eds) _Teaching and Learning Online: New Models of Learning for a Connected World_, Volume 2. New York: Routledge. **37**

Carroll, J. and Ryan, J. (eds) (2005) _Teaching International Students: Improving Learning for All_. London: Routledge. **161**

Clarke, A. (2008) _E-learning Skills_, 2nd edn. Basingstoke: Palgrave Macmillan. **23, 156, and 160**

Cochrane, T. (2013) M-learning as a catalyst for pedagogical change, in Z.L. Berge and L.Y. Muilenburg (eds) _Handbook of Mobile Learning_. New York: Routledge. **36**

Coughlan, S. (2014) **_Online Students Can't Help Being Sociable_**. BBC News. Available at: www.bbc.co.uk/news/business-26925463 (accessed 19 May 2015). **25**

Creme, P. and Lea, M.R. (2008) _Writing at University: A Guide for Students_, 3rd edn. Maidenhead: Open University Press. **146**

Cryer, P. (2006) _The Research Student's Guide to Success_, 3rd edn. Maidenhead: Open University Press. **178 and 188**

Davis, C. and Wilcock, E. (2008) **_Teaching Materials Science Using Case Studies_**. Higher Education Academy UK Centre for Materials Education. Available at: www.materials.ac.uk/guides/casestudies.asp (accessed 13 April 2015). **100**

Denscombe, M. (2014) _The Good Research Guide for Small-Scale Social Research Projects_, 5th edn. Maidenhead: Open University Press. **177**

Dickey, M.D. (2004) The impact of web-logs (blogs) on student perceptions of isolation and alienation in a web-based environment, _Open Learning_, 19(3): 279–91. **92**

Dyson, L.E., Andrews, T., Smith, R. and Wallace, R. (2013) Toward a holistic framework for ethical mobile learning, in Z.L. Berge and L.Y. Muilenburg (eds) _Handbook of Mobile Learning_. New York: Routledge. **87**

Entwistle, N. and Ramsden, P. (1983) _Understanding Student Learning_. London: Croom Helm. **31**

Entwistle, N. and Ramsden, P. (2015) *Understanding Student Learning* (Routledge Revivals). London: Routledge. **31**

Fisher, A., Exley, K. and Ciobanu, D. (2014) *Using Technology to Support Learning and Teaching.* New York: Routledge. **36**

Fleming, N.D. and Bonwell, C.C. (2006) *How Do I Learn Best? A Student's Guide to Improved Learning*, new edn. (See Further Resources, Study guides on the web for more information on VARK Guide to Learning Styles.) **33 and 134**

Glaser, B.G. and Strauss, A.L. (1967) *The Discovery of Grounded Theory: Strategies for Qualitative Research.* Chicago, IL: Aldine Transaction. **176**

Honey, P. and Mumford, A. (1992) *The Manual of Learning Styles*, 3rd edn. Maidenhead: Peter Honey. **30 and 32**

Honey, P. and Mumford, A. (1995) *Using Your Learning Styles*, 3rd edn. Maidenhead: Peter Honey. **32**

Honey, P. and Mumford, A. (2006a) *The Learning Styles Helper's Guide.* Maidenhead: Peter Honey. **32**

Honey, P. and Mumford, A. (2006b) ***The Learning Styles Questionnaire (80-item version).*** Maidenhead: Peter Honey. (The questionnaire is also available online at www.peterhoney.com – see 'Study Guides on the Web' in the Further Resources section for more details.) **32**

International Telecommunication Union (2014) ***The World in 2014: ICT Facts and Figures.*** Available at: www.itu.int/en/ITU-D/Statistics/Documents/facts/ICTFacts Figures2014-e.pdf (accessed 22 July 2015). **75**

Introna, L., Hayes, N., Blair, L. and Wood, E. (2003) *Cultural Attitudes Towards Plagiarism: Developing a Better Understanding of the Needs of Students from Diverse Cultural Backgrounds Relating to Issues of Plagiarism.* Lancaster: Lancaster University. **21 and 137**

Jenkins, A. (2004) ***Virtually Interesting Fieldwork.*** Oxford Brookes Teaching Forum. Available at: www.brookes.ac.uk/virtual/NewTF/48/tf_48jenkins.htm (accessed 13 October 2009). **170**

Khaddage, F. and Lattemann, C. (2013) The future of mobile apps for teaching and learning, in Z.L. Berge and L.Y. Muilenburg (eds) *Handbook of Mobile Learning.* New York: Routledge. **35 and 86**

Kolb, A.Y. and Kolb, D.A (2011) *Learning Style Inventory Version 4.0.* Boston, MA: Hay Resources Direct. **30**

Kolb, D.A. (1984) *Experiential Learning: Experience as the Source of Learning and Development.* Englewood Cliffs, NJ: Prentice Hall. **26, 29, 30 and 32**

Kolb, D.A. (2015) *Experiential Learning: Experience as the Source of Learning and Development*, 2nd edn. Upper Saddle River, NJ: Pearson Education Ltd. **26, 29 and 30**

Ladd, P.D. and Ruby, R. (1999) Learning style and adjustment issues of international students, *Journal of Education for Business*, July/August: 363–7. **161**

LaMaster, J. and Ferries-Rowe, J.D. (2013) So we had this idea: bring your own technology at Brebeuf Jesuit, in Z.L. Berge and L.Y. Muilenburg (eds) *Handbook of Mobile Learning.* New York: Routledge. **76**

Laurillard, D. (2013) Foreword, in H. Beetham and R. Sharpe (eds) *Rethinking Pedagogy for a Digital Age: Designing for 21st Century Learning*, 2nd edn. Abingdon: Taylor & Francis. **34 and 35**

Luey, B. (2010) *Handbook for Academic Authors*, 5th edn. Cambridge: Cambridge University Press. **194**

Macdonald, J. (2008) *Blended Learning and Online Tutoring: Planning Learner Support and Activity Design*, 2nd edn. Aldershot: Gower. **80**

Marton, F. and Saljö, R. (1976) On qualitative differences in learning: I – outcome and process, *British Journal of Educational Psychology*, 46: 4–11. **31**

May, T. (2011) *Social Research: Issues, Methods and Process*, 4th edn. Maidenhead: Open University Press. **175 and 177**

Modern Humanities Research Association (MHRA) (2013) *MHRA Style Guide: A Handbook for Authors, Editors, and Writers of Theses*, 3rd edn. London: MHRA. **124 and 192**

Neville, C. (2010) *The Complete Guide to Referencing and Avoiding Plagiarism*, 2nd edn. Maidenhead: Open University Press. **124, 137, 138 and 195**

Office for National Statistics (ONS) for the UK (2014) ***Internet Access – Households and Individuals 2014***. Available at: www.ons.gov.uk/ons/rel/rdit2/internet-access---households-and-individuals/2014/stb-ia-2014.html (accessed 13 May 2015). **76**

Oliver, P. (2010) *The Student's Guide to Research Ethics*, 2nd edn. Maidenhead: Open University Press. **178**

Orna, E. with Stevens, G. (2009) *Managing Information for Research: Practical Help in Researching, Writing and Designing Dissertations*, 2nd edn. Maidenhead: Open University Press. **188**

Pears, R. and Shields, G. (2013) *Cite Them Right: The Essential Referencing Guide*, 9th edn. Basingstoke: Palgrave Macmillan. (Details of both the printed book and the online version are available at: www.citethemrightonline.com.) **124**

Phillips, E.M. and Pugh, D.S. (2010) *How to Get a PhD: A Handbook for Students and their Supervisors*, 5th edn. Maidenhead: Open University Press. **174**

Quinn, C.N. (2013) A future for m-learning, in Z.L. Berge and L.Y. Muilenburg (eds) *Handbook of Mobile Learning*. New York: Routledge. **77**

Race, P. (2014) *Making Learning Happen: A Guide for Post-Compulsory Education*, 3rd edn. London: Sage. **31**

Rawlins, K. (1996) *Study Skills for Adult Learners*. London: Macmillan Magazines. **18**

Robson, C. (2011) *Real World Research: A Resource for Social Scientists and Practitioner-Researchers*, 3rd edn. Oxford: Blackwell. **175, 176, 177, 178, 179 and 192**

Robson, C. (2014) *How to Do a Research Project: A Guide for Undergraduate Students*, 2nd edn. Oxford: Blackwell. **177**

Rose, J. (2012) *The Mature Student's Guide to Writing*, 3rd edn. Basingstoke: Palgrave. **146**

Salmon, G. (2011) *E-moderating: The Key to Teaching and Learning Online*, 3rd edn. London: Taylor & Francis. **35, 81, 156, 157 and 169**

Salmon, G. (2013) *E-tivities: The Key to Active Online Learning*. London: Taylor & Francis. **35 and 162**

Sapsford, R. and Jupp, V. (eds) (2006) *Data Collection and Analysis*, 2nd edn. London: Sage and The Open University. **177**

Schön, D.A. (1983) *The Reflective Practitioner: How Professionals Think in Action*. London: Temple Smith. **26**

Simpson, O. (2013) *Supporting Students for Success in Online and Distance Education*, 3rd edn. Abingdon: Routledge. **50 and 97**

Thyer, B.A. (1994) *Successful Publishing in Scholarly Journals* (Survival Skills for Scholars series). Thousand Oaks, CA: Sage. **194**

Turabian, K.L. (1982) *A Manual for Writers of Research Papers, Theses and Dissertations*. Oxford: Heinemann. (Although there isn't a later edition of the British version, the American version published by the University of Chicago Press is now in its 8th edition, 2013.) **192**

Wheeler, S. (1999) Convergent technologies in distance learning delivery, *Tech Trends*, 43(5): 19. **17**

Index

Page numbers in *italics* refer to tables.

'3S model' of how to catch up 50–1
three 'Ss' model of m-learning 86
abbreviations 12, 192
ABI/Inform Global database 109
abstract ideas 29
abstracts 106, 109, 110, 128
Academic Conferences Worldwide 180
academic credentials 131
academic criticism 132–3, 163
academic knowledge 28
academic writing 128, 144, 164
Acceptable Use Policy (AUP), mobile
    technology 87
Access Management sign-in systems 111
accessibility
   buildings 71
   for disabled students 71–2, 97
   electronic resources 108
   Internet and mobile devices 75–6
   learning materials 97
   remote access to experiments 168
accounting, learning and assessment in 21–2
accreditation 37
active learning 23
administration
   course administrator 55, 68
   tasks 39–40
affective skills 22
alerting services 119
   RSS feeds/news feeds 94, 119
analysis *see* critical and analytical skills;
   data collection and analysis
anxiety 158–9
architectural education (UIA) 121
assessment
   feedback on 57, 64
   formative 24, 145
   group work 66
   learning by 24
   learning outcomes 21–2, 23
   online 91, 147
   responsibility for 25
   and screening test for dyslexia 72–3
   specifications 55–7
   submission of 56
   types of 55, 57

assessment criteria 56–7
   essay writing 141
   examinations 150
assignments 24, 25, 26
   submission of 55
   technology 80, 89
   time management 49–50
   see also essay writing
'assistive technology' software 96–7
Asynchronous Voice Boards 156
Athens Access Management sign-in system
   111
attendance requirements 54–5
Australia
   Australian Education Index 110
   Trove 183
autonomy 25

backing up work 95
balance, work/life/study 7, 12–14, 49
BBC *Bitesize* 167
bibliographic databases 108–11, 189
bibliographic information 104, 105, 106, 136–7
bibliographic software 122–3
bibliography 128
Blackboard 35, 71, 88–9
Blackboard Collaborate 34, 91
blind and partially sighted people 96–7
blogs and vlogs 92–3
Bloom's taxonomy 20–3, 34, 172
Blu-Tech/Blue lens 96
Booksellers Association database 105–6
bookshops 105–6
Boolean searching 114
brain-storming/thought-storming 142
'breadcrumbs' websites 129
breaks
   from computer 42
   from study 73–4
British Dyslexia Association (BDA) 72
British Library
   catalogue 104
   Document Supply Service (BLDSS) 104
   newspapers 112
   patent information 181
   Zetoc Service 118–19

British Newspaper Archive 112
British Newspapers Online 112
buildings, accessibility of 71
bulletin boards 89–90

CABI Abstracts 110
CABI Full Text 110
Canada: *Theses Canada* 183
case studies 100
    field work (Malta Virtual Field Sites) 170
    ReLOAD (Real Labs Operated at a
        Distance) 168–9
    research 176–7
    VLE 160–1
catalogues, library 103–5
CERUKplus (Current Education and
    Children's Services Research, UK) 180
citations *see* references/citations
cloud-based computing 88
cognitive skills 20–2
collaborative work *see* group work
communication
    online 162
    skills 156–8
community of practice 156, 160
Community of Science 120
complaints procedure 59
computer hardware/software 55, 78–9, 91–2
computer services helpdesk 124–5
computer/data security 87–8, 95, 124
computers (PC/laptops)
    breaks during use 42
    health and safety issues 96
    in libraries 76, 101
    see also technology
concentration 24, 39, 44
conference boards 89–90
conference papers 104, 109, 110, 118, 119,
    182
conference proceedings 180, 193
confidence-boosting 66
'connectivism' 36
constructive criticism 132, 145, 192
constructivist learning theory 23
contacts for support 53–4
continuing professional development 20
control
    and 'free-range learners' 33–4
    of learning 25–6
    m-learning 76–7
    of resources 79
COPAC online library catalogue 103–4

coping strategies 61–3
copyright 133–4
counselling/guidance service 71
course administrator 55, 68
course director 73
course materials 99–100
course-specific information 51–8
    assessment specifications 55–7
    attendance requirements 54–5
    contacts for support 53–4
    electronic learner support systems 55
    feedback/module evaluation by student
        58
    hardware/software requirements 55
    monitoring of progress 58
    programme information 52–3
    tutorial details 54
    university/college information 58
course/student handbook 51, 52–3, 54, 55,
    56, 57, 58, 59, 62, 74, 89
critical and analytical skills
    essay writing 143–4
    literature reviews 172
    reading 130–1, 132–3, 172
critical thinking 22
    multicultural group work 163
    see also reflection; *entries beginning*
        reflective
criticism
    academic 132–3, 163
    constructive 132, 145, 192
cue consciousness/cue seekers 31–2
cultural/religious groups 87
current awareness services 118–20
current research 180–1
cyber security *see* computer/data security

DART Europe 183
data collection and analysis 165, 167
data/computer security 87–8, 95, 124
databases 108–11
deaf people and technology 91
deep and surface learning 31
demands 12–14
demonstrations 91–2
design of notes 134–6
Developing Countries Initiative (DCI) for
    journals 111–12
diaries
    reflective 26
    research 188–9
    revision 147

Directory of Open Access Journals 112
Disability Officer 71
DisabilityRightsUK 71
disabled students 71–2
    accessibility to e-learning 97
    blind and partially sighted 96–7
    deaf 91
Disabled Students Allowance 73
discussion rooms, online 89–90
dissemination of research findings 193
dissertations and theses 182–3
distance learners 6–7
    potential pitfalls 10–14
    qualities, skills and attributes 9–10
    reasons for study 8
    student life 7–8
    successful 7
distance learning
    characteristics of 23–6
    definition and elements 5–6
    future of 36–7
Document Supply Service (BLDSS) 104
double reading 130–1
drafts
    electronic messages 158
    essay writing 144, 145
    research report 192
    research schedule 187–8
Dyslexia Action 72, 73
dyslexic students 72–3, 97

e-books 39, 96, 113
e-journals 111–12
e-learning 77–9, 94–5
    glossary 80–4
    required skills 79–80
e-moderators 35, 89–90
e-newspapers 112–13
E-print Network 182
electronic learner support systems 55
electronic learning environments *see*
    virtual learning environments (VLEs)
electronic mindmapping software 136
electronic resources
    current awareness services 118–20
    databases, bibliographic and full-text
        108–11
    evaluating websites 121–2
    information literacy 107–8
    IT support 124–5
    limits to access 108
    networking 120–1

references 122–4
search engines 114–15
search strategies 115–18
searchable lists of web resources 113–14
see also libraries
emails 85–6
    skills required 157
employment *see entries beginning* work
encryption 88
Endnote 107, 122–3
engineering
    Inspec database 109
    VLE case study 160–1
essay writing 140–6
    assessment criteria 141
    conclusion 143
    critical and analytical 143–4
    as exam practice 145
    introduction 143
    key points 146
    linking it all together 143
    literature research 142
    making your points 143
    note-making 142
    planning 142
    preparation and starting early 141
    read feedback 145
    read the question 141–2
    and report-writing, differences between
        164
    reviewers 145
    skills development 140
    sources of help 146
    use of drafts 144
    use of first person 144
    use of plain language 144
    word limits 141
ethics
    emailing 157
    mobile/m-learning 87–8
    research 178–9
Europe
    DART Europe 183
    patent libraries 181
European Higher Education Area 20
European Library 104–5
evaluation
    of information 21
    of modules by students 58
    of research projects 184–5
    of websites 121–2
evaluation reports 192

evidence 130, 131
examination revision 146–9
    choice of topics 148
    key points 149
    note-making 149
    planning 147
    reading 148–9
    schedule 147–8
examinations 150–4
    assessment criteria 150
    ending/last ten minutes 153
    essay writing as practice 145
    handwriting/spelling/grammar 150
    key points 153–4
    name and entry number/code 151
    planning 150, 152, 153
    preparation 151
    read whole paper 151–2
    strategic learning 31–2
    writing your answer 152–3
experience, personal 14, 28
experiential learning cycle 28–30
experiments
    home kits 168
    remote access 168

face-to-face support 65, 67
face-to-face teaching and learning 24–5,
        35, 49, 55
Facebook 23, 35, 67, 86, 93, 120, 124, 156
family and friends 13–14, 68–9
feasibility of research project 179
feedback
    assessments 57, 64
    essays 145
    experiential learning cycle 29
    module evaluation by student 58
    reading and responding to 24
feedforward 145
fees, payment of 60
field work, virtual 169–71
filing system 190
findings, research 190–4
first person in academic writing 144
FirstClass 89
fixed research 176–7
flexibility
    learning 30
    in studying 6–7
flexible research 175, 176–7
footnotes 123
formative assessment 24, 145

*Framework for Higher Education
        Qualification* (FHEQ) 19
friends and family 13–14, 68–9
funding/sponsorship of research 181, 190
future of distance learning 36–7

Gantt chart 44, *45*, 141, 187
goal-setting 8–9, 50
Google Alerts 119
Google Scholar 115
grammar and spelling 150
grey literature 181–2
grid for weekly planner *48*
grounded theory 175–6
group discussions 157–8
group work 155–6
    causes of concern, anxiety and
        frustration 158–9
    impact of technology 33, 34, 35, 156
    skills required 156–8
    strategies 159–61
    see also multicultural group work
guidance/counselling service 71

handwriting 150
hardware/software 55, 78–9, 91–2
Harvard reference system 123, 124, 137
health and safety issues of technology
        96
help, online 124–5, 132
highlighting 133

'I'/first person in academic writing 144
index cards 40, 136, 189
indexes
    and abstracts 106, 109, 110, 128
    of current research 180–1
    subject 113
information literacy 107–8
International Federation of Library
        Associations and Institutions (IFLA)
        105
International Non-Commercial Document
        Supply (INCD) Service 104
International Telecommunications Union
        (ITU) 75–6
international/overseas students 54, 108
Internet, using the
    for accessing bookshops 105–6
    for accessing library and other
        resources 101–5
    for assessment 24

for e-learning 88–94
for field work 169–70
for group work 156
for laboratory work 168–9
for networking 120–1
for research 180–3
hardware for 55, 78–9
skills for 85–6
support for 124–5
see also electronic resources; technology
interviews, research 186, 189
IT
  support 124–5
  see also electronic resources;
    technology

JiscMail 86
journals 106
  alert service 119
  e-journals 111–12
  library catalogues 103, 104

keeping in touch 63, 120
keywords
  essay writing 141, 142, 143
  examinations 151, 152
  note-making 129, 149
  searches 116, 117, 118
knowledge construction 34

laboratories
  virtual 169
  and workshops 168–9
language
  academic 65
  multicultural group work 162–3
  plain 144
learner autonomy 25
learner support *see* support
learner-centred learning 142
LearnHigher materials 132, 136, 137, 143,
    146, 164
  maths, data collection and analysis
    resources 167
  research skills 177
learning 18–19
  approaches, preferences and styles
    30–3
  definition of 18
  levels of 19–20
  outcomes and objectives 20–3
  process 28–30

sources of 26–8
see also e-learning; mobile/m-learning
learning by assessment 24
learning by doing 23
learning by reading and responding to
    feedback 24
learning by reflection 25–6, 29–30
learning by study days 24–5
learning flexibility 30
Learning Style Inventory (LSI) 30
Learning Styles Questionnaire 32
Learning Support Adviser 71
lectures 91–2
levels of learning 19–20
libraries
  catalogues 103–5
  patent 181
  registration 102, 108
  research compilations 181
  resources 100–3
  see also British Library; electronic
    resources
literature reviews 171–2
literature search and review 179–80
  current research 180–1
  grey literature 181–2
  theses and dissertations 182–3
logs
  blogs and vlogs 92–3
  reflective 26

mailing lists 86
management
  Access Management sign-in systems 111
  research *see under* research project
  time *see* time/schedule management
marking *see* assessment criteria
mathematics 166–7
  data collection and analysis 165–6
MathTutor 166
memory 149, 189
mentoring schemes 69–70
mindmapping *130*, 135–6
mitigating circumstances 95, 137
mixed-mode courses 49
mobile phones/devices 39, 40, 76–7
mobile/m-learning 86–8
  definitions of 34–5, 77–8
  future of 36–7
  glossary 80–4
  required skills 79–80
  security and ethical issues 87–8

moderators, electronic 35, 89–90
monitoring of progress 58
MOOCs 25, 37
motivation 8–9, 66
multi-disciplinary databases 109
multicultural group work 161–4
  critical thinking and academic criticism
    163
  language 162–3
  membership 161–2
  socialization 162
multimedia use 34
multiple-choice questions (MCQs) 24

National Academic Mailing (*JiscMail*) 86
national libraries 104–5
navigation tools, websites 129
netiquette 157
networking, electronic 120–1
news feeds 94, 119
newsgroups 120
note-making 133–6
  additional 134
  copyright 133–4
  design 134–6
  and essay writing 142
  and examination revision 149
  highlighting 133
  material used or not used 136
  physical means 134
  summarizing thoughts 134
numeracy *see* mathematics

online assessments 91, 147
online communication 162
online discussion rooms 89–90
online learning 33–4, 84–5
  see also e-learning; mobile/m-learning
open access
  journals 112
  reference styles 124
Open University
  home experiment kits 168
  mindmapping 136
  OpenLearn website 166, 167
organizing, practicalities of studying 39–40
outcomes of learning 20–3
overseas/international students 54, 108

pace of study 41
passwords and usernames 88, 110–11
patents 181

PATLIB centres 181
pedagogy 34, 36–7
peers/fellow students 64–7
periodicals *see* journals
periods of study 42
personal experience 14, 28
personal qualities, skills and attributes
  9–10
photocopying 102, 133–4, 137
pitfalls to avoid 10–14
place of study 38–9
plagiarism 137–8
  see also references/citations
planning
  essay writing 142
  examination answers 150, 152, 153
  examination revision 147
  study 46–9
podcasts 91–2
posters 171
postgraduates 20
Powerpoint 90, 91, 114
practical work 168
  demonstrations 91–2
presentations 171
professional association libraries 101
professional communities networking
  120–1
progress, monitoring of 58
ProQuest Central database 109, 110
*ProQuest Dissertations and Theses -
  Global* 183
*ProQuest Dissertations and Theses - UK
  and Ireland* 182–3
ProQuest UK Newsstand 112
psychomotor skills 22–3
public libraries 101
publication of research 193–4
punctuation 141, 192

qualifications framework 19
qualitative and quantitative research 175–6
qualities, personal 9–10
Quality Assurance Agency for Higher
  Education 19
quotations 138–9

reading 127–33
  abstract 128
  academic criticism 132–3
  bibliography 128
  chapters 129

conclusion 128–9
contents 128
cover 127–8
critical and analytical 130–1, 132–3, 172
double check 129
examination paper 151–2
examination revision 148–9
index 128
introduction 128
key points 133
learning by 24
lists 40
online help 132
order of 129
pre-course 127
relevance 127
speed 130
stopping 133
taking stock 129
see also literature search and review;
  note-making
record-keeping 118
references 122–3
research project 188–90
recording and using sources 136–9
bibliographical details 136–7
citation/plagiarism 137–8
quotations 138–9
references/citations 122–4
electronic resources 107, 115
and plagiarism 137–8
quotations 138–9
record-keeping 122–3
reporting research findings 192–3
searches 109
style of 123–4
see also bibliography; *entries beginning
  bibliographic*
reflection, learning by 25–6, 29–30
reflective diary/'log' 26
reflective writing 144
RefWorks 123
registration
library facilities 102, 108
and payment of fees 60
virtual learning environments (VLEs) 89
ReLOAD (Real Labs Operated at a
  Distance) 168–9
report-writing 164–5, 191–2
research funding 181, 190
research libraries 103–4
research project 173–4

ethical issues 178–9
evaluating other projects 184–5
feasibility 179
management 185–90
  plan/do/review 185–6
  record-keeping 188–90
  schedule 186–8
  time 186
preparation 174–8
  approaches 175–6
  choice of topic 177–8
  defining research and 'good' research
    174–5
  methodologies 175, 176–7
  research proposal 177
reporting findings 190–4
  audience 190–1
  citations/references 192–3
  content 191
  dissemination 193
  publication 193–4
  writing 191–2
see also literature search and review
residential sessions 65
resources
  abstracts and indexes 106, 109, 110, 128
  bookshops 105–6
  course materials 99–100
  see also electronic resources; journals;
    libraries
responsibility 25
Responsible Mobile-Use Policies (RMUPs)
  87
review
  essay writing 145
  literature 171–2
  see also literature search and review
review article 127
revision *see* examination revision
Royal National Institute of Blind People
  (RNIB) 96–7
RSS feeds 94, 119
rules and regulations 59

SAQs *see* self-assessment questions
schedule *see* time/schedule management
Scholarpedia 94
science: social science and natural science
  research approaches 175–6
Science Direct 112, 113
*Science Direct Personalization and
  Alerting Services* 119

Science.gov 182
SciVerse Scopus database 109
SCONUL Access scheme 101, 103
Scout Report 119
screening test for dyslexia 72–3
search engines 114–15
search strategies 115–18
   field searching 117
   keywords 116, 117, 118
   performing search 117
   record-keeping 118
   reviewing and refining search 117–18
   scope 116
   structure 116–17
   viewing results 117
searchable lists of web resources 113–14
security, computer/data 87–8, 95, 124
self-assessment questions (SAQs) 24, 91
self-directed learning 35
seminars 41, 44
   online 89
Shibboleth Access Management sign-in
   system 111
sickness certificate 55
simulations 91, 168
SKILL (National Bureau for Students with
   Disabilities) 71, 73
skills
   affective 22
   cognitive 20–2
   for data collection and analysis 165
   existing 14
   for e-learning 79–80
   for exams 150–4
   for information literacy 107–8
   for mathematics 166–7
   for m-learning 79–80
   for note-making 133–6
   for reading 127–33
   for report writing 164–5, 191–2
   for study (in general) 9–10, 70–1
   for working with others 156–8
   for writing 140–6
   psychomotor 22–3
Skills Plus 132, 163, 165, 171
Skills@Library 132, 171
skimming 129
social media 23, 67, 87
   Facebook 23, 35, 67, 86, 93, 120, 124,
      156
   'trolling' of 88
social networking services 120

socialization, in group work 162
software/hardware 55, 78–9, 91–2
speed reading 130
spelling and grammar 150
strategic learning 31–2
streaming lectures 91
student/course handbook 51, 52–3, 54, 55,
   56, 57, 58, 59, 62, 74, 89
students/peers, support from 64–7
study, definition and aim of 17–18
study days 24–5, 66
study schedule *see* time/schedule
   management
study skills support 70–1
subject information gateways/portals/
   trees 113, 114
summarizing thoughts, in note-making
   134
support
   breaks from study 73–4
   contacts for 53–4
   coping strategies 61–3
   for disabled students 71
   from course administrator 68
   from friends and family 68–9
   from other agencies 70–3
   from other students/peers 64–7
   from tutors 53–4, 63–4
   from work colleagues and mentors
      69–70
   IT 124–5
   through technology 67, 98
surface and deep learning 31

technology 75–7
   blind and partially sighted people
      96–7
   blogs and vlogs 92–3
   deaf people 91
   discussion rooms/conference boards/
      bulletin boards 89–90
   future of distance learning 36–7
   glossary of terms 80–4
   group work 33, 34, 35, 156
   health and safety issues 96
   impact on learning 33–6
   IT support 124–5
   lectures, demonstrations and podcasts
      91–2
   mailing lists 86
   maths and data collection and analysis
      165

online learning 33–4, 84–5
RSS feeds/news feeds 94, 119
security 87–8, 95, 124
self-assessment questions (SAQs) 91
and traditional texts, student
  preferences 97–8
videoconferencing 92
'wearable' 36
wikis 93–4
see also e-learning; electronic resources;
  email; mobile/m-learning; virtual
  learning environments (VLEs)
telephone conferencing 67
telephone support service 97
temporary leaver status 74
terminology 4
technology 80–4
textbooks 99, 106
theses and dissertations 182–3
thought-storming/brain-storming
  142
time
  and pace of study 41–2
  use 49–51
time/schedule management 43–9
  research project 186–8
  study schedule 44–6
  weekly planner 46–9
  work/life/study balance 7, 12–14, 49
touch-screen technology 80
'trolling' of social media 88
Turnitin software 107, 137
tutorials 25
  details 54
  suggested reading 145
  virtual training suite 113–14
  website evaluation 122
tutors
  as e-moderators 35, 89–90
  electronic resources 114
  role 155–6, 160
  support from 53–4, 63–4
  see also feedback

UKOP Online database 110
undergraduates 20
university/college information 58

URLs (Universal Resource Locators) 114,
  121, 131
username and passwords 88, 110–11

VARK questionnaire 33
videoconferencing 92
virtual field courses (VFCs) 170
virtual field work 169–71
virtual laboratories 169
virtual learning environments (VLEs) 88–9
  case study 160–1
viruses/virus checkers 95, 124
vlogs and blogs 92–3

'wearable' technology 36
Web of Science database 109, 118
WebEx 89
websites
  evaluating of 121–2
  navigation tools 129
  order of reading 129
  see also British Library; electronic
    resources; libraries
weekly planner 46–9
Wikipedia 94
wikis 93–4
word limits 141
work colleagues and mentors, support
  from 69–70
'work-based' learning
  mobile technology 88
  and 'work-related' learning 15
work/life/study balance 7, 12–14, 49
workplace
  continuing professional development 20
  learning 14–15
  as resource 28
workshops 168–9
writing
  emails 157
  report 164–5, 191–2
  see also essay writing; examinations

year planner 46

Zetoc Service 118–19
Zotero 123

Doing Your Research Project
A Guide for First-time Researchers
6th Edition

Judith Bell and Stephen Waters

ISBN: 978-0-335-26446-9 (Paperback)
eBook: 978-0-335-26447-6
2014

Step-by-step advice on completing an outstanding research project. This is **the** market-leading book for anyone doing a research project for the first time. Clear, concise and extremely readable, this bestselling resource provides a practical, step-by-step guide from initial concept through to completion of your final written research report.

Key features:

- A brand new chapter describing the benefits of using social media in research
- Tips on using online tools such as Delicious, Mendeley, Dropbox, EndNote and RefWorks
- Guidance on searching efficiently and effectively online

www.openup.co.uk

OPEN UNIVERSITY PRESS
McGraw - Hill Education